EXPLORATIONS IN SOCIOLOGY
British Sociological Association conference volume series

Published by Macmillan

Series Standing Order

If you would like to receive future titles in this series as they are published, you can make use of our standing order facility. To place a standing order please contact your bookseller or, in case of difficulty, write to us at the address below with your name and address and the name of the series. Please state with which title you wish to begin your standing order. (If you live outside the UK we may not have the rights for your area, in which case we will forward your order to the publisher concerned).

Standing Order Service, Macmillan Distribution Ltd, Houndmills, Basingstoke, Hampshire, RG21 2XS, England.

Fordism and Flexibility

Divisions and Change

Edited by

Nigel Gilbert
Professor of Sociology, University of Surrey

Roger Burrows
Associate Dean, School of Human Studies, University of Teesside

and

Anna Pollert
Senior Research Fellow, Industrial Relations Unit, University of Warwick

First edition 1992
Reprinted 1993, 1994

Published by
THE MACMILLAN PRESS LTD
Houndmills, Basingstoke, Hampshire RG21 2XS
and London
Companies and representatives
throughout the world

ISBN 0–333–56535–5 hardcover
ISBN 0–333–61815–7 paperback

A catalogue record for this book is available
from the British Library.

Transferred to digital printing 2001

Printed & bound by Antony Rowe Ltd, Eastbourne

Contents

List of Figures and Tables

Figures

Tables

Preface

The chapters in this volume originate from presentations at the British Sociological Association Annual Conference, held at the University of Surrey in April 1990 on the theme of Social Divisions and Social Change. The organisers of the conference were Nigel Gilbert, Roger Burrows, Sara Arber and Catherine Marsh. Some of the chapters are derived from a special session at the conference organised by Anna Pollert. All of the papers as presented have been rewritten in the light of reaction at the conference and editorial comment.

We thank Sheila Tremlett for her help in complicated negotiations, Alison Mill-Ingen for helping with the editorial work, and most especially, our two fellow conference organisers, Sara Arber and Cathie Marsh, without whom the whole escapade would have been no fun at all. The Institute of Manpower Studies is acknowledged for permission to reproduce Figure 5.1, originally published in *Manpower Policy and Practice*, vol. 1, 1985.

Three other volumes drawing on papers presented at the conference are being published simultaneously with this one: *Consumption and Class: Divisions and Change* (edited by Roger Burrows and Catherine Marsh), *Women and Working Lives: Divisions and Change* (edited by Sara Arber and Nigel Gilbert) and *Families and Household: Divisions and Change* (edited by Catherine Marsh and Sara Arber). Together they offer a picture of the state of sociology in the 1990s.

NIGEL GILBERT
ROGER BURROWS
ANNA POLLERT

Notes on the Contributors

James Anderson is a Senior Lecturer in Geography and chairperson of the Social Science Foundation Course Team at the Open University. His interests include nationalism and territoriality and urban and regional policy, with particular reference to enterprise zones and the New Right.

Roger Burrows is Associate Dean, School of Human Studies, University of Teesside and was previously Lecturer at the University of Surrey. He is the editor of *Deciphering the Enterprise Culture* (1990) and co-editor of *Consumption and Class: Divisions and Change*. He has published in *Sociology, Sociological Review, Work, Employment and Society*, the *Employment Gazette* and other journals.

Bernard Casey is a Senior Research Fellow at the Policy Studies Institute. He previously worked in the Labour Market Policy section of the Science Centre, Berlin. Major publications include *Temporary Employment: Practice and Policy in Britain* (1988) and *Work or Retirement* (1983), co-authored with Gurt Bruche.

Simon Clarke is Senior Lecturer in Sociology at the University of Warwick. His books include *The Foundations of Structuralism* (1981), *Marx Marginalism and Modern Sociology* (1982: Second Edition 1991), *Keynesianism, Monetarism and the Crisis of the State* (1988) and *The State Debate* (1991).

Tony Elger is a Lecturer and a member of the Labour Studies Group in the Department of Sociology at the University of Warwick. He has written extensively in the area of work and employment restructuring, focusing on the debates about flexibility and the recent impact of 'new' technologies. This builds on his earlier writing on the labour process. Recently, he and Peter Fairbrother have begun a long-term research project on workplace restructuring and union renewal.

Peter Fairbrother is a Lecturer and a member of the Labour Studies Group in the Department of Sociology at the University of Warwick. His main research interests are in the area of labour and politics, focusing particularly on the restructuring of work and employment and forms of union organisation and renewal. He has long had a concern with union organisation and activity in the state sector. His publications include *Flexibility at Work: The Challenge for Unions* and *Workplace Unionism in the 1980s: A Process of Renewal* as well as journal articles. His current research is on local trade unionism and workplace management in both the public and private sectors.

Philip Garrahan is a Principal Lecturer in Politics at the University of Teesside. With Paul Stewart he is the author of *The Nissan Enigma* (1991) and editor of *Restructuring for Economic Flexibility* (1990).

Nigel Gilbert is Professor of Sociology at the University of Surrey. His recent books include *Opening Pandora's Box: a sociological analysis of scientific discourse* (1984) and *Computers and Conversation* (1990). He has also written many papers on social stratification, the sociology of science, and cognitive science.

Jamie Gough is Knoop Research Fellow in the Management School at Sheffield University. He worked in the GLC's Industry and Employment Branch, and has published papers on local economies and local economic strategies. With Mike Macnair he is author of *Gay Liberation in the Eighties* (1985).

Glyn Holroyd studied sociology at Newcastle Polytechnic, graduating with First Class honours. He has been research officer at Durham University and the Polytechnic of East London. His publications are mainly in the field of industrial relations in the small firm. He is currently employed in the civilian branch of the Metropolitan Police.

David Kraithman is a Principal Lecturer in Economics at the University of Hertfordshire and a member of the Local Economy Research Unit. He has written articles and contributed to books in the area of location studies. He was a joint author of *Microelectronics: Capitalist Technology and the Working-Class.*

Frank Laczko is Senior Lecturer in Social Policy in the Department of Social Science and Policy Studies at Coventry University. He has worked as a consultant for the OECD for whom he has prepared a report on early retirement and older workers. Together with Chris Phillipson, he has written a book, *The Future of Work and Retirement: Social Policy and the Older Worker* (1991).

Steve Leman is a former primary school teacher and a postgraduate research student in the Department of Industrial Technology at the University of Bradford. He is a contributor to a forthcoming book, *Democratising the Workplace*, edited by J. Wintertom. He has written several conference papers and an article for the journal, *Industrial Tutor*.

Roger Penn is a Senior Lecturer in the Department of Sociology at Lancaster University. His recent projects include a study of Rochdale as part of the ESRC Social Change and Economic Life Initiative, modelling the effects of male unemployment upon female economic activity rates, and an analysis of the effects of technological change on skilled work in the British coal industry. He has written *Skilled Workers in the Class Structure* (1985) and *The Militant Craftsman: Skilled Workers in Britain and America* (1989).

Anna Pollert is Senior Research Fellow at the Industrial Relations Research Unit at the University of Warwick. She is the author of *Girls, Wives and Factory Lives* (1981) and the editor of *A Farewell to Flexibility?* (1991).

Al Rainnie is a Research Fellow at the University of Hertfordshire's Local Economy Research Unit. He has written extensively on the subject of industrial relations, restructuring and the small firm, and is author of *Industrial Relations and the Small Firm: Small isn't Beautiful* (1989).

Ian Roberts worked as an apprentice plumber in a Wearside shipyard, as a tax officer with the Inland Revenue and as a youth and community worker before beginning higher education. He subsequently obtained a doctorate at the University of Durham where he was a British Academy Research Fellow and is now a Lecturer in Sociology.

Stephen Lloyd Smith is a Senior Lecturer in Sociology, School of Social Science, Kingston University. He has published in the areas of urban political history, new technology in banking and retailing, emotional labour, power structure research, and collaborative high technology innovation.

Paul Stewart is a Lecturer at the Cardiff Business School, University of Wales. He is co-author with Philip Garrahan of *The Nissan Enigma* (1991) and editor of *Restructuring for Economic Flexibility* (1990).

1 Introduction: Fordism, Post-Fordism and Economic Flexibility

Roger Burrows, Nigel Gilbert and
Anna Pollert

Periodically the sociology of economic life is gripped by a set of concepts which function as organising principles for the whole area of inquiry. Crudely, work in the 1960s was largely concerned with debates about 'orientations to work' and 'embourgeoisement', whilst the bulk of work in the 1970s and early 1980s was little more than an extended response to Braverman (1974) and labour process theory. However, since the mid-1980s economic sociology has increasingly concerned itself with processes of 'economic restructuring' for which, until recently, no paradigmatic set of concepts have been forthcoming.

That 1980–9 was a decade of significant economic change is not in any doubt. However, how best to interpret these changes has become a source of much controversy. The literature on the restructuring of Britain has been marked by a plethora of often contradictory attempts to make some sort of social scientific sense out of the last decade. We have seen both liberal (Piore and Sabel, 1984) and Marxian (Aglietta, 1979) claims of transforma- tions in the dominant forms of production; both liberal (Saunders, 1986, pp. 289–351) and Marxian (Gamble, 1988) analyses of the supposed incom- patibility between market capitalism and more socialised systems of collective consumption; both liberal (Hall, 1985) and Marxian (Mandel, 1980) analyses of economic long waves. There have been more eclectic models claiming to be able to decipher shifts from 'organised' towards more 'disorganised' forms of capitalism (Lash and Urry, 1987); 'culturalist' representations, conceptualised in terms of shifts from 'modernism' towards 'postmodernism' (Harvey, 1989); New Right claims of an emerging 'enterprise culture' (Burrows, 1991); 'new' New Left claims of the advent of 'New Times' (Hall and Jacques, 1989); and so on and on.

For a while it appeared as if this babble of theoretical and political voices would remain disparate. However, of late three related concepts have emerged around which there has been an abrupt and dramatic crystallisation: *Fordism, post-Fordism*, and, supposedly linking the two, various manifestations of

1

economic *flexibility*. Dominant interpretations of the contemporary profusion of divisions and changes in the labour market and the organisation of work are now almost all discussed in terms of this conceptual triumvirate. A new orthodoxy of economic sociology is now well established (Pollert, 1991b).

There has been, it is suggested, a profound change in the labour process towards the 'flexible worker' and in the labour market towards a 'flexible workforce'. For some, this 'flexible workforce' is proof of a new, vigorous economy; for others, it is the product of a new 'manpower' policy to achieve a 'core' and 'periphery' workforce, with complementary 'functional' and 'numerical' flexibility; for others still it constitutes a 'two-nation' employment strategy designed to divide the workforce in order to bring about a wider transformation of society. For the Marxist-inspired French Regulation School, the significance of flexibility lies in a new form of capitalist control arising as the contemporary response to a crisis of Fordism. And for still others, 'flexibility' is part of the option provided by a 'New Industrial Divide' to transform both production and markets from a system based on mass production to one of 'flexible specialisation'. Finally, and relatedly, 'flexibility' lies at the heart of an all-embracing shift from Fordism to post-Fordism.

As already indicated, the conceptual and political sources of the concepts of Fordism, post-Fordism and flexibility are diverse. However, three positions are especially important and provide the major focus for the book: Marxist regulation theory; the notion of flexible specialisation associated with the 'new' institutional economics; and the model of the flexible firm derives from the managerialist literature.[1] In the chapters which follow, the diverse claims made by these three approaches are subject to various forms of empirical and theoretical investigation and their wider implications are examined in relation to emerging patterns of work in advanced societies.

SOME MODELS OF FORDISM, POST-FORDISM AND FLEXIBILITY

Marxist Regulation Theory

Marxist regulation theory is the most general and abstract position of the three.[2] It attempts to provide an analysis of processes of social change in a framework which links economic, social, political and ideological structures. It is concerned to explain the stability of capitalism over substantial periods of time in the form of 'regimes of accumulation' involving specific 'modes of regulation' which offer a resolution, albeit always a limited and provisional one, of the underlying contradictions of capitalism.

Regulation theory characterises the postwar boom in terms of a Fordist regime of accumulation based upon techniques of mass production buttressed by a mode of regulation consisting of mass consumption and the Keynesian welfare state.[3] The theory suggests that in recent years the process of restructuring we have been witnessing is a symptom of the 'crisis of Fordism' and the emergence of post-Fordism.

In contrast to the mass production, mass consumption, mass public provision and modernist cultural forms of Fordism, post-Fordism is characterised in terms of a homology between 'flexible' production techniques, differentiated and segmented consumption patterns, a restructured welfare state and postmodernist cultural forms. The breakdown of Fordism and the emergence of post-Fordism is conceptualised primarily in terms of a search for greater levels of economic flexibility. Boyer (1988), for example, lists five aspects of this new flexibility: adaptability of productive organisations; ability of workers to move from one job to another; laxity of legal constraints governing the contract of employment; adaptability of wages; and the possibility for companies to reduce some of their social and fiscal payments.

Flexible Specialisation

The theory of flexible specialisation is less holistic in its approach as it concentrates more narrowly on changes in the processes of production, rather than upon the wider context of these changes. As a theory of production it is based on a theory of competing technological paradigms: craft production and mass production. Mass production, the dominant 'system of industrial technology' (Piore and Sabel, 1984, p. 5) is based on the special purpose machine, organised as an assembly line, operated by a semi-skilled labour force, producing standardised products for a mass market. This production system, it is argued, is limited by the extent of the market; contemporary market fragmentation indicates that the mass market has reached saturation. Markets and new technology now drive a new form of flexible production based on flexible specialisation whose precise institutional form may, however, vary. The transition is at one level market and technology driven, at another, determined by political choice. Flexible specialisation is a new form of skilled craft production made easily adaptable by programmable technology to provide specialised goods which can supply an increasingly fragmented and volatile market. The 'industrial district' has been identified as the model of economic co-ordination and social integration for this new specialist production system; whether in the form of municipal local authorities, or in family networks, the innovative regional economy is seen to foster harmonious equilibrium between competition and co-operation between firms.

At the same time, restructuring along flexible specialisation lines has also been seen to apply to managerial shifts in larger firms to smaller units of more flexible production, which involve both technical changes in production and organisation, and changes of labour control away from Taylorism towards autonomously self-regulating work groups. In broad terms, the theory of flexible specialisation is based on the belief that it is possible to discipline the market economy and that capitalist social relations are not inherently contradictory: it is possible to choose whether to continue on the old, declining path of Fordist mass production, or to reform through flexible specialisation.

The Flexible Firm

The model of the flexible firm is the most concrete and specific of the three approaches. The most well known formulation is that of Atkinson and Meager (1986). The notion of the flexible firm is best treated as an ideal type which accentuates key elements of changing employment practices in some enterprises. However, this ideal typical description is also conflated with a prescription for 'good practice' in establishment restructuring. The model of the flexible firm, more than any of the other manifestations of the concept of flexibility, has acquired in the process of its dissemination, a place in the policy language of governments and employers: in practice, in legislation, in management consultancy and in industrial relations bargaining.

The ideal typical flexible firm is one which has attempted to secure three sorts of economic flexibility. First, numerical flexibility: the ability to change the size of the workforce quickly and easily in response to changes in demand. Second, functional flexibility: the ease with which workers can be redeployed to different tasks to meet changes in market demand, technology and company policy; and third: financial and pay flexibility to facilitate numerical, and, especially, functional flexibility.

The flexible firm attempts to achieve numerical flexibility in a combination of ways: there may be a peripheral category of workers without long-term security of employment; or such a group may be formed of employees on short-term contracts, in part-time jobs or job sharing and so on. Further numerical flexibility can be obtained by going outside the firm to secure the services of subcontractors, self-employed specialists, home workers or agency temporaries.

Functional flexibility operates by providing a core group of employees with a degree of security and high wages in exchange for their willingness to change tasks and to acquire and utilise new skills. Financial or pay flexibility involves adjusting pay structures to encourage functional flexibility and to match market rates for scarce skills.

CRITICAL ANALYSES

The chapters which follow are grouped into four sections which deal with: historical and theoretical critiques of the concepts of Fordism and post-Fordism; empirical studies of various localities; empirical case studies of specific industries; and empirical studies of emerging patterns of work and employment.

Historical and Theoretical Critiques

Clarke (Chapter 2) and Gough (Chapter 3) begin the volume with controversial historical and theoretical critiques of the concepts of Fordism and post-Fordism, both written from avowedly Marxist perspectives.

Clarke offers a polemic not only against recent theorisations of Fordism but also against the historical role that sociologists have played in the various attempts Ford, his company and its Foundation, have made to construct Utopias of a stabilised capitalism. He not only questions the validity of Fordism and post-Fordism as ideal types, but more importantly he subjects the regulation and the flexible specialisation theorists' history of Fordism to a devastating critique. Crucially, he questions the supposed homology between Fordism and Keynesianism as characterised in such accounts. He concludes that the relationship between the two 'was about as close and stable as we can imagine the relationship between Ford and Keynes would have been!' He is especially disparaging of recent sociological attempts to theorise the supposed demise of Fordism, viewing talk of post-Fordism as little more than an attempt by disillusioned socialist intellectuals to construct for themselves a Utopian vision of the future in which they themselves are to play a key historical role.

The chapter by Gough shifts the focus away from the history of Fordism towards the coherence of post-Fordist theories. In a technical paper which draws upon Marxist value theory he subjects various post-Fordist conceptualisations to a powerful critique. He argues that although technical and organisation aspects of economic restructuring are important, they need to be situated within their social forms represented in relations of value. Thus far, the notion of a regime of accumulation has tended only to be considered in terms of technical-organisational efficiency. However, a focus upon value-relations suggests that current forms of capital-labour relation are far more problematic for capital than purely technical-organisation discourses would suggest.

Locality Studies

The chapters by Rainnie and Kraithman (Chapter 4) and Penn (Chapter 5) examine empirically various aspects of the Fordism, post-Fordism and flexibility literature in relation to different localities in the UK.

Rainnie and Kraithman report on research carried out in 1989 in Hertfordshire, one of the relatively prosperous 'home counties'. They conclude that post-Fordist analyses exhibit an overly simplistic model of causality and tend to ignore the inherent element of contradiction in much management strategy. The development of dual labour markets is counteracted by the changes in the demographic structure of the workforce. The growth in 'non-standard' forms of employment, women's employment in particular, is so diverse that it cannot be unproblematically classified as a 'secondary' or 'peripheral' category. Moreover, for the most part employers' responses to demographic changes are largely *ad hoc* rather than strategic. The concept of flexibility is not a particularly useful one for coming to terms with the myriad of changes in the organisation of work and the labour market.

The concerns of Penn are more specific, although his data set is rather more extensive than the intensive semi-structured interview data of Rainnie and Kraithman. He examines both the methodological underpinnings and the evidence adduced in the Atkinson and Meager model of the flexible firm and then contrasts this with survey evidence from 954 establishments collected as part of the ESRC Social Change and Economic Life Research Initiative (SCELI). The data are from six localities across the United Kingdom: Aberdeen, Kirkcaldy, Rochdale, Coventry, Northampton and Swindon. Penn concludes that the Atkinson and Meager model is severely wanting on a number of levels. The analysis reveals no significant locality effects in relation to changing patterns of 'flexible' employment. There are, however, major industrial-sectoral effects which produce the initial impression of locality differences. Such an impression is, however, the consequence of differing industrial structures in the various localities. The results suggest that unemployment *per se* is not as significant a factor as suggested in the initial flexible firm model. There is strong evidence of a positive association between the size of establishments and the likelihood of the employment of at least some 'peripheral' employees. This result contradicts both the theoretical assumptions of Atkinson and Meager *and* their prognoses. Given that the average size of establishments has fallen over the last decade, we would expect that 'peripheral' employment (and thus 'flexibility') to be declining on the basis of the SCELI data. Atkinson and Meager's exclusive focus on larger establishments vitiates their claims of generalisability. Their ideal type does not provide a useful benchmark against which to compare the complex patterns of employment change in the UK.

Industrial Case Studies

The next three chapters all examine specific industrial case studies in order to explore the supposed increase in various aspects of economic flexibility. Elger and Fairbrother (Chapter 6) and Garrahan and Stewart (Chapter 7) look at the impact of the 'Japanisation' of work organisation at Lucas Industries and Nissan. The chapter by Leman shifts the focus away from manufacturing towards distribution by examining the gender, technology and flexibility changes in the UK mail order industry.

Elger and Fairbrother examine the process of modularisation at Lucas' Great Hampton Street works in the late 1980s. Although they find evidence of substantially altered patterns of work and occupational organisation which has posed serious challenges to established trade unionism, these changes and shifts provide little support for post-Fordist models of flexible working. The contested nature of the changes coupled with a reorientation and renewal of union organisation support the perspective that the changes are best viewed as a significant *reworking* of established capital-labour relations rather than any transcendence of these relations.

Garrahan and Stewart in their study of Nissan in Sunderland make four major points. First, the job enlargement which has taken place has usually meant enlargement vertically downwards, that is, the addition of less skilled tasks to a job. Second, task accretion has led to increased work intensity. Third, this work intensification is institutionalised through 'continous improvement' meetings and a system of worker peer surveillance, thus substituting worker-imposed for supervisor-imposed discipline. Fourth, extra-technical forms of subordination are constructed via company-centred ideologies of legitimacy based upon notions of 'togetherness' and 'co-operation'. They conclude that in Nissan, employees' autonomy, enhancement in skill and increases in knowledge are important elements in managerial strategies. The organisation of work at Nissan is not about employee empowerment, but rather the enhancement of employer power and control.

Leman reports that changes in the UK mail order industry conform only partially to the theoretical models of flexibility. Although he finds some evidence for increases in 'peripheral' part-time female employment, he finds little evidence of functional flexibility. There is some numerical flexibility, but this is not new; employment in the industry has always been cyclical, with obvious seasonal peaks towards Christmas and Easter. There is no evidence for the disaggregation of the industry; on the contrary, it remains highly oligopolistic with clear tendencies towards further capital concentration. The labour process is still best conceptualised in terms of the basic logic of Taylorist principles, albeit now in association with technological developments which allow for more precise control and monitoring of work. What is clear, however, is the gendered nature of the introduction of new technologies within the industry. Predominantly male systems designers have produced technologies which emphasise the control and surveillance of women's work.

New Patterns of Employment

The final section of the book examines various aspects of the restructuring of work and some emerging new patterns of employment. Casey and Laczko (Chapter 9) investigate what has happened, and what is likely to happen, to older workers within the labour market. Roberts and Holroyd (Chapter 10) reconsider the role of the family within industry, and they present empirical data on the material and symbolic functioning of family forms in small firms in the UK. Finally, Smith and Anderson (Chapter 11) consider the rhetoric and the reality behind new technology homeworking.

Casey and Laczko use data from the 1979, 1984 and 1989 Labour Force Surveys to show that the experience of older workers in the labour force has been highly influenced by the industry in which they were employed. There has been a growth in the proportion of older workers who are either self-employed, part-time or in temporary jobs, although most of this increase was accounted for by workers over normal retirement age. This development has led to older men's employment patterns coming to resemble more closely that of older women. They conclude that some of the changes they document might possibly promote greater levels of flexible retirement than changes in public policy.

Roberts and Holroyd examine the linkage between the family and industry in both historical and contemporary analyses. They conclude that the significance of the linkage in terms of both its material and symbolic import has been underestimated. In an empirical study of small firms they demonstrate that family owned and run firms have retained their historical importance through to the modern era, and that 'industrial relations' within such enterprises are often 'managed' by attempting to obscure the formal rationality of the cash nexus with a more traditional and affective rationality derived from the family form. Given the emphasis that the flexible specialisation model gives to small 'family firms' in industrial districts, this analysis is an important one in its disclosure of the reality of the experience of employers, employers' kin and employees within such enterprises.

Smith and Anderson conclude the collection by investigating new technology homeworking. Although predictions of future developments in this area are impossible to make, they conclude that the effects are unlikely to be dramatic. Face-to-face contact between members of organisations is likely to remain the paradigmatic practice for the large majority of the workforce. Current evidence simply does not fit any of the variety of 'post-industrialist' theses on the future of the home and work.

CONCLUSIONS

This collection of papers is necessarily a partial and selective attempt to offer a critical examination of the Fordism and 'flexibility' debate, providing alternative perspectives on the question of division and change within contemporary work and employment. If the rhetoric of the 'enterprise culture' has been held up as the panacea for the ills of modern economies at the level of popular discourse, the academic and policy analogue of this has clearly been the various manifestations of economic flexibilty. The papers presented here all demonstrate that the contradictory and complex nature of changes in the labour market and the organisation of work cannot easily be accounted for by either the 'binary histories' of the Fordism/post-Fordism variety or by supposedly unilinear social processes such as increasing 'flexibility'.

Notes

1. The best overview of this literature is Allen and Massey (1988).
2. For a detailed discussion and history of the approach see Dunford (1990).
3. See Jessop (1989, pp. 263–4) for a much more detailed twelve point ideal type of Fordism.

Part I
Historical and Theoretical Critiques

2 What in the F---'s Name is Fordism

Simon Clarke

FORDISM: REALITY, IDEAL TYPE OR UTOPIA?

There is a widespread belief that the 1980s marked a period of transition to a new epoch of capitalism, underlying which were fundamental changes in the forms of capitalist production. There is little agreement over the precise contours of the new epoch, or even over the term by which it is to be called, but there is a near universal consensus that it derives from the crisis and breakdown of something called 'Fordism'. There seems to be an emerging consensus that the 1960s marked the apogee of something called 'Fordism', the 1970s was marked by the 'crisis of Fordism', and the 1980s marked the transition to 'Not-Fordism', which will be realised in the 1990s.

Much energy has been expended in debating the diffuse characterisations of Not-Fordism. However, much less attention has been paid to the characterisation of Fordism. In this paper I want to ask the simple question 'What in the Ford's name is Fordism?'.[1]

The first issue to clarify is the scope and status of the concept of Fordism. As the term implies, it has something to do with the methods of mass production and social organisation of the labour process introduced by Henry Ford and developed by the Ford Motor Company. However, Fordism refers to much more than the technology and the social organisation of production. In the 1920s, particularly in Europe, Fordism came to be seen as a central component of Americanism, which was itself hailed as the herald of Modernism. The appeal of Fordism in Europe was that it promised to sweep away all the archaic residues of pre-capitalist society by subordinating the economy, society and even the human personality to the strict criteria of technical rationality. It was as such that Gramsci enthusiastically embraced the Fordist project in his essay 'Americanism and Fordism', and it was as such that Aldous Huxley equally vehemently rejected it in *Brave New World*, and Charlie Chaplin in *Modern Times*. However, this is not the sense in which Fordism is used today.

The term Fordism fell out of use during the 1950s and 1960s, in favour of Keynesianism and State Monopoly Capitalism, marking a shift in the focus of functionalist analysis from the labour process to macroeconomic and political relations. It seems to have been reintroduced into debate by the

Italian autonomists, who used it to draw attention to the narrow social base of the politics of the Keynesian Welfare State in the bureaucratic representation of the Fordist mass worker, seen not so much as an expression of the technology of production, but as the outcome of an historical process of class struggle (CSE/Stage One, 1976; Red Notes/CSE Books, 1979). It was then adopted by Aglietta and Palloix, as synonymous with the production of relative surplus value in the capitalist labour process, and was originally used in the same sense by Charles Sabel (Aglietta, 1979; Palloix, 1976; Sabel, 1982). While Palloix retained the autonomist focus on the class struggle, Aglietta developed his theory of capitalist regulation, according to which Fordist production is the basis of characteristic 'modes of regulation' of the reproduction of the social relations of production, distribution and exchange. According to Aglietta these modes of regulation together constitute a Fordist 'regime of accumulation' which underlay the relative stability and dynamism of the post-war boom.[2]

Aglietta's regime of accumulation was supposed to provide a way of overcoming the barriers to the sustained accumulation of capital which lie in the workers' resistance to capitalist attempts to raise productivity, on the one hand, and to disproportionalities between production and consumption, on the other. These barriers were overcome primarily by the institution of corporatist productivity bargaining, which provided both the means of accommodating workers to the intensification of labour and the means of securing a growing market for the growing product of consumer goods, while the welfare state and Keynesian macroeconomic policy ensured the stability of the system as a whole. Thus for Aglietta, Fordism was inextricably linked to the Keynesian Welfare State.

Aglietta attributed the crisis of the 1970s to the breakdown of this regime of accumulation, as Fordism reached its limits in manufacturing industry, with growing working class resistance to the intensification of labour, a slowing down of productivity growth, and a squeeze on profits, which provoked the 'stagflationary' growth of both inflation and unemployment. For Aglietta there were only two ways out of this crisis. On the one hand, there was the possibility of a neo-Fordist extension of the principles of Fordism to the state and service sectors, accompanied by an attack on the working class in the manufacturing industry, based on the 'decomposition' and 'recomposition' of the working class theorised by the autonomists, and introduced into the French debate by Palloix. On the other hand, there was socialism. The outcome could only be determined by an extended period of class struggle.

A third way out of the crisis was offered by Sabel and Piore, who saw the crisis of Fordism primarily as a crisis of mass production in the face of saturated markets, increasingly differentiated consumption, and the demands of the 'mass worker'. They saw the new methods of flexible specialisation, based on small scale, flexible, high technology production, exploiting the creativity and initiative of a multi-skilled and flexible workforce, as the basis of new co-operative relations of production. This approach was then incorporated by Robin Murray and *Marxism Today* (Hall and Jacques, 1989) into an eclectic version of the theory of regulation, as the basis of a post-Fordist regime of accumulation which supposedly provided the material foundations for a regeneration of social democracy.

Aglietta's regulation theory and the theory of flexible specialisation of Sabel and Piore have been extensively criticised elsewhere.[3] The core idea of both these theories is a post-Keynesian critique of the economists' conception of the market as the central regulatory institution of capitalist society, the modes of regulation (corresponding to a regime of accumulation) performing the role that economists assign to the market. The fundamental theoretical weakness of these theories is the fundamental weakness of Keynesianism: they criticise neo-classical mechanisms of *microeconomic* regulation, but then replace neo-classical microeconomics with a kind of *macroeconomic* sociology which simply cannot bear the explanatory weight placed upon it. Even if we grant the rather dubious proposition that Keynesian mechanisms can maintain the proportionality of production and consumption, there is no way in which they can maintain the proportionality between supply and demand for particular branches of production: wages may rise in line with productivity, but this provides no guarantee that the demand for shoes will rise in line with supply. For this reason alone the theories have to be judged incoherent.

These theories have also come under sharp attack on empirical grounds, as it has proved impossible to find any pure case of Fordism, post-Fordism, or flexible specialisation. The response of the proponents of these theories to such criticism has been to beat a strategic retreat, detaching their models from reality and presenting them as 'ideal-types'.[4]

The methodological device of the ideal-type is a favourite of sociologists, because it frees the sociological imagination from the boring constraints of empirical reality. However, it is also notoriously ambiguous. The ideal-type describes an objective reality which, while it might not actually exist, could at least conceivably exist, so that the device has some scientific value as a measuring rod against which to judge reality. Thus the ideal-type of the Fordist regime of accumulation purports to offer a model of a stabilised capitalism, in which the contradictions of the capitalist mode of production are, at least provisionally, overcome in order to secure sustained capital accumulation, social harmony and political tranquillity. Such a model may not actually be realised, but it can provide a measuring rod against which to judge the success or failure of particular societies to achieve such a stabilisation. However, to serve as a measuring rod it is essential that the ideal-type is itself coherent, which is certainly not a quality found in any of the models so far proposed.

However this is only one sense of the 'ideality' of the ideal type. The alternative sense is that of a model which describes not the objective reality of a potentially stable regime of accumulation, but an ideal, however incoherent, which significant social actors aspire to realise. As a Utopian project Fordism is undeniably a reality, or a series of realities, periodically renewed in the wake of the disappointment of failure. From this point of view sociological theories of Fordism have to be seen not as a theoretical reflection on Fordism, but as an integral part of the Fordist project. In the rest of this paper, which focuses on the succession of failed Fordist Utopias, we will see just what a central role sociologists have indeed had to play in the Fordist project. The repeated failures of Fordism have been as much as anything else the failures of the missionary project of sociology.

We need to begin our quest by looking at the Fordist revolution in production, which made possible enormous increases in productivity, but which has repeatedly confronted barriers to its expanded reproduction. The various Fordist Utopias have been attempts to overcome these barriers, on the basis of a wide range of diagnoses of the limits of Fordism. In developing the argument, therefore, we need to be alert to the question of the character of those limits: do they lie in the technology or the social organisation of Fordism, or do they lie in the wider society within which Fordism is inserted? The first point that needs to be established is that the limits of Fordism do not lie in the supposed technological 'inflexibility' of Fordist methods of production, which implies that the limits of Fordism are social, and call for social reforms to transcend them.

THE FORDIST TECHNOLOGICAL REVOLUTION

We must begin at the beginning, with the technical revolution which Henry Ford carried through at the Ford Motor Company. The story is well known, and doesn't need much re-telling.[5] There was nothing original in either the detail or the general principles which Our Ford applied to the production of motor vehicles. The decomposition of tasks, the specialisation of tools, the assembly of tools into the machine, and even of machines into the machine system, were all typical of the transformation of craft production into large-scale industrial production, a process which had already proceeded further in the US than anywhere else, spurred on particularly by the scarcity and organised strength of skilled workers.[6] The originality of Ford's project was that he applied these principles to a new branch of production, and he applied them with such a single-minded ruthlessness that he transformed the conditions of production of motor vehicles almost overnight.

Although Ford's achievement is popularly attributed to his introduction of the assembly line, and this certainly provided the most rapid and dramatic increases in productivity, this was only a small part of the revolution he carried through.

On the one hand, the introduction of the assembly line presupposed the mass production of standardised and interchangeable parts to a very high tolerance, which could only be achieved by specialist machines, which permitted both the deskilling of skilled work and the rigorous separation of production from assembly. Once this had been achieved the development of the assembly line was almost a formality. The most complex line, that of chassis assembly, took only six months to develop. Although this led to an immediate sixfold cut in the labour required to assemble the chassis, this only represented a saving of 10 hours of labour-time, or about two dollars fifty in wage costs, for a car which was selling for around five hundred dollars.

On the other hand, the development of an organic system of production internalised the sources of technological development. The fragmentation of tasks and of work processes meant that production bottle-necks were clearly and immediately identified, providing well-defined technological and/or organisational problems for Ford's engineers and production managers to tackle. It also meant that technological changes could be introduced discretely, replacing individual tools or machines or altering the organisation of particular shops, without having to transform the system of production as a whole. Thus Ford's revolution was not exhausted by the introduction of the assembly line. It did not mark a one-off technological change, but the internalisation of technological dynamism, and the incorporation of scientific and technical progress into the labour process. In this sense the Fordist fragmentation of tasks and standardisation of components introduced a new *flexibility* to the labour process which was the condition for technological dynamism, and so the culmination of the penetration of capital into production.

To avoid needless repetition the point probably needs to be emphasised once and for all: Fordism broke down what had been an extremely rigid technology, and an equally rigid organisation of the labour process, into its component parts, in order to reassemble it according to the principle of its own rationality. While there is no inherent virtue in flexibility for its own sake, and established methods may certainly become a barrier to further development, the constant technological dynamism inherent in the principles of Fordism implies a maximum of flexibility and adaptability of methods of production. Moreover, while Fordism deskilled large parts of direct production labour, it also created a need for new skills. On the one hand, to keep the line moving Ford needed a stratum of workers with polyvalent skills to fill gaps in the line, overcome bottle-necks and maintain machinery. On the other hand, the dynamism of Fordism, which had to be sustained to maintain a plant's competitive edge, implied the constant development of new tools, dies and machines which could only be developed by highly skilled workers, using flexible and general purpose machines.[7]

Ford's project was associated with a number of further characteristics which probably were essential to his own achievement, but which introduced elements of rigidity which soon proved to be a barrier to the further development of Fordism. In particular Henry Ford saw the vertical integration of production and the standardisation of the product as essential elements of his revolution. Vertical integration was necessary in the first instance because of the need to apply Fordist principles to the production of all the component parts of the motor vehicle. However, once these principles had been adopted by component producers, vertical integration presented a barrier to their further development because independent suppliers could achieve further economies of scale and of rationalisation by supplying identical components to a number of manufacturers.[8]

Similarly, the standardisation of the product was necessary at first in order to provide long enough runs to carry through the rationalisation of production and the standardisation of components. But once this was achieved standardisation of the product was a barrier to the further development of the technology of the factory. Ford's failure fully to appreciate that the key to his revolution lay in the standardisation of components, not the standardisation of the product, left open the gap which General Motors immediately filled by diversifying their model range. In this sense Sloanism cannot be counterpoised to Fordism since it is only the development of the principles of Fordism, removing barriers erected by the limited vision of Our Ford. It was the application of the principle of using standard components for the production of a range of models, and even as parts of quite different commodities, which permitted the rapid diffusion of Fordist production methods.[9]

If Fordism is to be identified narrowly with the production philosophy of Our Ford, we have to conclude that Fordism did not live beyond the 1920s. However, the principles which Ford introduced had a far wider significance than his own limited vision. Thus it makes much more sense to identify the technology of Fordism with the principles of the decomposition and recomposition of the labour process as the basis for the generalisation of industrial production methods and the internalisation of the sources of technological dynamism. In this sense Fordist technology is synonymous with the technology of the capitalist labour process, in which the social organisation of production is subordinated to the minimisation of labour-time.

THE FORDIST TRANSFORMATION OF THE LABOUR PROCESS

The attempt to minimise labour-time is not one which can be reduced to the technical organisation of the labour process. Thus the Fordist revolution involved not only a technical revolution but a simultaneous revolution in the social organisation of production. The primary barrier to the Fordist Revolution in production lay not in any technological inflexibility, but in the resistance of the workers to their subordination to the whim of the employer.

The Fordist revolution in the social organisation of work had, in the first instance, two elements. On the one hand, the rigorous decomposition of tasks, including the rigid separation of skilled from unskilled tasks, permitted the rigorous differentiation of the labour force. This was both conditioned by and reinforced the existence of a 'dual labour market' composed of a small stratum of skilled workers and a mass of unskilled immigrant workers.[10] On the other hand, the industrial labour force no longer comprised a more or less coordinated mass of discrete individual workers and work-groups, each of which was under the direction of a skilled or supervisory worker. Fordism sought to fuse the labour force into an organic whole, a genuinely collective labourer, in which the productive contribution of each individual and group was dependent on the contribution of every other. The distinction between these two aspects of the development of the industrial labour process is essentially the distinction between Taylorism and Fordism. Taylorism decomposes tasks and assigns those tasks to individual workers, while Fordism recomposes the tasks by welding the individual labours into a human-machine.[11]

The interdependence of tasks within the Fordist industrial machine makes the system very vulnerable to breakdown if any of its component processes are interrupted. Neither tasks nor workers can ever be perfectly standardised, so that a degree of flexibility has to be built into the industrial system to ensure that normal variations in the pace of work can be absorbed without bringing the whole system to a grinding halt. This may involve the holding of buffer stocks, reduction in the speed of the line, provision of a body of relief workers, permitting workers to move up or down the line, the breaking up of the process into discrete groups, and so forth. However this immediately implies that the willingness and ability of the worker to perform his or her allotted tasks cannot simply be imposed by the technology, for the flexibility which has to be built in to allow for individual variations and interruptions can easily be exploited by workers, individually and collectively, to re-create a degree of autonomy and to relieve the burden of work.[12] However, the benefits of the system for capital will be progressively eroded if it is simply adjusted to the needs and aspirations of the workers.[13] Thus the industrial system, far from providing a technological solution to the problem of regulation of labour, brings the problem of labour control to the fore. The resolution of this problem was the primary condition for the profitable introduction of Fordist technology.

The traditional method of controlling labour in craft production had been through the payment of piece-rates, with supervision achieved through skilled workers, on the basis of internal sub-contracting and the gang or helper systems. However such individualistic methods of payment were inappropriate to the new collective forms of organisation of labour in which individual productive contributions were subsumed under the whole. On the other hand, the technology could not in itself serve to impose a collective discipline on the workers. Thus labour control could only be based on a combination of the technical subordination of the worker to the machine, enforced by external supervision and reinforced by new methods of encouraging the worker's subjective motivation.

The destruction of craft unionism, which was based on job control, was the first condition for the Fordist socialisation of production, whose full development depends on the worker performing his or her allotted task, however skilled or unskilled it might be, in the allotted place, at the allotted time. In the United States employers had been able to achieve this, with Ford in the vanguard, by exploiting the mass influx of immigrant workers, and the very sharp sectional and racist divisions within the trades union movement, to destroy craft unions and, temporarily, to establish almost unchallenged capitalist control of production. However, the destruction of organised opposition was by no means sufficient to overcome the workers' resistance to their subordination to the imperatives of capital. Ford's Utopian sociological project derived from his attempt to overcome this barrier.

THE FORDIST SOCIOLOGICAL UTOPIA: THE FIVE DOLLAR DAY

The problem of workers' resistance appeared in a number of different forms: interruptions in production, deterioration in quality, absenteeism, sickness, labour turnover and the growth of trades union activity. All these problems threatened to undermine Ford's technical achievements. The first attempt to combat these problems, in late 1913, involved the creation of a new 'skill-wages' ladder, to reimpose a hierarchical structure on the labour force and to provide incentives, and a Savings and Loan Association, to combat insecurity, but this had little impact. In 1914 Ford introduced a much more radical scheme, which used higher wages and pervasive supervision in an extremely ambitious exercise in social engineering, the Five Dollar Day, which cut working hours and promised a more than doubling of pay, in the guise of profit sharing, for those who conformed to the standards set by Our Ford.

The Five Dollar Day involved a more radical restructuring of job categories, but more importantly it was used to set standards of morality and behaviour both on and off the job. Only mature workers with six months service whose moral and personal habits passed stringent tests were eligible for the bonus payments. To enable them to pass these tests, Our Ford set up churches and established a welfare and education programme to provide moral guidance, to teach English, to inculcate American values and to build the American Way of Life. Workers who failed the tests were allowed a period of probation before dismissal. The Sociological Department was set up to develop, monitor and enforce the scheme.[14]

The initial impact of the new scheme was dramatic. Absenteeism fell from 10 per cent to less than half a per cent. Labour turnover fell from nearly 400 per cent to less than 15 per cent. Productivity rose so dramatically that despite the doubling of wages and the shortening of the working day production costs fell. It seemed that Ford had found the answer.

In Europe the employers did not enjoy such favourable circumstances as had confronted Henry Ford. Not only did they face a less developed market, but they also confronted much more powerful craft unions. Although they had broken the power of revolutionary syndicalism by the mid-1920s, they still had to take account of the interests of skilled workers, and to organise the labour process in such a way as to reproduce and reinforce inherited divisions within the working class.[15] This in turn reproduced the differences in the skill composition of the working class and the institutional forms of class relations which distinguished Europe (and Japan) from the US.

The persistence of inherited forms of job control in European industry during the 1920s was widely seen as a primary cause of its relatively low productivity in relation to its American competitors. The destruction of such 'archaic' forms of industrial organisation was correspondingly seen as part of the wider Modernist project of Americanising Europe, sweeping away all institutions, cultural forms and social strata which marked European decadence in the face of the New World. Ironically this project was much more enthusiastically supported by ideologues (and sociologists) of the far Left and the far Right, including Antonio Gramsci (Clarke, 1990) than it was by employers, who had to cope with the reality of the class struggle over production. The problem was that the full Americanisation of industry could only have been achieved by confronting shopfloor power to establish 'management's right to manage', a right which skilled workers had never recognised. The dilemma faced by employers was that they could only impose such control through a destructive confrontational struggle. This was the primary consideration which underlay the resistance of European capitalists, as well as workers, to the Americanisation of European industry right up to the 1950s and beyond. While new technology could be introduced, healthy profits earned, on the basis of negotiation within the existing framework, there was no incentive to change. The fact that Fordist technology could be adapted to very different forms of social organisation of production was testimony to its flexibility.

Meanwhile the Fordist dream was not faring too well in the United States. Ford could not afford to pay high wages for very long. While inflation eroded the wage gains, the market for his car remained limited, despite the continued fall in price, and Ford faced growing competition from those who had followed his lead, but who had taken his revolution further. General Motors offered a greater product range, while the growing second-hand market undercut the model T. Nevertheless Ford remained convinced of the wisdom of his ways, and sought to meet growing competition by further cutting costs. However, technological improvements alone could not cut costs sufficiently to restore Ford's fortunes, the only alternative being wage cuts and the intensification of labour, enforced not by high pay, but by rigid and ruthless discipline, imposed by the re-named 'Service Department', with its private police force and its network of spies inside and outside the plant.

Other producers had been developing alternative, and more economical, systems of labour control. Ford's attempt to create a New Man (supported by a traditional woman) fit for his New Age bred only hostility and resentment, while incurring escalating costs of supervision and enforcement. While high unemployment enabled Ford to recruit labour through the 1930s, and he was able to use his wealth and power to keep out the trade unions, other employers were conceding union recognition and realising that new forms of industrial relations, built around collective bargaining, could reconcile labour control with industrial peace by trading acceptance of managerial prerogatives for better wages and working conditions. The development of more complex job classification and payment systems, including bonus, incentive and piecework payments, fragmented and divided the labour force, while providing a means by which individual workers could be subordinated to the discipline of their colleagues, reducing the costs of supervision. Such payment systems accorded the workforce a degree of collective control over the pace of labour, but at the same time, through productivity bargaining and the ideology of profit-sharing, institutionalised a common interest between the employer and the trades union, representing the 'collective labourer', standing above the daily conflict of interests between employer and individual workers or sections. Moreover the development of responsible trades unionism, with the ideological, financial and political encouragement of the state, proved itself a powerful force for political stabilisation during the New Deal, a stabilisation which was threatened by Ford's continued virulent opposition to the unions. Nevertheless, it was not until he was forced to recognise the UAW by a massive strike in 1941 that Ford conceded the failure of his divinely-inspired mission.

THE ROUTINISATION OF CHARISMA: OUR FORD AND HIS FOUNDATION

During the 1930s Fordism developed quite different forms of labour control from those initially advocated by Ford. A deformed version of the Fordist project of creating the New Man as the basis of a New Social Order persisted under authoritarian rule in Nazi Germany, in Stalin's Soviet Union, and, to a lesser extent, in Mussolini's Italy, in all of which the New Man was moulded not as the servant of the industrial machine but of the militarised state. Elsewhere, however, capitalists had been forced to develop new forms of control which abandoned the attempt to create the New Man, and which instead allowed a degree of negotiated autonomy to the workers' own organisations. The development of a stable industrial relations framework at plant-level was obviously closely associated with the development of industry-wide negotiating structures, and with the political recognition of the trades unions as the legitimate channel for the representation of their members' interests within a liberal pluralist political framework. The precise forms varied from country to country, depending again on the historically developed forms of trade union and political representation on which they were based. In the United States the Fordist Utopia had collapsed, to be replaced by the new dream of the New Deal. Although the New Deal has superficial similarities to the social democratic vision of the Keynesian Welfare State, it is important to be clear about the distinctiveness of the New Deal as a populist, rather than social democratic strategy (the difference was reflected within the working class in the struggle between the AFL and CIO). The Keynesian Welfare State was thus not a linear development of the New Deal, any more than the New Deal was a development of the original Fordist project.

The strategy of the New Deal could hardly be more different from Henry Ford's project, in according full political recognition to the working class. Social scientists again played a central role in developing and implementing the new Utopia of the New Deal, whose ideals were articulated by the (now largely forgotten) populist sociological theories of institutionalism. However, institutionalism rested on a naïve faith in the compatibility of capitalism and industrial democracy, which saw trades unions as the authentic representatives of the interests of the working class, and so as the bulwark of democracy within capitalism, but which failed to recognise any fundamental conflict of interests between capital and labour, so that a democratic political system could provide the framework for the rational resolution of class conflict. The viability of the strategy depended on the low level of development of the political organisation of the working class in the United States, on the limited development of trades unionism, and on the demoralisation of trades unions in the depths of the depression. Thus it was already running into difficulties in the wave of strikes and sit-downs in 1936–7, before it was given a new lease of life by the imperatives of war.

The limits of the Utopia of the New Deal became apparent immediately after the end of World War Two. The victors had to superintend the economic, social and political reconstruction of the vanquished, but they also had their own problems of conversion to peace-time, and these were their first pre-occupation. These problems centred on the appropriate forms of institutionalisation of class relations once wartime conditions had passed. Employers sought to reverse the gains made during wartime by the organised working class, while workers sought to take advantage of relatively tight labour markets, high profits, and potentially booming product markets, to secure further advances. The result, particularly in the United States, was a period of sharp, if episodic and fragmented, class struggle and marked institutional instability, whose political risks were symbolised by the left leadership of a number of powerful CIO unions.

The problem of stabilising the system of industrial relations in the US was acute, but abroad it was even worse, not least because of the naïvety of the first US attempt to export the New Deal to the defeated powers by encouraging the growth of trades unions as the bulwark of democracy and guarantee against a resurgence of fascism. They did indeed prove to be bulwarks of democracy but not, in non-American hands, dedicated to the realisation of Fordism and the American Way of Life. The rapid growth of militant trades unionism, often under communist leadership, threatened to hand Europe and Japan to the Communists on a plate.

While trades unionism would have a place in any democratic capitalist Utopia, so there could be no return to the crudity of Ford's original dream, it could not be on the terms of the New Deal and institutionalism. Trades unionism had to be depoliticised and shorn of its class character by reducing trades unions to the representatives of sectional economic interests, nego-tiating within the constraints of a legally regulated framework of collective bargaining, and represented politically only as interest groups within a pluralistic political system. Trades unionism had to be subordinated to the needs not of the working class, but of capitalism. It had to be rescued from the Reds and reincorporated into the ideals of Fordism.

Once again it was Sociology that rode over the horizon in the nick of time to provide the strategic perspective for the post-war reconstruction of capitalist class relations on a global scale. Not Ford's defunct Sociology Department, but a much grander institution, the Ford Foundation, with intimate links with the US government, and particularly the CIA. In 1948 the Ford Foundation commissioned a study on future policy whose report (the Gaither Report) was enormously influential in determining both the strategy of the CIA in its 'liberal' phase of the 1950s and the development of the social sciences. The most influential single project which resulted from the latter part of the initiative was the 'Inter-University Study of Labor Problems and Economic Development', which first bid for funds in 1951, and submitted its final report in 1975.[16]

We do not need to go over the familiar theory of industrial society, except to note that it defined an altogether more humanistic and optimistic Fordist project, which it was expected would sell better on world markets than Henry Ford's earlier offer of hard work and puritanical self-discipline. Kerr's was not a picture of industrial society as it is, even in the United States, but an ideal-type of industrial society, in which a happy, multi-skilled, well-educated, individualistic, achievement-oriented, socially, occupationally and geographically mobile, culturally homogeneous, psy-chologically healthy workforce constantly adapted to rapid technical and social change, resolving its conflicts peacefully through the appropriate channels of conflict resolution, and in particular an appropriate industrial relations system. Although for Kerr the development of such a functionally integrated society was ultimately inevitable, there were many barriers to be removed along the way, and the primary task of the Sociologist was to show how to remove them. While Ford's Sociology Department taught the New Man to behave in ways which accorded with the will of God and human nature, Kerr's Sociology Department taught the Newer Man (no – he didn't have any women either) to behave in ways which accorded with the will of Our Ford and the spirit of industrialism. Whether he (and his wife and two kids) liked it or not was irrelevant. Once he recognised its inevitability, he would accept it.[17]

STRANGE BEDFELLOWS: FORD AND KEYNES

It was one thing to draw up a blueprint of the new Fordist Utopia. It was quite another to implement it. The Sociologists and the Department of Labour, the CIA, the AFL/CIO, the ICFTU, and any number of initials and acronyms could all do their bit, but the restructuring of industrial and political relations depended on the ability of the capitalist system to offer secure employment, rising wages and adequate welfare benefits, none of which it had been able consistently to deliver in the past. Nor was it clear how such benefits could be delivered in the future, for there was a variety of diagnoses of the past limitations of capitalism, and a variety of panaceas for its reform.

In the immediate post-war period the predominant diagnosis and panacea offered by the more avant-garde intellectuals was one or another variant of Keynesian-welfarism. However, in the United States Keynesian-welfarism was associated with the New Dealers, and it was the New Dealers who bore the brunt of the blame for the post-war resurgence of class struggle in the US and the advance of the Left in Europe and Japan, so that within a couple of years there was little to distinguish between Keynesian-welfarism and communism. In Britain there was a Keynesian-welfarist strand in the Labour Party, but the primary emphasis of the latter was productivist. Welfare reforms were confined within the limits of production, while Keynesian measures were used to check inflationary pressure. The defeat of the Labour government in 1951 brought in a Tory administration which was certainly not committed to Keynesian full employment policies. As is well known, until the late 1950s Keynesian policies were used exclusively to contain inflation, not to sustain full employment by deficit financing.[18]

The framework of post-war reconstruction was by no means Keynesian. From 1947 it was unequivocally, both in theory and in practice, based on the rapid liberalisation of international trade and payments, culminating in the restoration of general currency convertibility in 1958. It was this liberalisation, not Keynesianism, which fuelled the post-war boom. The post-war boom made possible, and in turn reinforced, a 'post-war settlement' between capital and organised labour which permitted, and in turn encouraged, the generalisation of Fordist production methods. This post-war set-tlement included a greater or lesser growth of the welfare apparatus, whether publicly or privately funded, with the primary emphasis on contributory benefits for the best-paid and most secure sections of the working class, and markedly inferior provision for those without the necessary qualifying contribution record. For social democrats the achievements of the post-war years held out the promise of more: of more health, education and welfare, of better housing, of rising wages, and of a growth in democratic participa-tion. By 1960 McCarthyism and post-war liberalisation had apparently cleared the stage for the social democratic Keynesian-welfarism, which is nowadays identified as Fordism, to assume its historic role.

It soon became apparent that the growing economic and social problems were not just a few loose-ends that needed to be tidied up, but were rather a symptom of the re-emergence of the crisis tendencies of capitalist accu-mulation. Johnson's dream of the Great Society lasted only a couple of years before it was engulfed by the Vietnam War. Harold Wilson's project of technological and social modernisation barely got off the ground before it was swept away by economic crisis. The story of the crisis of Keynesianism is a familiar one, which doesn't need much retelling here.

Far from being the progenitor of the post-war boom, the growth of the Keynesian Welfare State was a symptom of the re-emergence of the crisis tendencies of accumulation from the end of the 1950s, marked by accumu-lating economic and social problems: inflation, unemployment, pauperism, urban decay, racism and an upsurge of class struggles. As we know, far from resolving these problems, Keynesian solutions only tended to in-tensify them. The rapid growth of state expenditure imposed a growing unproductive drain on profits. Expansionary policies fuelled inflationary pressures. Growing state intervention encouraged popular political mobil-isation and politicised economic decision-making. In short the relationship between Fordism and Keynesianism was about as close and stable as we can imagine the relationship between Ford and Keynes would have been!

The crisis of Keynesianism and the rise of neo-liberalism was particularly traumatic for social democrats and for the battalions of Fordist Socio-Therapists, who were threatened with demobilisation into the reserve army of Sociologists. They had to come up with a new Utopia, but one which cut all ties with the discredited past. The organised working class, temporarily cowed by defeat, could hardly provide the foundation for such a Utopia. Unable to find any other classes or strata on which to hang its vision of the future, where better to look than itself. The model of the new post-Fordist worker is provided by the new intellectual, playing at desk-top publishing, anticipating a lucrative home-based consultancy, graciously employing a

Filipino servant, and voraciously consuming artisanal products from the four corners of the globe.

There is no doubt that the world has changed during the 1980s, just as it changed during the 1970s, the 1960s and the 1950s. There is also no doubt that the social democratic, Keynesian-welfarist, version of the Fordist dream was shattered by the economic and political crises of the 1970s. However, the shattering of the dream must be sharply distinguished from the shattering of reality: the ideal of a stabilised capitalism has been a perennial sociological Utopia which has never been achieved, but has regularly foundered on the crisis-tendencies of capitalist accumulation which underlie the permanence of class conflict, whatever the institutional forms that conflict takes.

This does not mean that all Utopias are alike. The Utopias of Henry Ford, of Mussolini and of Stalin, of the New Deal, of the Ford Foundation, of Keynesian-Welfarism were Utopias which, for better or worse, seized on real historical tendencies, gripped the imagination of powerful political actors, and, for all their one-sidedness, constituted a significant historical force in their own right. The Utopias of Post-Fordism and flexible specialisation have no such vision, and can anticipate no such historical role. In this sense they do not define Utopias at all, but only vulgar ideologies, which do no more than rationalise the complacent self-satisfaction of a small social stratum trying to invent for itself an historical role.

Notes

1. I am very grateful to Tony Elger, Syd Houghton, Bill Taylor and Graham Taylor for helpful discussion of the issues explored in this paper.
2. Aglietta's theory was subsequently popularised by Alain Lipietz, and soon bred a range of vulgarised variants of the theme. A comparable, although theoretically less sophisticated, theory of 'social structures of accumulation' was developed in the United States by Bowles, Gordon and Weisskopf.
3. On Aglietta, see Clarke (1988a). On Sabel and Piore, see Williams *et al.* (1987).
4. This retreat was led by Lipietz and Boyer, who proliferated variants of Fordism with increasing rapidity. The obsequies were read over the corpses of flexible specialisation and post-Fordism by some of their foremost exponents at a conference at Arrowhead Lake in California in March 1990, which was supposed to celebrate their triumph. Paul Hirst and Jonathan Zeitlin ('Flexible Specialization versus Post-Fordism') declared that the theory of flexible specialisation proposed no necessary relationships between anything and anything else, but merely expressed the desirability of relations of trust and co-operation replacing relations of competition. Bob Jessop ('Fordism and Post-Fordism: A Critical Reformulation') declared that post-Fordism lacks both theoretical and empirical coherence. At the same conference Alain Lipietz and Danielle Leborgne proposed the ultimate in eclectic models,

based on the functional coexistence of an indefinite number of forms of Fordism and post-Fordism.

5. Beynon (1973, Ch. 1) gives a concise version of the story. Meyer (1981) is very useful. Ford (1922) is the sacred text.

6. The general principles were first systematically expounded by Marx in his unsurpassed discussion of 'Machinery and Modern Industry' in *Capital*, Volume 1, a discussion which could apply, with barely a word changed, to Ford's project. In this sense Fordism is 'a shorthand term for the organisational and technological principles characteristic of the modern large-scale factory' (Sabel, 1982, p.33).

7. 'On the flexibility of Fordism see Williams *et al.* (1987).

8. Thus the OEEC report on the development of the European motor industry after the Second World War warned against vertical integration on these grounds. The report is a fascinating glimpse of Proto-Not-Fordism, emphasising the decentralisation, multi-sourcing, sub-contracting of the US auto industry, and the centrality of the standardisation of parts to the ability of the industry to reconcile high productivity with a wide model range. Chrysler was typical in sourcing from 10000 suppliers of auto parts in 42 states, 75 per cent of whom employed fewer than 100 workers (OEEC, 1952).

9. Thus 'economies of scope', far from being incompatible with 'economies of scale', presuppose the large-scale production of components.

10. The idea that Fordism creates a homogeneous mass worker, to be replaced by the dual labour market of post-Fordism is patently absurd. Not only did Fordism create new categories of skilled manual worker, it also created a growing 'new middle class' of managerial, technical and supervisory workers.

11. Palloix (1976). In this sense too Fordism is only the full development of Marx's characterisation of the development of the capitalist labour process.

12. Thus Aglietta is quite wrong to claim that 'workers are unable to put up any individual resistance to the imposition of the output norm, since job autonomy has been totally abolished' (Aglietta, 1979, pp. 118–9) so that 'assembly-line work tends to unify workers in an overall struggle against their conditions of labour' (ibid., p. 121).

13. Of course this did not apply to the deskilling and routinisation of work to match tasks to the abilities of the large reserve of immigrant labour, an adjustment to the restricted needs and aspirations of an oppressed group of workers which proved extremely profitable to Our Ford.

14. For the details of the project see Meyer (1981).

15. Thus even Ford's attempt to import Fordism to Europe was not completely successful, despite every attempt to prevent the development of shop-floor trades unionism. C.f. Beynon (1973) Gambino (n.d.).

16. The final report listed 35 books and 43 articles as products of the project. The programme is best known from its theoretical summation, (Kerr *et al.* 1962). The original proposal was for a programme entitled 'Labour Relations and Economic Development', which sought to understand 'the position of the working class in a variety of societies' to assist 'the development of an effective American world-wide strategy'. The full story is chronicled in Cochrane (1979), which reprints the original proposal (pp. 61–73). Cochrane's work sought to establish whether Kerr's structural-functionalism had pre-

vailed over the institutionalist tradition on its intellectual merits, or on the crest of a wave of Fordist dollars. Fortunately Cochrane's research entirely vindicated the integrity of Sociology, even the 'British Marxist' John H. Goldthorpe's criticism of Kerr being interpreted as a 'form of flattery' (ibid., p. 134).

17.   The methodology of our contemporary theorists of post-Fordism is identical to that of Clark Kerr. Kerr and his associates started off with the hypothesis that all industrial societies shared a common core. However their researches soon showed an enormous variety of institutional forms of industrial society, forcing them to abstract their 'ideal-type' from any correspondence with reality, which they legitimated by distinguishing the universal 'logic of industrialism' from the imperfections of its implementation, determined by historical residues and by the character of the 'industrialising elite'. This eclectic combination of a technologistic structural-functionalism with a voluntaristic theory of history, whether in the hands of Clark Kerr or the theorists of Fordism and post-Fordism, can always cover its inadequacies by recourse to the contingencies of politics and history. However, at a certain point the accumulation of contradictions between theory and reality reaches such a pitch that elements of reality have to be reincorporated into the theory. Thus the theory of industrial society gave way to the equally gratuitous theory of 'post-industrialism', which in turn laid the ground for the theories of post-Fordism and flexible specialisation.

18.   On the whole question of Keynesianism and the State see Clarke (1988a). On the liberal framework of post-war reconstruction see Burnham (1990).

3 Where's the Value in 'Post-Fordism'?

Jamie Gough

Current debate on post-Fordism is centred on technical-organisational questions. These questions dominate discussion of the labour process, the organisation of the firm, inter-firm relations and the relation between production and consumption. Attention is focused on how, with given basic technology, the design, production and marketing can be organised in the most 'efficient' way; that is, to achieve some combination of cost minimisation, quality/variety maximisation, and responsiveness to markets. The prospects for the various forms of production organisation dubbed 'post-Fordist' are assumed to depend on whether they are efficient in this sense.

More grandly, it is supposed that the problems of the economy as a whole can be resolved by technical-organisational change. The stagnation of the world capitalist economy in the last twenty years is understood as a crisis of an old form of social organisation, Fordism, and the emergence of a new form, post-Fordism. In current discourse, these forms of organisation, sometimes termed 'regimes of accumulation', are seen as socio-economic and political structures connected to particular basic technologies, which enable sustained economic growth.

A crucial absence in this literature is consideration of how the technical-organisational questions fit with the social relations represented in value. In this chapter, I shall argue that Marxist value theory[1] is essential for giving an account of the phenomena addressed in the debate on post-Fordism and that most writing on post-Fordism illegitimately abstracts from value analysis.

My argument involves a number of central elements of Marxist value theory. I shall briefly summarise these here, and contrast them with the concepts dominant in theories of post-Fordism; their meaning becomes clearer in the subsequent discussion.

Firstly, labour in capitalist society, and hence capital itself, have both an (abstract) exchange value aspect and a (concrete) use value aspect. This duality underlies a contradiction of capitalist accumulation: for reasons of technical-organisational efficiency, that is, for use value reasons, capital tends to increase the socialisation of production, the web of interdependencies which cut across private property; but at the same time socialisation tends

31

to be broken up, in order to render labourers as abstract labourers and labour time as abstract labour time, that is, as value. Current discourse on post-Fordism focuses on the use value aspects of production, and neglects their inseparability from the exchange value aspects.

Secondly, the relation between capital and labour is not merely conflictual but contradictory in a number of dimensions. In particular, capital has both to use and to suppress the subjectivity of workers; and it has to treat workers both as concrete individuals and abstract labourers.

Thirdly, the faster the process of capital accumulation, the more it tends to overaccumulation with respect to surplus value produced, resulting in chronic tendencies to lowering of profit rate and economic crisis. It therefore cannot be assumed, as does most of the current literature on post-Fordism, that improved competitiveness, through improved technical-organisational efficiency, will lead to general economic revival.

Finally, these tendencies to crisis profoundly affect the capital-labour relation; the latter therefore cannot be understood merely through industrial sociology or management theory, as is done in most post-Fordist discourse.

This chapter puts flesh on these points. It argues that in abstracting from value relations, post-Fordist discourse greatly oversimplifies both the conditions under which new production paradigms emerge, and the conditions for overcoming general economic stagnation.

The current neglect of value is all the more remarkable given that a key text in the discussion, Aglietta's *A Theory of Capitalist Regulation* (1979), was concerned precisely to relate the labour process and forms of economic co-ordination, on the one hand, to value production on the other. For Aglietta, a 'regime of accumulation' was a social organisation of the accumulation of capital that can help to promote a sustained 'long wave' of accumulation: value and its contradictions were central to this conception. Whatever the inadequacies of Aglietta's original formulation (Davis, 1978; Clarke, 1988a and this volume), most of the present uses of the notion of a post-Fordist regime of accumulation vulgarise his conception by abstracting from the moment of value. In neglecting a whole domain of potential contradictions, they lend themselves to technical determinism and fatalism: post-Fordism becomes a 'fact', given prior to social action, to which we have to adjust.[2]

I first consider the aspect of post-Fordism which has been the most extensively discussed, the capital-labour relation within production. I argue that if this relation is regarded as one of value production, and is considered in the context of a crisis of capital accumulation, its dynamics are quite different to those that would be expected on technical-organisational grounds. The current forms of the capital-labour relation appear not as new 'models' for organising production but as expressions of multiple contradictions of value production; they are therefore subject to enormous variation, are unstable, and are open to struggle. I then widen the enquiry from relations in production to the articulation of the economy as a whole, and ask whether there is an emerging post-Fordist regime of accumulation, in Aglietta's sense of the term. I argue that the phenomena referred to as 'post-Fordism' do not add up to any such system; whatever else post-Fordism might be, it is not a 'regime of accumulation'.

My argument is compatible with the growing body of literature which criticises the post-Fordist thesis on essentially empirical grounds (for example Williams *et al*, 1987; Pollert, 1988a; Gertler, 1989; Amin and Robins, 1990). These authors point out that contemporary forms of production and co-ordination of the economy stubbornly refuse to fit any of the post-Fordist models. This paper will suggest one type of reason for the complexity of contemporary forms of restructuring: that the latter cannot be understood outside the contradictions of value production, and these tend to break up the technical-organisation models which post-Fordist theory proposes.

THE LABOUR PROCESS, CLASS RELATIONS AND VALUE

Post-Fordist theory argues that, at the heart of the new era of post-Fordism, are new forms of the capital-labour relation. These forms are able to overcome the problems for capital which have arisen within the Fordist labour process. Since they are said to be the basis for a qualitatively new era of accumulation, they are relatively stable and productive forms: they are able to suppress, or at least accommodate, conflict between capital and labour, and they enable relatively rapid increases in productivity and the incorporation of technological innovation in processes and products. What light does value analysis throw on this thesis?

I will have to consider something of an amalgam of the different views of what 'post-Fordist production' is, but this will not weaken the general line of the argument. Firstly, design, production and marketing are increasingly strongly integrated, both between firms and within them, using computerised machines linked electronically: 'flexible integration'. Within firms, the immediate control of the labour process occurs not through personal supervision but through the impersonal setting of targets and electronic measurement of output.

Most commentators propose that, within such systems of integration, and enabled by them, there is a division between 'core' and 'peripheral' workers. The core workers use advanced reprogrammable machinery and they can move between tasks. Their production is therefore flexible with respect to product change, thus enabling the short-run production of varied products at relatively low cost. They have secure employment contracts. The peripheral workforce may or may not use advanced machinery, but, at any rate, they tend to be less skilled than the core workers. Their production includes both the 'remaining' production of standardised products, and the overflows of production from the core during peaks in demand. Their employment contracts are insecure. The existence of core and periphery thus gives flexibility with respect to fluctuations in demand and with respect to different degrees of product variety. The division core/periphery often takes a geographical form.

These forms of organisation are regarded as able to stabilise class relations and to achieve consistent rises in productivity. The core workers, because of their security of employment and the possibility of rising wages associated with productivity increases, use their initiative day-to-day to resolve the problems thrown up by increasingly variable labour processes. In the longer term, they collaborate with management in restructuring the labour process, and indeed will themselves suggest changes to it. The new craft worker is born. The peripheral workers, on the other hand, are controlled by the ease with which they can be replaced.

My criticism of this argument will be internal, and falls into two parts. I shall initially assume the empirical validity of the post-Fordist account, in the sense that capital is attempting to introduce some such forms. But I shall (a) question the supposed stability and productiveness of these forms: the post-Fordist model is fraught with contradictions and instabilities associated with value relations. This suggests (b) a different interpretation of the empirical forms. The instabilities of the model are due to the fact that the post-Fordist forms of the capital-labour relation are not based simply on technological and organisation rationality, but represent forms of class struggle in a particular conjuncture. Let us take these two arguments in turn.

(a)   The Contradictions of the Post-Fordist Model

Consider first 'flexible integration'. The high degree of interdependence involved in such systems makes them very vulnerable to shocks (Elam and Borjeson, 1989), in particular, to industrial action by workers. Some of these systems involve the spatial proximity of different stages of production, as in 'just-in-time' systems of subcontracting or in the new industrial districts. This concentration and inflexibility of location gives workers in these complexes considerable potential bargaining power (Gertler, 1989).

To the extent that the labour process involves skills generalisable across firms, proximity tends to produce underinvestment in training and under-supply of skilled labour. This can increase the bargaining power of skilled workers. Thus the highly socialised form of production implied by flexible integration gives workers strong potential points of resistance – in other words, inflexibility for capital.

The class relations of the 'core' have specific contradictions. To the extent that security of employment is guaranteed by capital in the interests of collaboration, labour can use this security to resist intensification. The high organic composition characteristic of the core gives labour the power to immobilise expensive plant. High wage differentials between core and peripheral workers may help in establishing control, but to the extent that they do not correspond to productivity differences they disrupt the role of value in establishing proportionalities across the division of labour (Aglietta, 1979, pp. 144–6). Within each firm, the high integration of tasks and stages of production makes it difficult to apportion rewards according to output or effort, just as it is in flow line production. This produces a tendency to hourly and uniform payment rather than output-related payment (ibid., pp. 147–50); yet this conflicts with the individualisation of terms and employment and incentives to individual initiative which are said to be characteristic of post-Fordism. In other words, the major contradictions of the Fordist labour process (ibid., pp. 120–1) are equally present in the post-Fordist labour process. This is because the essential characteristics of the labour process remain the same: an ever increasing substitution of dead for living labour and an ever increasing socialisation of the production process in order to increase labour productivity.[3]

In the periphery, insecurity of employment produces low commitment from workers and low investment in training from employers. These tend to limit the volume of production per worker and, especially, the quality of production. In both core and periphery, then, capital faces the problem of simultaneously obtaining co-operation from workers and imposing control. The emphasis of the problem may be different in core and periphery, and is certainly different between different labour processes, but the tension between the two aims is present in all cases (Friedman, 1986, pp. 98–100).

In reality, the forms of the capital-labour relation are much more varied and complex than are pictured in the model. This is because of the con-tradictions just discussed, which tend to shift capital away from the 'pure' core/periphery solutions. For example, there are many contemporary ex-amples of workers who are skilled, have high task flexibility, or who use expensive plant, but who are subjected to insecure contracts of employment. This is done either to provide incentives to effort which security of employment is seen as undermining (for example, this is becoming common with managers), or to limit the ability of the workers to bargain over wages and conditions (for example current changes in the contracts of British journalists and TV workers). But this strategy itself has contradictions. Flexible employment contracts undermine the accumulation of knowledge specific to the firm's particular work. Flexible hours and rewards can undermine morale and thus productivity (for managers, see Scase and Goffee, 1989). Each solution has its own contradictions.

(b)   Capital-Labour Relations and the Crisis

Both the construction of 'core' and 'periphery' and their contradictions need to be theorised in terms of the particular period of crisis. I shall suggest this through a number of discrete points:

(i) A period of crisis itself tends to lead to increasing differences in the capital-labour relation. When the average rate of profit is low by historical standards, and the overall processes of capitalist reproduction are disrupted, the dispersion in the rate of profit tends to increase (more numerous losses; but some sectors/forms of capital/firms still making high profits). As a result, the wages that firms can afford become increasingly differentiated. Moreover, differences are widened by wages becoming increasingly dependent on intensity of work, willingness to accept restructuring, and firm performance. The tendency towards increased differentials is exacerbated by the increased level of unemployment; the pressure of the unemployed on the employed is always highly uneven, and tends to be greatest on workers with least skills.

These simple mechanisms, arising directly from value relations, are sufficient in themselves to explain, not so much a core/periphery *dualism*, but increasing *differentials* in wages and conditions. But they also explain the instability of the place of particular groups of workers on this continuum. In the present period, higher-than-average profits of companies, and even of whole sectors, are very unstable; and levels of unemployment of particular sections of the workforce can fluctuate markedly. Since it is dependent on these variables, the hierarchical placing of groups of workers can change quite rapidly.

(ii) Stagnant and uneven accumulation tends to have a disciplining effect on all workers. But for skilled workers there are also processes which tend to *increase* their bargaining power. In periods of low average profitability and/or high uncertainty of future profits, capital and the state tend to economise on investment in training, producing shortages of skilled workers.

Low investment in housing and other social infrastructure lowers the spatial mobility of (skilled) labour power. A lower rate of investment, in particular to introduce innovative processes, reduces the disruptive effect on labour organisation that such investment nearly always has, and also weakens a major means used by capital to deskill jobs. The reluctance of capital to invest thus can paradoxically increase the bargaining power of skilled workers, in spatially uneven ways, again exacerbating differentiations.

(iii) A period of crisis is a contradictory time in which to attempt to introduce highly integrated and/or fixed-capital-intensive labour processes. On the one hand the disciplining effect of the crisis can facilitate the introduction of such processes. On the other, the co-operation of workers, on which such systems are strongly dependent, is undermined by the need for wage restraint or wage cuts, by resentment over widening or otherwise altered wage differentials, and by insecurity of employment. Moreover, instability of employment undermines learning-by-doing.

(iv) In a period of crisis the contradiction between the spatial mobility and immobility of capital becomes sharpened – but not resolved. This contradiction has the following form (Harvey, 1982). The social nature of capitalist production tends to produce spatial concentration of production (that is, employment of living labour, including administrative, design, and similar work). Aspects of this social nature are: the mutual dependence of different branches of production, the dependence on immobile infrastructures and skilled labour power, the local circulation of knowledge, and the long depreciation time of many types of fixed capital and of 'human capital' which require complementary investments to be maintained over similar times in the same site or locality for the investment to be realised. In times of crisis, the competitive advantages to be derived from these aspects of agglomeration tend to become particularly important. As we have noted, some characteristic contemporary forms of production are strongly 'social' in this sense. But this immobilisation of capital has its contradictions. These are manifested directly in exchange value terms in inflation in land values, in the price of infrastructures, and in the price of labour power. In fact, the immobility of capital prevents it from adequately commensurating labour in different places, and thus from adequately rendering labour as abstract labour and labourers as abstract labourers. There is thus also always a tendency towards spatial mobility of capital. In times of crisis, this tendency, too, is accentuated. Spatial mobility enables capital to remove the particular, concrete ties that labour has to it, and thus to subordinate labour more effectively. Here, again, we see the production of core/periphery in a geographical form. But we also see that this is a highly unstable division:

capital is liable to decentralise from the core, or to recentralise from the periphery. The recent history of capitalism shows plenty of examples of both these processes.

Two conclusions can be drawn. Firstly, the phenomena said to represent post-Fordist capital-labour relations can be theorised more coherently through value analysis. Secondly, this analysis suggests that the present forms are episodic, a function of the period of crisis, rather than features of a long-term regime of accumulation.

Throughout this section we have seen various contradictions of the contemporary capital-labour relation. These contradictions suggest a reason why theorists of post-Fordism differ so much on what this animal actually is. Under the pressure of crisis, firms are attempting to balance many different demands of the process of value production, including conflicting demands arising from the various elements which they would like to render 'flexible' (tasks, products, quantities, employment hours, employment rewards, and so forth). Not surprisingly, the outcomes are unstable, varied and 'impure'.

'POST-FORDISM' AS 'A REGIME OF ACCUMULATION'

The claim of post-Fordist theory is not merely that there are new, stable forms of the capital-labour relation but that these are the basis for a new 'regime of accumulation'. For the meaning of this term we need to go back to Aglietta. Aglietta argued that certain social structures during the era of 'Fordism' facilitated a long period of sustained accumulation, from the later 1940s to the late 1960s - early 1970s. Aglietta did not regard the particular arrangements of Fordism as overcoming or ending the fundamental contradictions of capitalist value production but rather as giving them particular form; these contradictions would therefore eventually break out as overt crisis, and Aglietta gave an account of the crisis of Fordism in these terms. In other words, Aglietta's original formulation of the notion of regime of accumulation was rather modest compared with most contemporary usages. If, therefore, we want to ask whether a new post-Fordist regime of accumulation can be discerned, in Aglietta's meaning of the term, one is not looking for arrangements which remove contradictions of value production but merely ones which transmute them and thereby postpone the outbreak of open crisis.

Here I shall give an internal critique of the notion of a 'post-Fordist regime of accumulation', which accepts Aglietta's formulation of the concept as applied to Fordism. I do this not because I agree with Aglietta's theorisation (Clarke, 1988a and this volume), but because it is Aglietta's term 'regime of accumulation' to which theorists of post-Fordism appeal, and because Aglietta's formulation of the concept is the most sophisticated available, in that it sets out to understand the technical-organisational aspects of the economy as moments of value production. A use of Aglietta's notion at least enables us to address the questions for post-Fordism posed by value production.

A crude summary of Aglietta's argument is the following. The Fordist labour process has two crucial aspects: a high and increasing organic composition of capital, and the potential for rapid increases in productivity achieved not simply through new process technology but through intensification of work. In the 1930s and 1940s, a system of industrial relations was established around this labour process, whereby real wages increased (more or less) in line with increases in productivity. These wage rises helped to win toleration by workers of the intensification of work. The rising organic composition of capital upset the proportionality between the two departments (capital and intermediate goods, final goods) and tended to depress the rate of profit, only partly offset by decreases in the value of labour power enabled by rising productivity in consumer goods industries. This process is expressed in a devalorisation of capital, which then serves to raise once more the rate of profit. In the Fordist era this process of devalorisation of capital took a particular form. The ever-rising consumer expenditure (from wages supplemented by social security incomes), and the growth of credit underpinned by the international monetary system of Bretton Woods, enabled firms to set their prices at a high enough level to pay for a rapid depreciation of fixed capital. Devaluation of the total capital was thus carried out, not through abrupt crises as in pre-Fordist capitalism, but through continuous devalorisation. The short business cycle was attenuated, and in cyclical downturns there were few outright bankruptcies. But the consistent setting of prices above those implied by the average socially necessary labour time resulted in creeping inflation. The contradictions of accumulation were therefore displaced from their nineteenth century form, bankruptcies and abrupt devalorisations, to a different form which facilitated a long period of more-or-less uninterrupted expansion, but at the cost of increasing inflation. This inflation would become the kernel of the eventual crisis of Fordism, but since we are here concerned with regimes of accumulation as means to sustained upward long waves, we need not consider the modalities of this crisis.

What are the implications of this account for the capitalist economy now, and for emergence of a new regime of accumulation around the 'post-Fordist' labour processes and employment relations discussed in the last section? I shall discuss four elements of such a potential regime of accumulation: (i) the overaccumulation of capital; the organisation of devalorisation through (ii) the wage-price relation and (iii) the use of credit; and (iv) the wage-productivity relation.

(i) There is no less of a tendency to overaccumulate capital with respect to surplus value produced in the present period than in the 1950s and 1960s. There is no reason to suppose that the organic composition of capital is any lower, or any less likely to increase in the long term. Microprocessor-based process technologies have the ability to increase greatly, in some cases massively, the productivity of labour. Unlike the situation in the postwar boom, these technologies are being used to cut the use of labour power in office work, consumer services and design as well as manufacturing and raw materials processing. It is true that the values of machines of given capabilities are in some cases falling very fast, due to rapid advances in microprocessor technology, something which tends to counter the rise in the ratio of values of fixed capital to labour power. But in many areas these machines are being introduced into previously essentially unmechanised labour processes and, more importantly, the advances in microprocessor technology are being used not primarily to purchase and use machinery of fixed capabilities at lower prices but rather to use machinery with greater and greater capabilities, at the same or rising cost, in order to dispense with more and more labour power.

Moreover, the infrastructure requirements of the new labour processes are large: telecommunications, investment for training in the use of new technologies, the urban infrastructures needed for new concentrations of control activities, and the transport facilities needed for the ever more elaborate world division of labour. Investment in these physical and human infrastructures increases the ratio of dead to living labour. There is therefore no reason to suppose that current labour process changes have altered the classical tendency for the organic composition of capital to rise, and the consequent tendency of capital invested to increase relative to surplus value produced per unit time.

In the short to medium term the tendency to overaccumulation is governed by the processes of capitalist competition. New, more competitive fixed capital investments are made by each firm irrespective of the limitations of aggregate demand, on the assumption that these will maintain or increase the firm's market share. The aggregate effect of these investments is a constant tendency to overcapacity. There are various features of the new labour processes which accentuate rather than diminish this tendency.

First, there is a rapid rate of innovation in process technology in many branches and rapid technical depreciation of fixed capital.[4] This requires hectic investment in qualitatively new fixed capital, exacerbating the tendency to overcapacity (Clarke, 1988a). Secondly, and consequently, changes in the labour process and in inter-firm relations encourage relocation of production, either to side-step opposition by workers to restructuring, or to obtain more suitable supplies of labour power, infrastructure and so forth. Moreover, rapid depreciation of fixed capital facilitates this mobility. These shifts in location involve installation of new capacity and infrastructures. All these processes tend to sharpen the tendency to overaccumulation in the short to medium term.

An offsetting tendency is that a given rate of change in product specification may require installation of new fixed capacity at a lower rate than in the postwar boom, due to the potential product-flexibility of some new technologies. However, theorists of post-Fordism generally argue that the rate of change in product specification has increased, since the new process technologies are being used to increase the range of products offered and their rate of obsolescence. It is not evident, then, that this provides a strong counter-tendency.

We can conclude that the tendency to overaccumulation both in the long term and the short to medium term has not been decreased by current changes in labour processes. In fact, it may well have increased. Note, moreover, that this tendency, over both time spans, is the stronger the greater the 'technological dynamism' of the economy. The idea that the rapid technological innovation of post-Fordism shows that 'it' is beginning to overcome the root of the crisis is the reverse of the truth. What, then, of the mechanisms which Aglietta argued transmuted the tendency to overaccumulation during the postwar boom?

(ii) Firstly, one mechanism which Aglietta argued to be central has disappeared: wage rises across each sector of the economy are no longer increasing in parallel to average productivity rises (if indeed they ever were: Clarke, 1988a). For example, in both the US and Japan since the mid-1970s rises in average real wages have been very small and have been far less than productivity increase. Moreover, wage differentials have increased (for the US see Davis, 1986, pp. 208–9; for Japan see Itoh, 1990). The pattern of consumer incomes which Aglietta argued to be crucial for continuous rapid depreciation of fixed capital, namely incomes rising continuously and at more or less equal rates for all wage and salary earners, has therefore disappeared (Itoh, 1990). Yet, as we have just seen, if a new regime of accumulation is to emerge, some such mechanism is necessary, just as much now as it was in 1950.

Proponents of the notion of a post-Fordist regime of accumulation might argue that the relation of wages, productivity and prices obtaining during

the last 15–20 years is an episodic one, a function of a period of crisis, and that a new regime of accumulation which accomplished a new boom would involve a different wage-productivity-price relation. However, any such new mechanism is a matter of pure speculation, all the more so as the regulation theorists have been at pains to emphasise that the installation of a new regime of accumulation is largely a matter of chance (Lipietz, 1987).

Moreover, this argument concedes a lot, since it implies that the supposed new regime of accumulation cannot be read off from current trends. Indeed, one can agree wholeheartedly with the premise of the argument: that the wage relation in the 1970s and 1980s has been constructed by a crisis of accumulation rather than by post-Fordist changes in the labour process as such. The lagging of wage rises behind productivity increase, thus increasing the rate of exploitation, is a classic process in such a crisis. I have already argued that an increase in wage differentials is an aspect of the crisis of profitability. But if the current relations between wages and productivity are at least partly to be understood in terms of the value relations of the present period, they cannot be taken as representing part of a new more permanent regime of accumulation.

(iii) A second mechanism which Aglietta saw as central to sustaining the boom of the 1950s and 1960s was the expanded role of credit. Here there has been no decisive change: the credit system is no less capable now than in the postwar boom of funding inflationary expansion and accelerated depreciation/devalorisation. It is true that the means by which credit can be expanded have changed: dollar convertibility, which played an important role in maintaining international liquidity during the boom, ended with the end of the boom. But the 1980s has demonstrated that a system of floating exchange rates, with no overwhelmingly predominant currency, is compatible with massive expansion of credit and a safeguarding of the credit system. The extension of credit to companies, consumers and states played a central   role in the expansion of the world capitalist economy since 1981. In the advanced capitalist countries, especially the US, despite a generally deflationary strategy, the state has continued to guarantee private credit, particularly through the bailing out of bankrupt financial institutions.

If one used the typical method of post-Fordist theorising, one would then conclude that a 'loose' credit system is part of the new regime of accumulation. However, this would go against the predominant view of post-Fordist theorists, that post-Fordism constitutes a sharp break with Keynesianism, including Keynesian monetary and credit systems. It would mean that certain central features of the regime of accumulation did not change decisively from one regime to the next.

Alternatively, the credit expansion of the 1980s could be seen, not as a permanent feature of a new regime of accumulation, but as episodic, as part of a particular stage in the crisis of accumulation. The low rate of productive investment (especially of extensive investment) gives rise to a vast pool of money capital which seeks valorisation through interest-earning lending and speculation. Companies deal with losses or low reinvestable profits by borrowing and consumers deal with their more stagnant incomes by borrowing. The effect of this has been different from the effect of credit expansion in the postwar boom à la Aglietta. Rather than enabling accelerated depreciation of capital, it has tended to preserve the value of productive and commodity capital (fixed capital, stocks of goods) and to increase fictitious capital values (the stock market, property, and so forth). It has thereby postponed necessary devalorisation. But this argument, as with the analogous argument around the wage-productivity relation, shows that current developments are more coherently theorised by value theory than they are by positing an emergent new regime of accumulation.

(iv) A central element of Aglietta's Fordist regime of accumulation was the place of the wage-productivity relation within the labour process (as distinct from its place in the system of realisation). Aglietta argued that intensification of work, changes in the technical division of labour, and deskilling were won by employers through rises in real wages, and the expectation that these would continue. We have noted above, (ii), that this relation has not obtained in the last two decades. But we also saw in the previous section that the current forms of the capital-labour relation by no means ensure harmony. The concept of a regime of accumulation, however, requires some such mechanism.

Three broad conclusions can be drawn from this discussion. Firstly, value relations and their contradictions continue in the contemporary economy to produce crisis tendencies which hinder any new period of sustained accumulation. The claim of current post-Fordist theory, that renewed expansion can result from increases in competitiveness and 'efficiency', can only be made by abstracting from value analysis. The latter has demonstrated that competition is only a surface form (that is, real but misleading) of capital accumulation, and that increased productivity does not necessarily produce economic expansion.[5]

Secondly, the existence of a new 'post-Fordist regime of accumulation', even in embryo, is unproven. Regulation theory proposes mechanisms for transforming and postponing the crisis-prone nature of capitalist accumulation, linked to the dominant labour processes. We have seen that these mechanisms are no less necessary with post-Fordist than with Fordist labour processes, yet we do not know what such mechanisms might be. Indeed, in his state-of-the-art presentation of the regulation approach, Boyer concedes that the nature of a post-Fordist regime of accumulation is unknown (1986, pp. 114, 125, 128) (though he is nevertheless confident that it is emerging! (ibid., pp. 125–9)).

Thirdly, some important contemporary phenomena, namely the relation of wages to productivity and structures of credit, which are commonly regarded as aspects of post-Fordism, can actually be more plausibly theorised as aspects of a particular period of crisis of capital accumulation. One does not need the notion of post-Fordism to understand these phenomena.

CONCLUSION

In this chapter I have sought to stress the importance of considering value relations in discussion of post-Fordism. This is not to say that technical-organisational aspects of the question are irrelevant or uninteresting; rather that they need to be placed within their social forms represented in value relations. I have argued that a consideration of value production shows that technical organisational efficiency is insufficient to constitute a regime of accumulation, in Aglietta's sense. It therefore remains to be shown how the phenomena said to constitute post-Fordism could facilitate a long period of sustained accumulation, and thus inaugurate an era of post-Fordism. Moreover, consideration of the current forms of the capital-labour relation as value relations suggests that they are far more problematic for capital then technical-organisational discourses would suggest. One could extend the type of critique and reinterpretation given here to other phenomena dubbed post-Fordist, such as inter-firm relations and concentration of ownership. For the phenomena discussed in this paper, at least, their reconstruction in terms of value theory suggests that their trajectories are not governed by technical-organisational efficiency but by the concrete development and mutual articulation of various contradictions of capitalist social relations. These contradictions allow the eruption of consciousness, choice and struggle.

Notes

1. For a contemporary exposition and review, see Harvey (1982).
2. *Marxism Today*'s (October 1988) presentation of the 'New Times' is a gross example of this fatalism. But this can be found also further to the left (for example GLC, 1985) and on the extreme left (for example Geddes, 1988). For critiques see Levidov (1990) and Pelaez and Holloway (1990).

3. For Aglietta, the extraction of relative surplus value ('intensive accumula-
    tion') through these means defines the Fordist labour process, in contrast to
    earlier labour processes used to extract absolute surplus value ('extensive
    accumulation'). In Aglietta's terms, then, there are only two possibilities;
    there cannot be a new, non-Fordist labour process; and current developments
    in the labour process are eminently Fordist. I owe this point to Simon Clarke.
4. The rapid rate of depreciation of fixed capital has been noted by Williams *et
    al.* (1987) as a reason for the use of machinery which is technically product-
    flexible to produce relatively long runs: the large cost of the machinery, and
    its rapid moral obsolescence, require it to be in use for a high proportion of
    the week, and this typically requires long runs. This is a striking instance of
    contradiction between the technical aspect of production and its value form.
    It is however distinct from the argument I give here, since it concerns inter-
    firm competition, whereas I am concerned here with capital accumulation in
    aggregate.
5. The 'institutionalist' method of most current post-Fordist theory, of seeking
    to add a social dimension of economics, fails to construct a critique of
    economic appearances, in particular competition.

Part II
Locality Studies

4 Labour Market Change and the Organisation of Work
Al Rainnie and David Kraithman

The current ·fixation with flexibility rests on the twin assumptions that management will react clearly and strategically to a set of external stimuli and that there will be one best way of resolving difficulties thrown up by changed circumstances, producing a strategy that can be unproblematically implemented. This latter assumption holds largely because workers in this approach are treated rather like a pliable lump, able to be dissected and shaped at management's command with little resistance.

However, we should not assume that management is all seeing and all knowing. Hyman (1987) suggests that the key to understanding the notion of managerial strategy is that of contradiction: there is no single best way to overcome the contradictions between the forces and relations of production on the one hand and the production and realisation of surplus value on the other. This leaves management strategy as a programmatic choice among alternatives, none of which will prove satisfactory. The outcome, Rose and Jones argue, is that 'much management policy making and execution is piecemeal, uncoordinated and empiricist' (1985, pp. 98–99). This leaves a situation whereby the *ad hoc* tends to rule over the strategic and, further, what strategy does exist in a particular area, say industrial relations, can clash with objectives in others. As we shall see, vital here is the notion of time. Managerial tactics themselves (if not strategy) drawn up in one particular time frame can take an inordinate length of time to translate themselves into practical action at workplace level. By that time the external circumstances that 'demanded' the shift in strategy, assumed to be timeless, can change. Thus what appears at one point to be rational can, by the time of implementation, be counterproductive. To put it another way, changing external circumstances over which management have little or no control, can act to highlight the contradictions inherent in any managerial strategy far more quickly than their own internal logic would suggest.

Much of the recent literature on the flexibility debate has been based on two further assumptions:

49

1. The major stimulus for change in work organisation is, currently, change in product markets:

    > But in the early 1970s, as international competition increased and world markets fragmented, firms became more and more wary of long term investments in product specific machinery. The product market often disappeared before the machinery costs were recovered. The more volatile markets became, the more firms experimented with flexible forms of organisation which permitted rapid shifts in output (Sabel, 1989:18).

2. Emerging from these changes at the level of the workforce is a core-periphery distinction. Skilled (usually male) workers operating general machinery to meet flexible production needs become the core and various forms of marginal labour (part-time, temporary) and marginal workers (women, minorities, disabled, and so forth) bear the burden of the new flexibility and form the periphery.

    > In future, work in manufacturing will be about flexible team working with much smaller, more skilled workforces. Services will continue to provide the main source of new jobs, fuelling the continued rise of womens' part-time employment which will be at the core of the 1990's economy (Manifesto for New Times, 1989, p. 33).

We wish to question all these assumptions. In particular we wish to restate the importance of labour and labour markets as a factor inducing change in work organisation. We question the validity of the emergence of a dual labour market. Finally we cast doubt on the image of an omniscient and omnipotent management that emerges from some contributions to the recent debate.

Briefly, we wish to suggest that:

1. Post-Fordist analysis exhibits a simplistic interpretation of causality and ignores the element of contradiction in management strategy.
2. Moves towards a dualistic labour market are counteracted by the realities of the changing demographic structure of the labour force.
3. Growth in non-standard forms of employment, women's employment in particular, cannot be unproblematically lumped into a secondary or peripheral category.
4. Employer's responses to demographic change are *ad hoc* and knee jerk rather than strategic.

The chapter is based on research we carried out in Hertfordshire in 1989 concerned with demographic change and economic development in the local economy. Hertfordshire is one of the relatively prosperous 'home counties' abutting the north of London. Semi-structured interviews were undertaken with senior executives (usually personnel managers or managing directors) in twenty-nine organisations chosen to reflect the sectoral and size composition of the local economy. This is reported in more detail in Kraithman and Rainnie (1989).

CONFUSING AND DEFUSING DEMOGRAPHICS

The explosion of the 'demographic time bomb', the dramatic decline in the number of 16–24 years olds in the UK population, has been accompanied as much by hot air as fatal fall out, although in the boom counties the potential for disaster is certainly there. In Hertfordshire unemployment standing at under three per cent is roughly half the national average. The local labour market is therefore tight, and this is reflected in the decline in unemployment rates for 16–18 year olds from 17.3 per cent in January 1984 to 5.4 in January 1988. Movement into the County to counteract labour shortages is hindered by high house prices. In the first quarter of 1989 average house prices in the South East (excluding Greater London) stood at just over £81000, compared to a UK average of £52076, and £30038 for Scotland.

Local evidence (Hertis, 1988) pointed to a number of emerging trends including poaching of skilled labour, difficulty in hiring young workers, the lack of unskilled labour and upward pressure on wages. A list of job categories considered to be difficult to fill ranged from software engineers, through office staff to labourers.

Employers tend to use the notion of 'skill shortages' to account for recruitment difficulties as diverse as demographic change, low pay and regional housing market imbalances. Skill shortage is therefore a term to be used with some delicacy, often used by employers to blame anyone but themselves for recruitment difficulties. Despite these reservations it is clear that severe structural change in the labour market could cause problems.

Hertfordshire Demographics

The number of 16–19 year olds in the County will fall by 28 per cent (that is, more than the national average) between 1986 and 1993, a decline from 60000 to around 46000. Even though the decline is going to bottom out in the middle of the next decade, it seems highly unlikely that there will be a rapid return to the youth labour market conditions of the 1970s. In 1986 there were around 140000 people in the County in the 16–24 ago cohort and by 2001 that number is projected to decline to around 100000, a fall of some 40000.

It must however be stressed that though there will be a dramatic decline in the number of young people entering the labour market, overall the population of working age is expected to rise from around 628000 in 1988 to over 638000 by the year 2001 (Kraithman and Rainnie, 1989).

School Leavers

The number of 16 year olds in the County is expected to decline from 12170 in 1989 to a low point of 10304 in 1993, rising thereafter to 11447 in 1995. Retail and office work dominated the employment profile of the County's fifth year school leavers in 1988, particularly for women, with construction and engineering being as important for young men. These then are the industries that can expect to come under pressure first from demographic changes.

Employment Trends

Two trends are of importance:

1. Employment in the County is expected to decline from 393000 in 1989 to 388719 in 1995.
2. There will be an increase in demand for employees with technical, professional and managerial qualifications, in both manufacturing and services.

Employment decline can largely be explained by the fact the despite deindustrialisation the County still has a greater proportion (28 per cent) of employees in manufacturing industry than the national average (24 per cent). Major job losses in this sector (13900), primarily associated with defence and defence related industries, will not be offset by a rise in service sector employment (9900) (Kraithman and Rainnie, 1989).

We have then a complex situation whereby a decline in the number of 16–19 year olds is going to be offset by a generally static overall demand for labour, but within that, an increasing demand for qualified personnel.

The Hertfordshire Response

Although Hertfordshire employers were aware that there is some sort of problem, knowledge of the actual extent of that problem is remarkably uneven. As a general rule, bigger organisations were better informed than small, with one small employer in engineering rather optimistically believing that:

> I haven't been particularly worried about the drop in the number of young people. Anyway I always thought that it was going to pick up again after 1990.

Although the level of awareness of the full extent of the current labour market changes was mixed, every organisation visited was experiencing recruitment difficulties of one form or another. However, echoing a general feeling that emerged from the study, the Health Authority acknowledged that staff and staffing problems had been largely taken for granted until the problems became critical:

> The Health Service has a great advantage because people have large emotional feelings about the NHS and we exploit it mercilessly. For years we just relied on it. People like working for the NHS, so we pay them peanuts, treat them badly and they still come.

This was a common problem and reinforces a basic point, that even in organisations that felt the shock waves of demographic change relatively early, reaction was slow, *ad hoc* and far from being strategic.

Graduate Recruitment

Graduate recruitment is important for two reasons; first because there is going to be an increasing concentration on qualified staff into the 1990s; and second, because problems that organisations face in recruiting graduates echo many of the more general problems to be faced by employers.

One retail chain argued that the working culture within the organisation was anti-graduate and there was therefore no resistance to examining whether the company actually needed graduates. However, graduates were needed and difficulties were being experienced recruiting them. The response was two-fold; firstly, a move was made away from general graduate training to a much earlier identification of the particular area that the graduate was to focus on; secondly, responsibility was offered much earlier and promotion speeded up. This was a theme echoed across all sectors, not just those recruiting graduates. There was a perceived need not only to provide better salaries and the possibility of accelerated progression through the company, but also to advertise the fact that this was the case. In other words, good retention policies were going to be an essential element of any recruitment package, as a pharmaceutical company made clear:

> The problem is to show people that staying in the industry will give them the opportunity to be at the forefront of science research, have a good steady progression and that the money will be at least reasonable.

And the effect that this was having on wages was obvious:

> We've been putting up graduate and Ph.D. starting salaries dispropor-tionately to others for many years now. Graduates are now in at around £13500 with bonus, Ph.D.s around £16000 and we're not the best payers in the industry, though we are in the upper quartile.

In most organisations the first reaction to recruitment difficulties was simply to raise wage levels. However as sector after sector followed suit this could have no more than a short term effect. For most small and medium sized firms this first reaction was their only one. A more strategic response was usually only exhibited by large organisations.

One alternative reaction was to review whether recruitment of graduates at previous levels is actually necessary. A local authority described it as the necessity of re-examining credentialism, especially given that:

> We are trying to take in lesser qualified people. It's been forced on us in accountancy. Qualified accountants don't exist and we're having to pay qualified rates to get unqualified people. If we get qualified staff we pay the earth.

'The earth' meant around £19000 for fairly newly-qualified staff in law and accountancy. The tactic of this local authority became 'grow your own', sponsoring people through university and into proper, long-term, career paths, coupled with restructuring work so that some could be done by non- or semi-qualified staff, overseen by qualified employees. It has to be ac-knowledged that this tactic had not yet progressed beyond the good idea stage.

Further advanced was a pharmaceutical company who are intent on examining skills profiles, particularly at the graduate technician interface. The question was, were graduates doing work that could be done by tech-nicians? If so, by shifting work down the ladder, this change could be described as job enrichment for able people who chose to come straight into the company from school. On the other hand they would free existing graduates for more demanding and thus more interesting work as well as perhaps relieving the upward pressure on graduate recruitment. The process was bringing the technician and scientist grades side by side and thus providing an opportunity for technicians to cross over what was previously an unbridgeable gulf.

This, as we shall see, was not an isolated example and calls into question the development of a clear dual labour market within organisations. Difficulties in recruiting qualified staff are forcing organisations to examine and develop career paths from lower points of entry into the organisation. The necessity of retaining and developing current personnel is a countervailing tendency against any sort of dualism.

Young Workers

Given the complexity of the problem confronting employers in Hertfordshire, one could reasonably expect, firstly, a cool review of the facts and, secondly, a strategic review of appropriate policy responses. With one or two exceptions, this has not happened. Most organisations have settled for a short-term response which seems largely to consist of throwing money at the problem, followed by beating a path to the office door of the local headteachers, coupled with an almost mystical faith in woman returners as the saviours of the labour market of the 1990s.

There is no doubt, as the recruitment agencies confirmed, that a wage spiral is developing across broad sections of the local market. There are, however, a number of different forces contributing to the upward pressures and, equally, a number of contradictory elements in the picture

The first element is simply to stay ahead of the pack by leading the bidding for young workers. An example of this is Tesco, a major food retailer, who offered pay increases of up to 22 per cent for young workers as part of an overall 8 per cent wages settlement. The increases were 20 per cent for 17 year olds and 22 per cent for staff aged 16. Tescos in particular and retail stores in general, are particularly reliant on young people. Tescos have 41 per cent of their staff aged under 25. Their strategy is partly aimed at keeping labour, not just recruiting it more successfully. It is also aimed at being competitive across the whole wage/age range and therefore is increasing rates of pay overall, though more quickly for young people. The idea being a move generally towards a single adult rate.

However, the resort to competitive bidding assumes that companies know both who their competitors are and what they are paying. Even in the case of major companies we cannot assume this to be the case:

> I thought we paid well, but we don't. We pay well at the young end, but not at the more mature end and how we will stand with back to work mums I don't know. . . . We've done no work on what other people in the local economy are doing. It's that element of market intelligence that we have not got.

The local wage growth spiral is reinforced by another phenomenon: the emergence of poaching as a recruitment strategy in the local economy. Although small firms were the loudest in their complaints about wage spirals, the evidence of this and earlier studies of the Hertfordshire labour market (Rainnie *et al.*, 1989) suggests that small firms view poaching staff from large organisations as a legitimate tactic, and perhaps reflects the tendency for small firms to see training as someone else's responsibility. A small engineering firm in this study, despite complaining about the wage levels set by large firms, argued that,

> We have no difficulty recruiting skilled staff because we get them all from British Aerospace.

And another small company involved in engineering complained that:

> We have problems with the recruiting agencies pestering staff at home and in the office. They are a pain and unethical.

And yet the self same firm argued that they would always take on good engineers and were using agencies to find them. Their complaint seemed to be:

> Even the people who are recruiting for us are searching us for people that they can filch.

The knock-on effect is that other firms are drawn inexorably into the same mesh. The spiral has two accelerating tendencies. The first is that firms tend to raise wages as a defence in the face of the actions of recruiting agencies, as a first attempt to stabilise the firm and avoid losing expensive and difficult to replace staff. Secondly, firms are drawn into the process of using agencies themselves.

Competitive bidding, based on inadequate knowledge, and producing little result leads to attempted short cuts, for example recruitment agencies, which may provide partial answers in the short term but has the effect of adding another twist to the wage spiral.

The London Effect

Poaching is not the only phenomenon accelerating the wage spiral. Proximity to London has complicated but important effects. The first element is experienced by local firms trying to recruit professional staff in demand in the City. One recruitment tactic adopted by a firm in the south of the county was to offer London salaries and compete on the basis that professional staff would then have all the advantages of London salaries without the expense and hassle of travelling in and out of London. This simply has the effect of exporting London wage rates up the M1 and A1, the main motorways from the Capital, through the County, to the North.

This effect is being exacerbated by the trend toward the use of location allowances to combat labour shortages in specific areas, with many companies moving away from use of strict geographical boundaries in favour of targeting particular groups of workers or towns where recruitment and retention pressures are most acute. Flat rate increases in local allowances have been supplemented by both the extension of existing boundaries and the introduction of new allowances to other areas experiencing staffing difficulties (IDS, 1989).

Tescos, the major supermarket chain, is moving towards greater flexibility, adding a third rate to its London and provincial, designed to cope specifically with problem stores that don't qualify for the London rate. The number of these is, apparently, growing all the time. However the uneven nature of these developments can cause problems for organisations with a national profile. For example, one of the major banks pays regional allowances but not throughout the whole region of which Hertfordshire is a part. In Watford, the allowance is £1500 per annum, in Corby, nothing. This causes problems for internal transfers, particularly where the bank's policy is to recruit at base level and rely thereafter on internal promotion. This requires a large degree of local mobility. However, a move from Milton Keynes to Northampton, no great distance, would mean losing a regional allowance of £700 per annum. Therefore, the personnel department has felt unable to move anyone in this way except on a promotion, which would mean an increase in salary anyway. So moves to cope with local labour market variation can have the effect of blocking flexibility at a national level.

So far, we have concentrated on the wage spiral effect and the factors contributing towards it. The assumption has been that firms are aware of the extent of the problem and are reacting to it. This is not always the case. There are sectors that cannot compete on the basis of wages and there are those where there appears to be considerable resistance, if not antagonism, to the necessity of competing. For both, the prognosis is dire. For example, a sector dominated by small organisations, hairdressing, faces disaster. Ten years ago, the hairdressing industry was recruiting one in every forty-six of all 16 year old school leavers, an intake of some 15000 each year. If the intake to the industry were to remain at the same level, by 1993 the industry would need to recruit one in every twenty-eight school leavers.

The Government's much criticised Youth Training Scheme (YTS) is now the most common route into the industry, with around 80 per cent of entrants taking this road, but the intake is falling. Recruitment to one agency in the South-East was less than 400 out of a target of around 700 in 1989.

This is hardly surprising given that YTS pays £29.50 per week in the first year and £35.00 in the second year, compared to an average wage of £78.20 for 16 year old women manual workers in 1988. The industry is dominated by young people, with half the labour force being under 22 years of age, but shows little signs of adapting to the 1990s.

The Death of Sweaty Betty Salons

The Chief Executive of one of the hairdressing industry's major training organisations has argued that there is very little evidence of women returning, largely because the industry itself will not tolerate women wanting to finish work at 3.30 and refusing to work Saturdays. He argued that the industry was going to have to look at taking in adults and therefore flexible hours, but the message was not well-received.

> We've got an industry that sees the £29.50 YTS allowance as quite adequate. The industry has an appalling low pay record . . . we're really talking about an industry that's in the dark ages as far as its attitude to flexible working is concerned, and I think we've got a major problem and I don't see it going away without a lot of trauma for the industry.

The industry is moving slowly on the question of wages, now offering employed status to trainees, a three-year fixed term contract, and specifying a minimum wage of £40 per week in the first year, as well as contributing to trainees' travel costs. This is insignificant beside average pay rates for 16 and 17 year olds, and does not even reach the first twist in the wage spiral that Hertfordshire currently experiences.

The Chief Executive of the training body believes that the lack of response from the industry will primarily hit small firms, forcing the 'Sweaty Betty salons' out of business:

> I don't think the industry as such will pull itself round. One trend that has grown is franchising and these will take the necessary action . . . And a lot of others – backstreet hairdressers – will go out of existence.

Faced with an inflexible response to the need to introduce flexible forms of work designed to meet the needs of a particular segment of the labour market, not employers' concerns, many industries, hairdressing especially, fail the test.

The future, then, looks bleak for an important part of the consumer service industry, and the outlook overall in terms of the wage spiral effect is not much better unless you happen to be a member of the scarce sections of the Hertfordshire labour market. The unions have not let this fact go unnoticed.

WOMEN RETURNERS AND OTHER FORMS OF SALVATION

After increasing wages and industry/school links, women returners were advanced as the saviours of the local economy. In the eyes of one engineering firm:

Women returners are the great white hope of the 1990s.

It is symptomatic of how little thought has been put into this that women returners as a category, in the eyes of many firms, remain an undifferentiated mass, a simple substitute for cheap youth labour. As one organisation in financial services explained:

Someone has got to replace the young people who aren't there. Someone has got to do the work. A lot of administration is basic clerical routine and the over-25s won't do it, so we look for young people who are not seeking to set the world on fire. Part-timers coming back can exactly replace that group.

Women who are intending to come back to work in the next few years constitute an heterogeneous group, with many different skills and backgrounds and complex needs defined in terms of training and support (Healy and Kraithman, 1989). However, there is little evidence that employers in the County are aware of the nature of the new entrants or the need to restructure and reform their working, training and recruitment practices.

The results of our research would seem to suggest that although most large organisations are claiming to be or striving to be equal opportunities employers, in reality they show little practical evidence of such intention. Small employers seemed largely unaware of the existence of equal opportunities policies.

It is not just the attitudes to be found within firms that cast doubt on their ability to draw upon women returners as a source of labour. Their current form of organisation can create blockages. There is a belief among personnel staff at 'grassroots level' in national organisations that the centre neither reacts quickly enough to perceived problems, nor allows local management sufficient flexibility of response to the peculiarities of local labour market conditions:

We want to offer a menu of contracts, and not have to stick so rigidly to the limited variation of hours on offer by the company.

On the other hand, at national level, it was argued that there could be no move towards store-specific pay scales because of the need to move staff, particularly managerial staff, between stores. There are two elements to this problem: the first is that the local-national dichotomy is inherently irreconcilable. The second is more general and refers to the length of time that it takes to analyse situations and implement policies. A number of mainly national organisations have set up working parties to examine the nature and implications of the problem. However, there is a feeling that by the time their deliberations have been translated into a response at local level it will be too late:

> We can't change overnight, but to turn it [the organisation] on its head now will take ten years, by which time we will have got through the 90's and will have too many staff again.

Many organisations are experiencing resistance to the examination of traditional working techniques, never mind the implementation of new practices, and the resistance is from management. Discussing the introduction of a more flexible working hours system, a major science-based concern commented that:

> We have the expectation that support staff will be there at times when we need them. We've said we want people from 8 am to 6 pm., maybe not every day, but we need to call on that facility. I'm not confident that changes will be made in time because line management doesn't understand the need for change.

Equally, there has been resistance within the financial services to the introduction of part-time working and job-sharing:

> Managers are very anti-job splitting. Two bodies are more problems than one. . . . There has been resistance from managers who think that older people cause problems, assume they have kids and will want time off. They want someone to come in at nine and stay there.

To be fair, it is not simply managerial attitudes that are causing blockages to the introduction of work systems that might help attract women back to work. There are also structural blocks. The first is accounting procedures based on headcounts that do not differentiate between part-time and full-time staff. One manager explained the tensions involved:

> Our accounting systems are such that we still cannot take on two halves and call them one. But nevertheless our need is so great that we will take a part-timer because it is better than nothing at all.

Obviously such systems militate against flexible working hours systems. This was encountered in engineering, and in another variation, within the retail sector, in the shape of productivity indices. Viewed from the centre, a personnel director argued that:

Local management has quite a bit of flexibility subject to meeting productivity indices . . . but there is a problem with managers and productivity indices, only wanting people when they require them, not when the workers wish to work. It's a balance, it's about between when people want to work and when we need them and we have control mechanisms which show when we have gone too far.

On the other hand, a local store's personnel manager, in a different retail chain, put forward a contrasting view:

We have no official vacancies right now, but if anybody walks in then we will take them on. We had an awful argument with the region on the basis that we must recruit on a basis other than immediate need. But if we do then we won't meet our turnover per head targets because we will be 'overstaffed'. It's very difficult to convince head office that set manning targets have to be superseded.

There is strong evidence (Healy and Kraithman, 1989) that the number of women proposing to return to work in the County would increase with the availability of better and cheaper childcare including after school care. The same research suggested that the provision of childcare facilities would lead to an increase in the number of hours women could and would work.

However, although some larger organisations were exploring childcare provision, none of those visited in the course of this research actually provided any. One bank commented that:

I'm sceptical about crèches. I can't imagine how we would make it work to be honest. We would have to employ all sorts of people, nurses, doctors and so on, and I'm not certain how well it would be used. This is the biggest problem, not knowing. I suspect that all the other banks are sitting back, watching and waiting and seeing. . . . It's not a cheap operation and I'm not certain that the return would justify the expense and neither does anyone else, and that's why were sitting around and waiting.

More seriously, crèches were dismissed because:

We could fill it today with the kids of existing staff. It wouldn't give me one extra recruit and that's not what I want. . . . Whatever we offer we have to offer to existing staff. A crèche would only have the long term effect of getting people more readily back from maternity leave.

Very few organisations had started to think of the implications of attracting women returners for their training programmes. This could be disastrous, given that research on women returners in the north of the County

(Healy and Kraithman 1989) concluded that access to the right form of training was one of the principal demands of women wishing to re-enter the labour market. Specifically, training programmes would have to include aspects of confidence building and personal development, as well as skills related to new technology. One of the few organisations to confront this issue was a science based company who suggested that:

> A change in focus towards returners will mean different training needs, because they have a different orientation. School leavers for example are quite happy with the new technology, but older workers haven't been introduced to computers at school and may have left work just as word processing was starting. It's going to be difficult getting people to adapt, which throws up a lot of selection and training issues. A lot of it will have to do with confidence and reintroducing people to technology to build that confidence.

Retention

Retention is vital:

> Because it is so difficult to recruit, even losing one person is disastrous. The length of time needed to replace someone of particular skill and experience has really been extended because there is so few people to choose from.

And it is not simply money that will tie people to a company. A recent survey (Beaumont, 1989) pointed to the fact that twice as many people left organisations to get more experience than left to get more money. The survey concluded that

> the challenge for organisations lies in enabling their managers and executives to widen their experience and knowledge within their existing company rather than letting them seek it elsewhere (Beaumont, 1989, pp. 44).

And there is evidence that firms are aware of this for all workers, not just managers and executives.

In attempting to construct what one firm described as 'golden handcuffs', packages that would tie individuals to a particular organisation, managers were aware that there are contradictory forces at play:

> We give people transferable skills which means that they are poachable. But in a labour market shortage situation it is dangerous to make people tightly bound into the organisation, because you don't engender commit-

ment. The argument is that by equipping people with skills to judge our standards against others, we're giving them the freedom to choice to elect to stay with us. People locked in can be damaging.

Moreover, it is not just that unimaginative or restrictive golden handcuffs can adversely affect those that they bind. Recruitment and retention strategies aimed at new employees can also have a disruptive effect on long established sections of the workforce:

> So we have people in the organisation who've been struggling away in a particular grade for years, but some new soul comes right in at the top. And that causes disharmony right the way down through the rest of the staff.

Indeed, nearly all organisations stressed the importance not only of constructing good career paths with adequate related training, but also of publicising the existence of such schemes. However, as we have seen, it is doubtful whether the blockages to implementation in terms of structural defects and managerial attitudes will allow this to take place. For example, work reorganisation, unrelated to demographics, can raise obstacles. A financial services group described how the growth of routine, computer-based data processing jobs had opened up a void in the company's career structure with the threat of a two-tier structure developing; routine jobs at the base, highly qualified staff at the top and nothing in the middle. The task then would be to construct artificial bridges across that gap. On similar lines, in retail, the move to uniform store layout ('the manager is just given a photograph and told that's how shelves should look. We decide how often to change the design and it's not as often as previously') allied to new ordering systems, have caused problems. Stores are moving towards systems that closely resemble Just-In-Time systems, but:

> Technical change has led to a drop in job satisfaction. For the business, it's a positive step, for the individual it's negative. For example, heads of department used to be responsible for lots of things, ordering, layout, and had far more control and greater contact with the customer. Now there is no stock in the store, so she can't even decide what to substitute if one line runs out. My fear now is that the upshot will be that we will only be able to recruit people with less calibre and less ability.

Once again, work reorganisation had opened up a void that the personnel department was going to be forced to bridge. There may indeed be a dual labour market structure straining to emerge from current work reorganisation, but labour market conditions are forcing personnel departments to construct training programmes and career paths that transcend any growing divide. Furthermore, flexible working systems have to be offered simply to attract and retain people within the organisation, often in the face of management resistance. The terms of the new flexibility with respect to fringe benefits, career prospects and so forth means that both the jobs and the workers doing them cannot easily be confined to a secondary or peripheral sector.

Relocation

Moving work systems completely out of the County is also not an easy option, through there is evidence that labour market conditions are so critical that it is gaining popularity. The case of Tescos moving 700 administrative and clerical jobs from Cheshunt to South Wales has been well-publicised. The company is moving what it describes as its 'paperwork factories', large volume data handling, but recognises that even this is only a short-term solution, given that demographic change in South Wales threatens to present similar problems in the near future. This tactic is not restricted to retail, with one financial services organisation devolving as much work as possible to Ireland. If labour market conditions in the County do not ease in the foreseeable future, we must expect the trickle of organisations abandoning the area to become a fast-flowing stream.

CONCLUSIONS

In general we suggest that the flexible specialisation/post-Fordist analysis, amongst other faults, exhibits too simplistic an interpretation of causality. Moves towards a single dominant paradigm are viewed as being a uniform unopposed march in a particular direction. This ignores the element of contradiction that is central to the notion of management strategy. There may be an underlying trend in management philosophy and work organisation in a particular direction, but it cannot be assumed that this can be simply and unproblematically implemented.

We have seen with sectors as diverse as retail, pharmaceuticals and financial services that moves toward a clear dual labour structure within the individual organisation run up against the realities of the external labour market. Recruitment difficulties require the construction of internal career ladders that transcend any growing divide. This serves to reinforce the point made by Edwards and Sisson that, in opposition to post-Fordist analysis,

the growth in non-standard forms of employment may reflect not so much a conscious strategy on the part of employers as a response to changes in the supply of labour, especially shortages of young people and the need to replace them often with married women (Edwards and Sisson, 1989, p. 2)

However, employer reaction was *ad hoc* and based on partial and often misleading information. For example, it is clear that employers' perceptions of the character of women returners, viewed primarily as cheap and simple substitutes for increasingly scarce young labour, are well removed from the actual wants, needs and aspirations of potential women returners ·(Healy and Kraithman, 1989). It is hardly surprising to find that most employers' reactions are slow, non-existent or appear to fly in the face of labour market realities.

Such moves that are being made in the direction of workplace and child care provision, managed career breaks, and so on call into question the validity of lumping all part time work and workers into a single category of peripheral work forms. The necessity for personnel departments of having to cope with adverse effects of work organisation (JIT) systems by constructing complex training and career progression programmes undermines the dualistic structure and reinforces the point that managerial strategies in particular areas can throw up contradictions in others. Flexibility is being demanded, but as much by the need to cope with a recruitment crisis as by a change in the nature of competition (though we do not underestimate the power of this stimulus). However, flexibility in this sense is encountering resistance from management as much as from workers and the outcome is a form of work that is increasingly parting company from the image suggested by any of the accounts of flexible specialisation.

We have then a situation whereby flexible working patterns are being introduced, albeit in a piecemeal fashion, as a means of attracting a particular segment of the labour market. In some sense it is flexibility in the interests of labour rather than being part of the construction of an homogenous secondary sector. This must call into question the validity or usefulness of the concept of flexibility as either a global description or an analysis of current changes in labour market structure.

5 Flexibility in Britain during the 1980s: Recent Empirical Evidence

Roger Penn

In recent years there has been an increasing literature that has argued that Britain is experiencing an increase in 'flexibility'. Newspaper commentaries[1] and various surveys[2] have suggested that the 'Thatcher decade' has been characterised by the advent of the 'flexible firm'. This line of reasoning received a major boost with the publication of a report by the Institute for Manpower Studies at Sussex University for the National Economic Development Office (NEDO) in 1986. The NEDO Report, *Changing Working Patterns* by Atkinson and Meager, has become the cornerstone of an increasingly ideological, polemical and fractious debate about the nature of contemporary socio-economic structures.[3] However, few, if any, have scrutinised either its empirical evidence or its central methodological underpinnings. The purpose of this chapter is to provide a careful examination of the evidence provided by Atkinson and Meager and then to contrast their theses with the results of a survey of 954 establishments undertaken as part of the UK Economic and Social Research Council's (ESRC) Social Change and Economic Life Research Initiative in 1986 and 1987.

Atkinson suggests that firms, 'are really looking for three kinds of flexibility – functional, numerical and financial' (Atkinson, 1984a, p. 28). He presents his model of the flexible firm in a famous diagram that has been reproduced in most of his subsequent publications (Figure 5.1).

Atkinson argues that functional flexibility or 'multiskilling' is sought amongst core employees within the firm. Other categories of employment are subject to strategies of 'peripheralisation'. This can involve numerical flexibility with its possibilities for increasing the numbers of part-timers, short-term contractees, Youth Training Scheme trainees or job sharers to maximise the 'fit' between a firm's needs and its employment practices. He suggests that pay flexibility is also sought, partly to purchase the functional flexibility outlined above and partly as the key to a global transformation of the effort-bargain within the firm.

The causes of these developments are laid out clearly by Atkinson at various stages in his argument. They can be characterised as 'generic' and

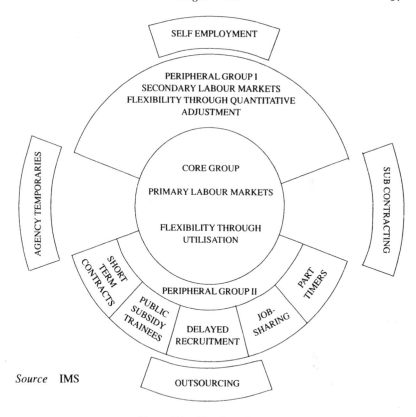

Figure 5.1   The flexible firm

'conjunctural'. Figure 5.2 displays the logic of Atkinson (and Meager's) model in its essential form. According to the argument, British firms have experienced greater competitive pressures and greater uncertainties[4] during the 1980s. This has both caused *and* been affected by technological change. The rational response of a firm to such pressures will be the implementation of a strategy of flexible employment. These take a variety of forms but, in Atkinson's eyes, they are essentially *additive*.

There are a series of methodological problems with Atkinson and Meager's NEDO research. The first centres upon their exclusive focus on large firms. The authors state that this 'was agreed with the sponsors of the study on the simple grounds that small firms are by their very nature more "flexible" than large, more informal, more bureaucratic organisations' (Atkinson and Meager, 1986, p. 90). However, in terms of their own

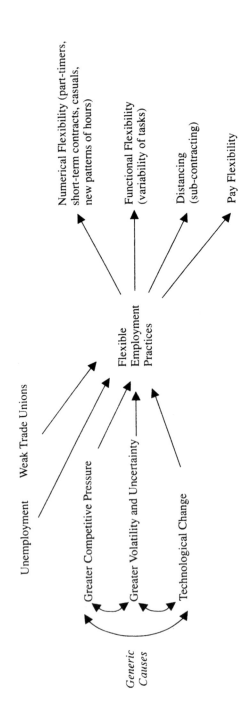

Figure 5.2 Atkinson and Meager's model of the flexible firm

operational definitions of flexibility outlined earlier, such an assertion makes little sense. Considerable organisational capacities are likely prerequisites for a managerial strategy of widespread flexibility. The managerial time and effort required for the organisation of part-timers or for the monitoring of sub-contractors are both obvious examples of this point. 'Flexibility' in the authors' own definition is not necessarily synonymous with formality. Furthermore, Atkinson and Meager fail to examine the effects of variations in size upon flexibility within their own data set. Indeed, their research displays a remarkable lack of clarity about the precise unit of analysis utilised. Sometimes it would appear as if the focus on large units refers to establishment size, sometimes to corporate size and, on occasions, to divisional size within companies.[5]

There are also considerable peculiarities surrounding the sample itself. This cover 72 firms in four industrial sectors. The sample includes engineering, food and drink, retail and financial services. It is not clear why these sectors were selected nor which parts of engineering – itself a very broad set of related industries – were selected. Atkinson and Meager provide no proper defence for these arbitrary industrial selections nor any estimates of their typicality. In additional, there is a considerable geographical bias to the sample. Only one out of the 72 companies studied was identified as being from North-West England. On the other hand, ten were clearly from the South-East/South.

Finally, Atkinson and Meager often utilise odd base referents for their empirical analysis of flexibility. They generally exclude firms not seeking flexibility from both their tabulations and subsequent discussions. In fact, they normally contrast 'successful' with 'unsuccessful' firms within the sub-set of firms that are seeking flexibility, rather than 'flexible' from 'non-flexible' firms. This sleight of hand facilities a systematic exaggeration of the actual levels of flexibility within the 72 firms that they examined.

The debate about the flexible firm has become bogged down in an ideological and value-laden debate. Atkinson and Meager themselves encourage such a discursive 'turn' by their own prescriptive use of their model. Nevertheless, the model of the flexible firm is a useful heuristic tool. It does possess *prima facie* a certain degree of plausibility. It is certainly amenable to operationalisation and, therefore, to critical empirical scrutiny. Nevertheless, commentators have not, in the main, adopted such a strategy. The main purpose of this chapter is to fill this gap and to examine Atkinson and Meager's arguments in detail in order to assess their empirical validity.

The analysis in this chapter is structured around an attempt to discover the extent to which there has been a general movement towards flexibility in Britain in the 1980s. It is focused explicitly on establishments in six localities – Aberdeen, Coventry, Kirkcaldy, Northampton, Rochdale and Swindon. Such a sample has the advantage that it permits an examination of locality variations in the extent of flexibility, something completely ignored by Atkinson and Meager. The sample of 954 establishments covers all the major Standard Industries, thereby permitting an assessment of the relationship between industrial sector and flexibility. The focus of the analysis is mainly upon part-time and other 'peripheral' forms of employment. In the latter section, the chapter also provides data on the extent to which new forms of management had emerged in Britain by early 1987. This chapter does not discuss functional flexibility or sub-contracting since these have been dealt with elsewhere.[6]

THE MAIN PARAMETERS OF THE DATA

The data comprise 954 completed telephone interviews with establishments employing twenty or more employees collected by the Policy Studies Institute (PSI) for the ESRC's Social Change and Economic Life Initiative in the winter of 1986 and 1987. The interviews were conducted in Aberdeen (217), Coventry (156), Kirkcaldy (126), Northampton (157), Rochdale (122) and Swindon (176). The firms were selected from a list of employers taken from 1000 interviews with adults between 20 and 60 years of age conducted in each of the localities for the Initiative by Public Attitude Surveys earlier in 1986.

As is clear from Figure 5.3, the six localities varied considerably in terms of the effects of the economic depression which struck Britain after 1979. At one extreme, unemployment in Rochdale rose from 6.0 per cent in 1979 to around 18 per cent throughout the period from 1981 to 1986. At the other, unemployment in Aberdeen oscillated around 6 per cent throughout the period between 1981 and 1988. This paper uses the variable 'locality' as a proxy for these variations in employment trajectories during the 1980s.

The establishments surveyed by telephone covered a wide variety of sizes. Size of establishment also varied to some degree across the six localities (see Table 5.1).

As is clear from Table 5.1, there were relatively few larger establishments in Rochdale and relatively more in Coventry. This reflected the differing structure of manufacturing industries in the two towns. Coventry contained a significant number of very large assembly plants, many of which were connected with the automobile industry, whereas Rochdale remained a centre of medium-sized specialist machinemakers and industrial

% UNEMPLOYED

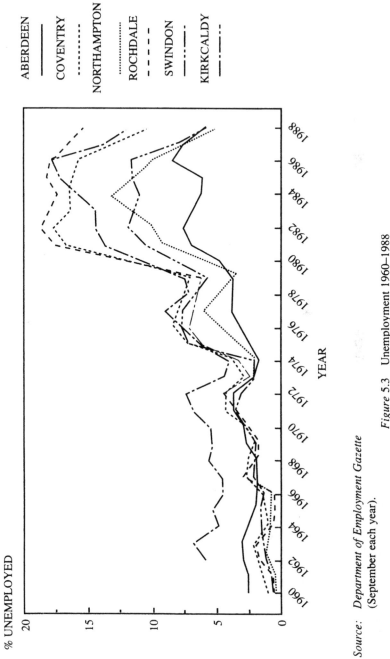

ABERDEEN ——
COVENTRY – – –
NORTHAMPTON ·····
ROCHDALE – –
SWINDON –·–·–
KIRKCALDY –··–··–

Source: *Department of Employment Gazette*
(September each year).

Figure 5.3   Unemployment 1960–1988

Table 5.1   The relationship between size of establishment and locality (percentages)

	20–99	100–499	500+	N
Aberdeen	51.4	38.4	10.2	216
Kirkcaldy	50.8	38.1	11.1	126
Rochdale	52.5	41.8	5.7	122
Coventry	48.4	34.8	16.8	155
Northampton	47.1	39.5	13.4	157
Swindon	46.0	41.5	12.5	176

textile manufacturers. Nevertheless, the broad pattern of establishment sizes was similar across the six localities.

There was a significant difference between the six areas when the industrial profile of their sampled establishments was examined as is evident from Table 5.2.

Aberdeen contained almost all the primary (oil) and energy-related establishments. Likewise, two-thirds of the textile establishments were located in Rochdale. The Coventry sample contained a relatively high proportion of metalworking establishments. These patterns confirm the continued historical specificity of employment in these localities. In the case of Rochdale, textiles have been heavily concentrated there since the mid-nineteenth century. Similarly, engineering has dominated employment in manufacturing in Coventry throughout the twentieth century. The prominence of oil in Aberdeen is far more recent. Overall, therefore, we can conclude that there is a statistically significant relationship between locality and industrial sector within the Policy Studies Institute telephone survey.

Nearly half of the establishments reported increases in the number of employees over the previous five years (Table 5.3). The size of establishments had risen most in Swindon and Northampton, both of which have been relatively buoyant economically during the 1980s (see Figure 5.3). Decreases were nearly as common as increases in the other four localities. In the cases of Rochdale, Coventry and Kirkcaldy this partly reflected the general high levels of unemployment during the 1980s and in the case of Aberdeen it reflected the difficulties in the oil and oil-related sectors at the time of the survey.

There was also a strong relationship between changes in numbers employed and industrial sector (Table 5.4). Expansion of numbers was most marked in private sector services such as financial, business, retail and wholesale services. On the other hand, contraction of numbers was most

Table 5.2 The relationship between locality and industrial sector (establishments employing 20 or more persons)

	Primary/ minerals	Metal-working	Textiles	Other manu-facturing	Construction	Government & public services	Financial/ business services	Retail/ wholesale	Other services
Aberdeen	36	15	3	17	17	56	18	26	29
Kirkcaldy	1	23	2	22	7	38	6	15	12
Rochdale	–	18	14	27	5	29	1	12	16
Coventry	3	43	4	19	3	36	6	23	19
Northampton	–	20	–	36	5	45	13	22	16
Swindon	3	29	–	27	5	47	11	29	25
N	43	148	23	148	42	251	55	127	117

Table 5.3   Establishment size, 1981/2 to 1986/7, by locality (percentages)

	Increasing	Decreasing	Constant	Don't know
Aberdeen	41.3	38.3	18.4	1.9
Kirkcaldy	40.2	32.5	24.8	2.6
Rochdale	39.8	38.9	17.7	3.5
Coventry	42.7	37.1	15.4	4.9
Northampton	55.9	23.4	19.3	1.4
Swindon	56.2	20.4	19.1	4.3
N	410	281	168	27
%	46.3	31.7	19.0	3.0

Table 5.4   Changes in numbers employed by industrial sector (percentages)

	More	Less	Same	Don't know
Primary/minerals	42.5	40.0	17.5	–
Metalworking	37.9	47.0	12.9	2.3
Textiles	42.9	38.1	19.0	–
Other manufacturing	45.3	33.8	19.8	1.4
Construction	28.6	54.8	14.3	2.4
Government & public services	44.4	26.8	22.8	6.0
Financial/business services	59.2	12.2	24.5	4.1
Retail & wholesale	55.2	27.6	14.7	2.6
Other services	56.7	20.6	21.6	1.0
N	410	281	168	27
%	46.3	31.7	19.0	3.0

evident in construction and metalworking. Expansion was reported more often than contraction throughout the service sector and within textiles and 'other manufacturing' plants. In the case of textiles such results are explicable in terms of the specific chronology of employment change within the industry. The major contraction of textile employment in Britain took place between 1978 and 1982 and by 1986 the industry had become one of the most profitable in Britain and was expanding from the depths of the earlier depression (Penn, Scattergood and Martin, 1991).

The PSI data covered almost 1000 establishments in six localities in Britain in 1986–7. The locality samples are similar in terms of the relative size of establishments within each sample but quite dissimilar in relation to the industrial composition of such establishments. Such data provide a powerful base from which to assess the validity of claims that Britain has witnessed an expansion of flexibility during the 1980s. Indeed, the PSI data permit an analysis of three sets of inter-related themes, all of which are integral to the flexibility debate. The questionnaire posed questions to respondents about the following issues:

1. The extent of and changes to the numbers of part-time employees between 1981–2 and 1986–7.
2. The extent of and changes to the numbers of other 'peripheral' employees during this period.
3. The extent of 'flexible' employment practices by management.

The following section will examine each of these sets of changes in turn.

ANALYSIS OF THE RESULTS

Part-Time Employment

It is clear from Table 5.5 that in every locality the number of part-timers had remained the same between 1981–2 and 1986–7 more often than it had changed. The relative stasis of part-time employment contrasts with the changes in the total numbers employed (see Table 5.4). Part-time employment expanded the most within establishments in Swindon and Northampton and least in Kirkcaldy and Coventry. Indeed, in the latter case there were almost as many establishments reporting decreases in part-time employment as reporting increases. However, these apparent locality differences were mainly explicable in terms of the industrial mix of the six locality sub-samples.

As is evident from Table 5.6, there are a series of major sectoral differences in the trajectories of part-time employment. In the primary/minerals sector (most of which comprised the oil industry in Aberdeen) part-timers either rarely or never exist. The textile establishments (most of which are located in Rochdale) have witnessed a dramatic elimination of part-time

Table 5.5   Changes in the number of part-timers 1981/2 to 1986/7 (percentages)

	More	Less	Same	Never had any	Don't know
Aberdeen	21.7	11.6	45.9	17.4	3.4
Kirkcaldy	17.9	12.0	48.7	13.7	7.7
Rochdale	20.4	16.8	49.6	8.0	5.3
Coventry	19.6	18.9	39.2	14.0	8.4
Northampton	27.8	15.3	45.1	9.0	2.8
Swindon	28.3	9.4	42.6	15.1	4.4
N	202	121	397	118	45
%	22.9	13.7	45.0	13.4	5.1
Private Sector	18.9	15.9	43.4	18.1	3.6
Public Sector	31.4	8.9	48.2	3.2	8.2

Table 5.6   Changes in the numbers of part-timers by industrial sector (percentages)

	More	Less	Same	Never had any	Don't know
Primary/ minerals	5.0	5.0	45.0	40.0	5.0
Metalworking	11.4	14.4	47.7	22.0	4.5
Textiles	9.5	47.6	38.1	4.8	–
Other manufacturing	8.6	19.4	49.6	19.4	2.9
Construction	16.7	14.3	35.7	31.0	2.4
Government & public services	32.7	9.7	47.2	2.4	8.1
Financial & business services	26.5	14.3	42.9	12.2	4.1
Retail & wholesale	39.1	11.3	37.4	7.8	4.3
N	202	121	397	118	45
%	22.9	13.7	45.0	13.4	5.1

employment. This is part of a longer secular trend that has witnessed the elimination of much part-time employment in textiles (Penn, Scattergood and Martin, 1991). Overall, throughout manufacturing establishments in the sample, part-time employment has decreased far more often than it has increased.

Such results are consistent with other recent research that has demonstrated a significant decline in part-time employment in manufacturing industries in Britain since 1971 (Elias, 1989). This is in dramatic contrast with both retail and wholesale, and government and public services where part-time employment has expanded far more often than it has decreased (by a factor of around three and a half). The reasons given by respondents for such expansion of part-time employment contrast interestingly between these two sub-sectors of service employment. In the case of retail and wholesale, 'pressure on wage costs', 'rationalisation' and the explicit drive for 'flexibility' were most often mentioned. In government and public services, 'workers' preferences', 'company strategy' and 'flexibility' were the most frequent responses. However, amongst textile establishments new forms of shift work, 'rationalisation' and 'company strategy' were also the reasons most often provided for the elimination of part-time employment! Clearly, 'company strategy' and 'rationalisation' can be seen as leading to either an increase *or* a decrease in the employment of part-timers depending upon the specific industrial context.

'Peripheral' Employment

The PSI telephone questionnaire also sought answers about other forms of 'peripheral' employment apart from part-time employment. Respondents were asked about the employment of agency workers, contractors' staff working on the establishment's premises, workers on short-term contracts, casual workers and homeworkers or outworkers. It is evident from Table 5.7 that workers on short-term contracts, contractors' staff and casual workers were common in establishments in all six localities. Home or outworkers were generally infrequent and agency workers featured relatively often in Swindon and to a lesser extent in Northampton, Coventry and Aberdeen. Nevertheless, apart from the one exception concerning agency workers and contractors' staff in Swindon, it is apparent that the majority of the establishments in each locality did not employ people in each of the specific category of peripheral employees at the time of the survey.

There are, nevertheless, tremendous variations between establishments in differing industrial sectors across the six localities (Table 5.8). The employment of agency workers was the rule in primary/minerals (that is,

Table 5.7 Peripheral employees in the six localities (percentages)

	Aberdeen	Kirkcaldy	Rochdale	Coventry	Northampton	Swindon
Agency workers	40.5	27.7	30.3	42.9	47.8	58.0
Contractors' staff	44.7	38.8	45.1	49.3	45.8	52.8
Short-term contracts	45.2	50.0	39.3	53.2	47.8	44.3
Casual workers	32.7	33.3	35.2	42.3	40.8	44.3
Home/outworkers	3.7	4.8	7.4	6.4	13.4	8.5
Total	217	126	122	156	157	176

Table 5.8 Peripheral employees by industrial sector (percentages)

	Primary/ minerals	Metal-working	Textiles	Other manu-facturing	Construction	Government & public services	Financial/ business services	Retail/ wholesale	Other services
Agency workers	74.4	53.4	21.7	52.7	64.3	23.9	61.8	37.8	35.0
Contractors' staff	65.1	54.7	56.5	50.7	52.4	43.0	36.4	42.5	35.9
Short-term contracts	48.8	45.9	30.4	41.2	40.5	62.9	45.5	34.6	37.6
Casual workers	25.6	25.7	34.8	41.2	33.3	42.2	41.8	40.2	44.4
Home/ outworkers	2.3	9.5	26.1	15.5	7.1	2.0	7.3	4.7	6.0
N	43	148	23	148	42	251	55	127	117

Table 5.9   Peripheral employees by size of establishment (percentages)

	29–49	50–99	100–249	250–499	500–999	1000+
Agency workers	22.9	38.6	47.1	53.4	67.6	77.3
Contractors' staff	32.4	36.7	50.2	61.2	72.1	72.7
Short-term contracts	31.7	41.0	51.4	52.6	70.6	81.8
Casual workers	29.4	38.5	40.4	43.1	41.2	54.5
Home/outworkers	4.2	10.5	8.2	5.2	7.4	9.1
N	262	210	255	116	68	44

Table 5.10   Peripheral employees by changing size of establishment (percentages)

	Size increasing	*Size decreasing*	*Size constant*
Agency workers	55.3	52.8	43.4
Contractors' staff	55.6	68.9	46.5
Short-term contracts	59.9	56.6	51.2
Casual workers	49.7	40.4	48.8
Home/outworkers	9.9	8.5	7.0
N	342	235	129

oil) and construction sites. Their use was very infrequent in both textiles and government and public services. Contractors' staff were again the norm in the oil industry and common in manufacturing plants. They were less frequently employed in the service sector. Almost two-thirds of government and public services' establishments utilised employees on short-term contracts. Apart from this, there was little difference between other industrial sectors in the employment of such workers. Casual employment was infrequent in oil and engineering plants and, rather surprisingly, on construction sites. Homeworkers only featured to any extent in manufacturing plants, particularly within textiles. Most of the latter employees were involved in the 'making-up' area of textiles which merges into the clothing industry.

There was a strong relationship between the size of the establishment and its likelihood of employing all categories of 'peripheral' employees apart from home- or outworkers (Table 5.9). In the case of agency workers, contractors' staff and short-term contractees, there was a monotonic rise in the likelihood of the employment of such employees as the size of establishment rises. For casual workers, there was also a similar broad trend overall. However, there was little evidence of any significant relationship between the employment of 'peripheral' workers and the *changing size* of the establishment itself (Table 5.10). Overall, such employees were just as likely to be found in expanding as in contracting sites of employment.

Flexible Management

Establishments were asked a series of questions about flexible forms of management. They were asked whether they had introduced a series of specific changes during the preceding two years (Table 5.11). Few establishments had increased shift working or increased the use of work measurement and method study. Almost half the establishments had increased their use of individual pay incentives but far fewer had increased their use of group pay incentives. On each of these items (apart from work measurement), private sector establishments were more likely to have promoted such changes than public sector ones. However, in the case of the replacement of full-timers by part-timers the converse was true, although most establishments reported no such changes (Table 5.12). There were significant differences between establishments in different industrial sectors. In-

Table 5.11   Flexible management in the 1980s: changes between 1984/5 and 1986/7

	% Yes		
	Total	*Public*	*Private*
Increased shift working	21.4	8.2	25.9
Increased use of group pay incentives	21.3	16.8	22.8
Increased use of individual pay incentives	45.7	34.2	49.5
Increased use of work measurement/method study	27.4	30.4	26.4
Replacement of some full-timers by part-timers	16.6	29.9	12.2
Replacement of some employees by agency, contract, casual or temporary workers	14.1	12.0	14.8
N	733	184	549

Table 5.12 Flexible management in the 1980s: changes by industrial sector

	Primary/ minerals	Metal-working	Textiles	Other manu-facturing	Construction	Government & public services	Financial/ business services	Retail/ wholesale	Other services
Increased shift working	12.8	33.9	44.4	23.4	2.9	10.0	24.4	31.3	13.9
Increased use of group pay incentives	7.7	30.6	16.7	25.8	11.4	16.3	17.8	31.2	10.1
Increased use of individual pay incentives	43.6	45.2	50.0	46.8	48.6	28.8	51.1	57.8	58.2
Increased use of work measurement/ method study	12.8	23.4	22.2	33.9	28.6	28.1	26.7	31.2	25.3
Replacement of some full-timers by part-timers	0.0	3.2	11.1	7.3	5.7	33.1	13.3	25.7	22.8
Replacement of some employees by agency, contract, casual or temporary workers	5.1	11.3	22.2	16.1	22.9	13.1	22.2	11.9	13.9
N	39	124	18	124	35	160	45	109	79

creased shift-working and increased pay incentives were far less frequent in government and public services than in manufacturing or service sector sites. On the other hand, the replacement of full-timers by part-timers was relatively most frequent (albeit infrequent absolutely) in government and public services.

CONCLUSIONS

Size of Workforces

The size of establishments' workforces had changed considerably during the period between 1981–2 and 1986–7. More establishments reported increases in size than reported decreases. Overall, almost 80 per cent of establishments interviewed reported changes in size. There was a pronounced tendency for establishments to have increased in size more often in Northampton and Swindon. This was primarily the result of the sectoral balance of establishments in the respective locality sub-samples. Northampton and Swindon had a relatively large proportion of employment in the three industrial sectors with the highest rates of increase – financial and business services, retail and wholesale and 'other services'.

Part-Time Employment

Unlike overall employment, part-time employment was far more likely to have remained static during the preceding five years. Where part-time employment had changed, it was almost as likely to have fallen as it was to have risen in the various localities. The small locality effects were again mainly the result of the differing sectoral mixes of the sub-samples and, by extension, of the differing overall employment profiles in the six towns. Part-time employment was more likely to have fallen in manufacturing (particularly in textiles) and more likely to have risen in the service sector (notably in retail and wholesale). Such results parallel a range of research findings that has revealed this to be the general pattern of recent employment change in Britain (Martin and Roberts, 1984; Corry and Blanchflower, 1987; and Elias, 1989). The reasons given by respondents were interesting insofar as the same rationale could be provided for increasing the number of part-timers as for decreasing the number. Such findings about part-time employees strongly support the notion that there is *no single economic logic or rationale that underpins managements' employment policies in contemporary Britain.*

Peripheral Employment

There was considerable evidence to support the notion that many establishment utilised most types of peripheral employment apart from home or outworkers. Nevertheless, apart from agency workers and contractors' staff in Swindon, the majority of establishments surveyed did not utilise each of the types of peripheral employment examined. Whilst there was only a small locality effect, there were dramatic industrial-sector and size effects. Agency workers were routinely used in oil where unions are scarcely recognised but infrequently utilised in government and public services and textiles, both of which are highly unionised sectors (94 per cent of government and public services' establishments dealt with unions, as did 79 per cent of textile plants) where trade unions oppose the use of agency workers. Contractors' staff were again the norm in oil and common in manufacturing plants. Subsequent research on a sub-sample of manufacturing establishments in Rochdale has shown that, whilst contractors' staff are not uncommon, they are marginal to production and are normally utilised for annual shutdowns or specialist maintenance (Penn, 1991b). Contractors' staff are less frequently used in the service sector and where utilised they are, once again, marginal to main forms of service provision. Two-thirds of government and public services' establishments employed people on short-term contracts. This is very much a phenomenon of the 1980s and results not from a universal imperative towards flexibility as *the* rational form of management but from a series of methods of coping with central Government fiscal pressure within these localities.

This chapter has examined the extent to which peripheral forms of employment are being used in contemporary British establishments. However, it is necessary to pose two further questions concerning the novelty of such employment practices and the pervasiveness of their use. Our case studies of 32 of the establishments taken from the original 122 surveyed by telephone in Rochdale suggested that, in the main, these kinds of peripheral employment are by no means new. There is little evidence, therefore, of any fundamental trend towards peripheralisation of employment in the 1980s, as argued by Atkinson and Meager. Nor are such forms of peripheral employment, where they do exist, pervasive. They are marginal to the main patterns of employment in most establishments. Indeed, most employment is either full-time or part-time involving people employed on standard long-term contracts working either at or directly from their employing establishment.

Flexible Management

Most establishments reported no changes along the various trajectories of flexible management during the preceding two years. The main area of change was in the sphere of pay. However, this mainly involved an extension of conventional individualised payment systems rather than the advent of group-related pay.

Overall Conclusion

The analysis reported above revealed no significant independent locality effects in relation to changing patterns of 'flexible' employment. There were major industrial-sectoral effects which produced the impression of locality differences. However, such an impression was primarily the result of the differing industrial mixes within the six localities. Such results suggest that unemployment *per se* is not as significant a factor as that suggested in Atkinson and Meager's model. There was powerful evidence of a strong positive relationship between the size of establishment and the likelihood of the employment of at least some 'peripheral' employees. This relationship starkly contradicts both the theoretical assumptions of Atkinson and Meager and their prognoses. Given that the average size of establishment has fallen during the 1980s, we would expect *de facto* that 'peripheral' employment and, as a corollary, flexibility, would also be declining on the basis of the data reported in this paper. Furthermore, the strong positive association between size of establishment and the likelihood of 'peripheral' employment means that Atkinson and Meager's exclusive focus on larger establishments vitiates their claims to generalisability. Put in a nutshell, their analysis is heavily biased towards the likely discovery of 'flexibility' and cannot be used as an empirical benchmark from which generalisations about employment patterns in modern Britain should be derived.

Appendix 1

The Questions Asked in the SCELI Telephone Survey of Employers

Q8a. In *total*, are there more people on the payroll now than five years ago, or less people, or about the same?

Q9a. Have the numbers of part-timers, working less than 30 hours a week, changed compared with five years ago?

Q13a. Do you *ever* make use of any of the following kinds of workers:
Workers employed by agencies?
Contractors' staff working on your premises?
Workers on short-term contracts?

Casual workers, given just a few days or weeks' work?
Homeworkers or outworkers?

Q13b. Considering these types of workers as a whole, how many are doing work for you currently?

Q13c. What was the total number two years ago, roughly?
Higher. Lower. Some. Don't know.

Q13d. Why has the total changed over the period?

Q24.   Thinking of all sections of employees, have any of the following steps been taken over the past two years:
An increase in shift working?
Increased use of group or collective pay incentives?
Increased use of individual performance assessment?
Increased use of work measurement or method study?
Replacement of some full-time employees with part-timers?
Replacement of some employees with contract or agency staff or casual or temporary workers?

Notes

I should like to thank Angeliki Papantonakou for her help with the data analysis in this paper.

1. See, for example, the following articles in the *Financial Times*: Michael Smith, 'Flexibility deals vital for survival, unions told', *Financial Times*, 22 June 1988; Charles Leadbetter, 'Qualitative Flexibility', *Financial Times*, 10 October 1988; Philip Bassett, 'Flexibility deals viewed as part of long-term industrial change', *Financial Times*, 25 October 1988; John Gapper, 'British Gas Flexibility Plan Dead and Buried, Says Union', *Financial Times*, 24 December 1988; John Gapper, 'Survey Finds Flexibility Important to Mothers', *Financial Times*, 22 May 1989.

2. See, for instance, N. Meager (1985), Incomes Data Services (1986), ACAS (1987).

3. The flexible firm thesis has been elaborated by Atkinson in various publications (Atkinson, 1984a, 1984b, 1985; Atkinson and Gregory, 1986a, 1986b) and by Hakim (1987). The most assiduous critic of the Atkinson approach to flexibility is Pollert (1988a, 1988b).

4. Atkinson and Meager neither provide any evidence to support these claims nor any guidance as to what they might mean operationally.

5. It is worth noting that there are virtually no retailing establishments that employ over 500 employees at establishment level. Furthermore, in Rochdale (for example) there were only three establishments in 1981 with over 1000 employees and less than a dozen with over 500 employees. In terms of most people's experience, employment in a large establishment is relatively unusual. Therefore, even if flexibility were happening in such large establishments, this could not demonstrate a general trend.

6. See Penn (1991a and 1991b).

Part III
Industrial Case Studies

6 Inflexible Flexibility: A Case Study of Modularisation

Tony Elger and Peter Fairbrother

A major feature of the current debate about work reorganisation and corporate restructuring has been a concern with the emergence of new sorts of relations between management and workers. These new relations have often been interpreted as exemplars of a wider process of transformation, involving major departures from earlier patterns of Fordist mass production (Sabel, 1990). However, other commentators have viewed such innovations more sceptically, suggesting that these developments have involved an often uncertain, contested and crisis-ridden recomposition of enduring class relations (Gough, this volume; Clarke, this volume).

A distinctive variant of these arguments has focused on the significance of Japanese models of work reorganisation, particularly as these have been adopted or adapted by innovative transnational corporations. Many commentators have argued that the methods developed by Japanese enterprises have increasingly served as models of economic efficiency and employee integration to be emulated by other transnationals (Bassett, 1986; Oliver and Wilkinson, 1988). There are several strands of argument, however, which offer a more sceptical appraisal of the so-called Japanisation of British industry. One important theme is that this pursuit of economic efficiency is at the cost of increased worker exploitation (Turnbull, 1989; Garrahan and Stewart, this volume). Another theme is that any such innovations have been extremely uneven and fragmentary, characterised by the piecemeal adoption of selected facets of flexibility (Pollert, 1991b; Elger, 1990).

One of the major examples of work reorganisation ostensibly inspired by the Japanese model is Lucas Industries plc. At Lucas during the 1980s management adopted an explicit policy to restructure employment relations, involving a systematic reorganisation of manufacturing using such methods as Just In Time and Total Quality control. Within the Lucas factories the most notable development has been the introduction of modular or cellular production techniques, involving flexible work practices, batch production and team work.

These developments have been publicised and analysed by both Lucas management and outside commentators. The emphasis of in-house analyses has been on the substantial achievements of radical restructuring (Parnaby, 1987a, b, c). In particular, John Parnaby, the Group Director for Manufacturing Technology for Lucas Industries plc since 1983, has been a leading and enthusiastic exponent of an approach to Manufacturing Systems Engineering which owes much to 'modern methodologies applied so execellently in Japan' (Parnaby, 1987c, abstract). He has gained a high'profile in the engineering profession as an advocate of these ideas, and has been a moving force orchestrating the decentralised restructuring of the Lucas factories in the Birmingham area and elsewhere.

Some outsiders have also provided a sympathetic exploration of the managerial logic of these initiatives in the context of the restructuring of capital (Oliver and Wilkinson, 1988). More sceptical commentary, however, has focused not only on the systematic character of managerial strategies but also on the resultant intensification of work (Turnbull, 1986 and 1988). One problem with all these analyses is that they recognise but do little to explore the complexity and variety of these developments. To remedy this deficiency and develop the analysis further it is necessary to present a fuller account of the dynamics of relations between labour and capital and the forms of differentiation within each.

Accordingly this chapter addresses three interrelated concerns: managerial policies and approaches; the often mundane but varied character of change; and forms of trade union organisation and activity. Firstly, it will be suggested that, while both corporate and operational management have sought to restructure in response to the international market and competitive pressures, management decisions have been rather less certain and comprehensive than has usually been suggested, and have involved considerable unevenness and uncertainty in practice. Secondly, the implications of modularisation have been quite varied, reflecting in part the local peculiarities of production and the specific relations between workers and their managements. The result has been a redrawing of the frontiers of accommodation and control rather than the establishment of co-operative work relations. Thirdly, the resulting policies and practices have had distinctive and threatening ramifications for collective organisation as well as involving an engineering logic of reduced overheads and stock in progress. In particular the marginalisation of certain types of craft employment neutralised specific union groups, while the end of piecework removed one key basis of union organisation.

This chapter reports on the practical experience of corporate restructuring and work reorganisation at one Lucas factory, at Great Hampton Street in Birmingham. It draws particularly on detailed interviews conducted on site by the authors with key union and management informants, including the business unit director as well as past and present convenors. These interviews focused on the bargaining and implementation of modular production during the 1980s. This evidence is supplemented by published and unpublished documentary material and responses to questionnaires completed by a panel of section stewards. The first round of research was completed in 1986, just after the introduction of the first module, and included the questionnaire survey and the collection of archival data, as well as an extensive interview with one of the convenors. Further work was done in 1990, including a series of interviews with key informants together with additional archival research.

MANAGEMENT STRATEGIES

Lucas Industries plc is the parent and holding company for a large number of wholly and partly-owned companies engaged in the production of electrical systems, principally for the vehicle and aerospace industries. A large transnational based in Birmingham and with companies in many parts of the world, it was founded in the nineteeth century and manufactured lighting and accessories for bicycles and motor cycles, subsequently broadening and diversifying its interests in the twentieth century. In the postwar period the company expanded its operations overseas, and by the early 1980s an increasing proportion of its production and employment was outside Britain (Gaffikin and Nickson, n.d., p. 137). By this time the company operated in aerospace, automotive and other related industrial markets. Against this background Lucas employment in the UK fell from over 69000 in 1979 to under 46000 by 1987 (Gaffikin and Nickson n.d.; Oliver and Wilkinson, 1988, p. 45). During the early 1980s there were closures of UK plants, short-time working and also threats that closure could only be avoided by radical increases in productivity. By 1989 for the first time more than half the group's sales were from subsidiary companies overseas and, when direct and indirect exports were taken into account, 77 per cent of sales were to end-customers overseas (Lucas Industries plc, 1988).

The plant studied was largely dedicated to production for the aftermarket, which involves the recovery, rectification and rebuilding of such items as starter motors and alternators for sale through the garage trade. This contrasts with the other major automotive activities of the corporation covering the manufacture of new products (Turnbull, 1989). It should, however, be noted that while the bulk of the work at Great Hampton Street involved remanufacture, there was also some initial manufacturing of products, such as Emergency Beacons. The Great Hampton Street factory is the base for Lucas Aftermarket Operations, which until 1987 was a wholly owned subsidiary of Lucas Electrical Limited. This then became a shadow company and the Aftermarket Operations were transferred to Lucas Automotive Limited, a major wholly owned subsidiary of Lucas Industries plc.

Historically, the production and rectification of alternators and starter motors has involved standardised techniques with a workforce divided according to task. Try (1985) argues that the dominance of Lucas Electrical in the components industry allowed the introduction and maintenance of flow-line mass production. This was a method of manufacture where operators assembled products on a production line and craft workers were concerned with design, component production and the maintenance of the flow of work. As a result these plants employed considerable numbers of specialist craft workers. At the same time this organisation of work was characterised by a significant sexual division of labour: the workforce at the Great Hampton Street plant was about equally split between men and women, with the skilled workers predominantly male and the production workers female. It should also be noted that overall approximately 10 to 15 per cent of the workforce were black.

Traditionally, the major market and profit base of Lucas Electrical Limited had been the British vehicle industry. In 1980, however, for the first time in 100 years, the company failed to make a profit. The main reason for this was the ending of protection for the British vehicle market during the 1970s (Dunnett, 1980, pp. 90–1) accompanied by the increase in foreign competition in the vehicle components industry. This had distinctive implications for aftermarket operations in that an increasing proportion of their work has been the reconditioning of non-Lucas components, initially concentrating on those of cognate design but now embracing all competitor models.

These developments prompted a management restructuring of Lucas which involved a series of crises and reorganisations. Oliver and Wilkinson (1988) recount how during the 1980s top management adopted a ruthless programme of restructuring which required each business unit to perform or be sold off. This involved a 'policy of vigorous decentralisation with an active programme of measuring up, in every detail, to each company's or division's particular competitor' (van de Vliet, 1986, p. 41), which was embodied in a programme of Competitiveness Achievement Plans (CAP). By 1986 one critical consequence was that around forty business units had been closed or sold. Though the CAP was implemented somewhat belatedly at Great Hampton Street, it stimulated critical scrutiny of markets and operations, the relocation of work within and between plants, and a major programme of work reorganisation.

The company has increasingly sought to introduce flexible production methods and qualify the operation of standardised high volume flow-line production. In particular, from the early 1980s modular systems of operation have been introduced into this and other Lucas plants. The increasing competitiveness of the car markets, together with the experience of a profit squeeze, stimulated corporate management to seek changes in work organisation across Lucas Industries plc. At Great Hampton Street changes in the aftermarket provided a distinctive impetus because efforts to sustain a substantial market share required the capacity to reprocess smaller volumes of components from an increasingly diverse range of manufacturers.

The Great Hampton Street site had, for a long time, been organised largely in terms of a flow of work through a series of specialised production areas, each dedicated to particular stages of production. Direct production workers in these areas were complemented by substantial groupings of indirect craft and technical workers, concerned with such service functions as machine maintenance and the routing of components through the factory. Modularisation involved major changes in these aspects of the organisation of production, as it created mini-factories with specific objectives and budgets. The change was described as follows:

> Before the module there were stores, works engineers, a toolroom, all the principal support services in various departments. At the Great Hampton Street works they picked one particular product . . . foreign unit starter motors and alternators. They bought old units from scrap merchants. The units are stripped down and cleaned. Before the module, they were stripped down into bits at another site and then sent over to our site where they were built up and made into reconditioned units in various departments. The new proposal was that the stripping, cleaning, and building would all be done in one area and there would be no outside support from any other area. So what happens is that you have a unit coming in, an old scrapped unit, and it is stripped, cleaned and new parts are put in, all in one area (McDivitt, 1987, p. 68).

Lucas sought to reorganise work relations and redefine job tasks in a quite radical fashion:

> [The company] took a sharply different approach from the traditional one of trying to fit work around long established categories of employees. The company also placed great emphasis on having as many people as possible employed directly on production within the new modules, cutting back on indirect jobs and support functions (IRRR, 1984).

The company claimed that this innovation meant that:

> in effect we are re-designing our factories by using the expertise of the people on the shopfloor, solving problems at their source and achieving high standards of efficiency (Lucas Industries, 1984).

Thus it is evident that the company was embarking on a pioneering trajectory.

As indicated above, Parnaby was central to the process of modularisation and projected a radical and systematic break with low variety, specialised mass production. He was sharply critical of established features of management, identifying manufacturing management as inadequately professionalised and over-specialised, and advocated that change should be achieved using multi-disciplinary project teams trained in manufacturing systems engineering. The basic organisational units of the resultant modular production process were to be simple cellular structures, constituting natural groupings of activities and involving:

> new flexible job structures with multi-skilled staff and with indirect control activities being carried out by direct staff on-line (Parnaby, 1987b, p. 2).

Workers within each cell were to be actively involved in implementing the details of production, whilst being guided and assessed against a set of tightly defined yardsticks. The cell leader became responsible for microcomputer-based scheduling procedures; the cell and individual operators became accountable for quality; and all members participated in 'team-based and cell-focused continuous improvement procedures supported by structured training programmes' (Parnaby, 1987b, p. 2).

FROM FLOW-LINE TO MODULES

In practice, the development of modules at the Great Hampton Street site has been much more mundane and variegated than Parnaby's overview suggests. The implementation of these plans carried something of the style of management by *dictat*, with an apparently quite single-minded pursuit of the modular conception as an unproblematical solution. However, while this eventually forced almost all areas of the factory into some variant of modularisation, it also led to substantial variability of practice and the (re)surfacing of persistent tensions within modular organisation. Indeed, in retrospect the only common denominator of what became labelled as modular production appears to be a regrouping of equipment and workers to locate complete processes within specific areas, to facilitate low volume batch production, but with very variable and often quite conventional implications for the organisation of production activities. In particular there is little evidence of any cumulative movement towards a workforce of cohesive teams of flexible generalists.

It should be noted that modularisation was introduced against a background of widespread feelings of uncertainty and insecurity. Workers and unions at Great Hampton Street had seen the broader programme of corporate rationalisation lead to major reorganisations, redundancies and closures at related Lucas factories. Furthermore, on the site itself, modularisation was preceded by a wide spectrum of less dramatic moves which needed monitoring and negotiation by the unions, such as self-inspection by operators; subcontracting and contracting-out work; short-time working; redundancies and redeployment between sites; and communications exercises and quality circles. Some of these developments involved isolated incidents but they nevertheless had a cumulative impact (compare Penn, this volume). They fueled anxiety and engendered a sense that senior management were trying out possibilities with the broader objective of acquiring a flexible workforce. Work reorganisation reinforced feelings of vulnerability and an awareness of the need for union vigilance, though management's commitment to new developments was seen as a necessary basis for the survival of the factory, with positive benefits for some categories of workers.

Patterns of Modularisation

A major feature of the management approach was the forceful implementation of central management policies, communicated through the personal style of senior site management. This involved a complex combination of features, including a vigorous commitment to a programme of change, a skilful selectivity in dealings with unions, symbolic rewards to pioneering work teams, and 'being seen to be tough' through occasional threats of dismissal. The company also took steps to develop a managerial structure and ethos to facilitate the introduction and operation of modules. Specifically, the general manager of the plant was replaced in 1986 by two business managers, for remanufacturing and for manufacturing respectively (Lucas Co. Annual Report) and supervisory roles were reorganised. This was accompanied by management training and induction programmes about modularistion and its benefits.

A Task Force to introduce the modules was established in mid-1985, involving technical and managerial staff from within the plant as well as managers and consultants from outside. Later specific Task Forces focused on the implementation of changes in particular product areas. In May 1985, the Joint Shop Steward Committee (JSSC) met the relevant Task Force following rumours that Foreign Unit Rectification (FUR) and related specialist processes were to be the first area of modularistion. Subsequently, in November 1985, the Task Force recommended a module for Foreign Units, to be established in 1986. By February 1986 the unions were involved in formal negotiations with management and meetings with their FUR members about the implications of modularisation. Meanwhile the company proceeded with the technical and physical reorganisation of the area.

At this juncture, in June 1986, the company opened formal negotiations on the establishment of a module for the manufacture of Emergency Beacon Lighting. This sought to integrate phases of the production of a product which had been dispersed through different floors and areas of the factory. As a specialised manufacturing product, it represented a somewhat atypical part of the site's operations, but one which, according to market research, offered the prospect of independent commercial success.

After a two-month period of preparation this module was established for a management-designated six-month trial period, and senior managers put particular efforts into the motivation and organisation of the workforce. This involved a comprehensive training programme for a section of the workforce, high-profile communications exercises using videos, team T-shirts and token rewards for team performance such as cream cakes and champagne.

While the major preoccupation of the unions remained with the re-organisation of FUR, management sought to use what they termed 'the Beacon experiment' as an exemplar for modularisation:

> The pilot was important because it allowed us to put definition to our purpose in terms of how we wanted to work in the future and of course what we needed was flexibility, mobility, commitment, and an understanding of the concept of ownership [of production responsibilities] (management informant, 1990).

According to union informants management did succeed in nurturing a sense among the module workforce of being an elite, and this served to marginalise the unions during this period. Despite this there was a persistent catalogue of complaints from the workforce about production-related problems during the experimental period.

The process of work reorganisation in the FUR module was contested and more gradual. The scope and terms of any assimilation of maintenance and stores workers into the module remained the subject of long-standing disputes which blocked such changes until 1987. Meanwhile production workers initially continued to perform their established tasks on transfer to the module, and thereafter the moves towards flexibility were largely confined to job rotation within specific cells of three to five workers, rather than being more wideranging. A union respondent commented in retrospect:

What we thought was that it would be flexibility within the module [but] somewhere along the line it got lost and it became flexibility in the module within the cell you work in (1990).

Such arrangements combined specialist operator expertise with limited flexibilities, and appear to have suited management as they sought to cope with the reconditioning of smaller batches of more diversified products.

As part of the introduction of modules, the company moved to end the previous piecework arrangements and establish flat rates. This meant that all fifty workers in the FUR module were paid at the same basic rate, initially £123. The implication was that this would lay the basis for widespread task flexibility, though initially people were to continue with tasks similar to those they had before. In this context many were attracted by higher wage rates for similar work, while those who would have taken a wage cut were protected with variable personal allowances to guarantee previous wage levels.

Another critical feature of the reorganisation was that first-line supervisors were regarded as a pivotal part of the module workforce. Their designation was changed from 'foreman' to module controller. In part, the organisation of the module around the module controller represented the resurrection of a previous fruitless attempt to introduce quality circles, rejected by the unions some four or five years earlier. With the introduction of the modules there was a move to define them as quality groups. This took the form of the module controllers calling the module workforce together and talking about output, problems and so forth (union informant, 1986).

It is evident that within the overall programme of change the Beacon Cell and the FUR module represent disparate but characteristic outcomes of the process of modularisation. Each case was conditioned by somewhat different production and commerical contingencies, and such features helped to sustain a spectrum of procedures and organisation which came to distinguish one module from another. The different trajectories of change involved in the establishment of these two modules were also the outcome of varied processes of bargaining and a managerial concern at the prolonged nature of the negotiations surrounding the FUR. Thus this became the occasion for introducing more speedy and conspicuous changes in Beacons, according the Beacon Cell exemplary status in the overall process of modularisation.

Workers' Experiences of Modules

The introduction of modules promised changes in the daily experience of work. Traditionally flow-line production has involved the tight specification of a series of distinct tasks with limited opportunities for movement between them (Kelly, 1982). In her study of a comparable electricals factory, Cavendish graphically captures the experience of such work:

> Each operator had to perform several tasks on the UMO [component] as it made its way down the line. Management was in charge of grouping these jobs, and laid down the number of seconds and split seconds allowed for each. . . . Whenever I could finally do a job, it became very very boring. You had to look at it and concentrate all the time, so your mind had to be on the work (Cavendish, 1982, pp. 17 and 35–6).

This can be contrasted with the proposals for Great Hampton Street. One convenor's expectation was that:

> Everybody in this module [FUR] will do every job on the production side, which the operators wanted. Instead of just standing there all day just screwing one screw in, they will go onto stripping, they will go onto cleaning, they will go onto spraying and they will move around, and also there was one rate of pay for the job (interview, 1986).

This expectation was, however, qualified in practice.

While stewards' comments at the time indicate many common concerns, especially about the impact of modularisation on production workers, they also provide hints of significant differences in experience and response (steward questionnaires, 1986). These differences are consistent with comparisons drawn by a senior craft steward, between production and indirect craft workers. He implied that the latter grouping were a source of problems for the stewards as well as for management:

> Production workers were more flexible than the craft based workers. The problems that we had were with the indirect workers, that is, the works engineers, stores, toolrooms, where from the start they said they were not going to participate in the module . . . they would serve the module from outside (McDivitt, 1987, p. 69).

Thus, when management created a new manufacturing craftworker category the skilled engineers initially would not apply for these new positions. As a result, management:

> ended up recruiting people who were not really capable of doing the tasks they wanted them to do. So management, under pressure, allowed the toolroom to service the module plants from outside and that is the situation until now. The works engineers and the toolroom still continue to service that department from outside (McDivitt, 1987, p. 69).

Nevertheless, over a longer period of time and following further negotiations, much of the maintenance and setting work was devolved to the modules, largely in the form of responsibilities allocated to manufacturing craftworkers but also through extending the remits of production workers.

By comparison with the experiences of many indirect groups, the changes experienced by the direct production workers were rather undramatic. The abolition of piecework was a common denominator, but beyond this there were substantial variations between modules in such features as improvements in facilities, investment in new machinery and the reorganisation of work routines. Thus in one module a new rest area was provided, but work routines changed very little. Even rotation between jobs within the module hardly changed, though potentially made easier by the abolition of piecework. The previous practice had been to move workers quite frequently, despite frictions over different earnings potentials and learning times. For this group of workers the most obvious increase in flexibility was that which cut across the module, and involved loaning workers to other modules!

In FUR, there was a more substantial reorganisation of the production process around batch production by groups of three or four workers, whose work was now paced more evenly by batch scheduling, thereby avoiding a mixture of piecework pressures and idle waiting time (interview 1990). However, any modernisation of the working environment appeared superficial, largely restricted to large notices defining the various module areas. Modules were spilt into several cells, and then into various benches, and these were serviced by subgroupings of internal craftworkers and setters, thus retaining substantial task specialisation.

As the modular form was gradually extended to cover virtually the whole range of production activities on the site, the patterns of task allocation and flexibility became increasingly varied. In this context informants noted that some sets of workers had been given quite extensive training on a wide variety of standard production tasks and this was sometimes paralleled by rather broader job rotation than in the FUR module. At the same time the company's commitment to off-the-job training remained sporadic and *ad hoc*, and the usual (but contested) expectation was that operators should train one another in their different tasks. Thus many workers thought the establishment of modules a desirable development and appreciated the wider range of tasks potentially associated with modularisation (McDivitt, 1987, p. 72). However, many found themselves confined to a more limited repertoire of activities, and most felt that the modules were insufficiently resourced, both in terms of expertise and rewards for responsible staff. There was also scepticism about such matters as the incorporation of quality inspection into production routines, since cost and especially output pressures remained paramount (interviews, 1990).

The major changes in relations between direct and indirect workers meant that the reorganisation of store work followed a particularly complex trajectory. Following the computerisation of stock control and the introduction of modules, management proposed merging stores and progress-chasing in a new job of material controller. The Amalgamated Engineering Union (AEU) bargained successfully to keep the job as a manual one, and then the stores workers fought to gain skilled grading. They were successful in this, but only after several strikes.

A key consequence of modularisation was the intensification of staff work. This was the result of continuing pressure to shed indirect staff, coupled with the creation of small module-based multidisciplinary staff teams whose expertise is now stretched over a wider range of activities. Indeed the reorganisation of indirect work, particularly on the staff side, had involved a dispersal of expertise, both through the shedding of experienced workers and the scattering of specialists across modules (interview, 1990). In these circumstances the priority has been the immediate utilisation of available skills, but this has undercut the considered development and dissemination of skills and experience, both through training and the sharing of expertise. Furthermore, the shift from a structure of departmentalised staff specialisation to multidisciplinary teams has clearly been experienced as a disruption of the established occupational cultures which, among other things, provided an important matrix for informal dissemination of expertise.

The introduction of modules took place in the context of wider corporate restructuring and against a background of a variety of changes in working arrangements and employment conditions at the Great Hampton Street site. Modularisation was a key element of management's reorientation towards more diversified production and their pursuit of increased workforce flexibility. Nevertheless, the process of innovation was quite protracted and resulted in a very variegated pattern of work organisation, with little evidence of the emergence of a cadre of flexible generalists. This reflected both management efforts to tailor modules to the specific production requirements and skill levels of the workforce, and workplace union initiatives aimed at modifying changes to protect workers' interests.

UNIONS AND CHANGE

It will have been evident that, in the face of the challenges and pressures involved, workplace unionism played an active role in the detailed development of restructuring. At the same time, corporate rationalisation and work reorganisation substantially altered the terrain of union activity, especially in regard to the relationship between craft and non-craft unionism and the gendered composition of the unionised workforce. As a result, union members at Great Hampton Street inevitably became engaged in a process of regroupment and renewal of trade unionism.

Historically trade union organisation and representation has been characterised by pressures towards centralisation of representation for Lucas factories in the area, together with fragmentation along occupational lines. Up until 1974 production workers at the Lucas factories were represented site by site. From that date until very recently negotiations about wages and conditions were conducted on a group or regional basis between union representatives and the Central Personnel Department (Try, 1985, p. 54). This centralisation of negotiations was enabled by the company recognition of the Senior Stewards Committee (SSC), comprising factory convenors and senior stewards from the different sites that made up Lucas Electrical in the Birmingham area. Cutting across these arrangements, and to a certain extent limiting this process of centralisation, was the long-standing recognition of the Toolgroup as a distinct bargaining unit (Meacham, 1972, p. 28). Over time other groups also gained such recognition, so that by 1985 there were, in addition to the SSC, five separate negotiating groups with distinct bargaining arrangements.

The process of central negotiations had grown out of, and remained rooted in, substantial workplace steward organisation, which nevertheless embodied some of the sources of fragmentation already outlined. At Great Hampton Street there was an active JSSC covering the shop floor unions. In 1986 three unions participated in the JSSC: AEU with fourteen representatives, Transport and General Workers' Union (TGWU) with sixteen representatives, and Electrical, Electronic, Telecommunication and Plumbing Union (EETPU) with one. Meetings were held monthly and according to one informant attendance averaged 24. In addition to this the convenors of each union attended a monthly SSC meeting for all Lucas plants in the Birmingham area. Alongside the manual unions, the non-manual workers were organised into three unions: Association of Professional, Executive, Clerical and Computer Staff (APEX), covering approximately 250 clerical workers; Technical, Administrative and Supervisory Section (TASS), covering approximately 75 technical staff; and Association of Scientific, Technical and Managerial Staffs (ASTMS), covering 20 supervisors. Subsequently, in 1989 TASS and ASTMS merged to form Manufacturing, Science and Finance (MSF), and although the plant organisations maintained distinct identities there was evidence that a closer working relationship had been achieved. Unlike the manual union negotiations, which were usually conducted in the absence of full-time officials, the non-manual unions tended to bring their full-time officials into site negotiations, particularly on wages.

In the last fifteen years the predominantly male craft groups gradually lost their pre-eminence in wage negotiations, although they still retained an advantage on bonus and related special payment items. Basic wage levels were increasingly negotiated by the SSC on behalf of the production workers, the majority of whom were women workers (Try, 1985, p. 66). The practice developed that the production worker negotiations were settled first with the craft groups negotiating and settling subsequently. Some of the resultant tensions were evident in stewards' comments on the course of wage negotiations, as they were seen from Great Hampton Street. In debating the idea that there should be unified negotiations, one craft steward stated that this would remain difficult 'as long as production workers continue to sell themselves cheaply' (union records). On another occasion, the proposal that 'production workers should be the last group to submit their claim' met the response that production 'are not always the first to go in but they are the first to settle' (union records).

The refocusing of trade unionism took place in the context of an apparent 'toughening' of the company approach to industrial relations. The method increasingly adopted by the company was to 'soften up' the workforce with rumour and suggestion so that the eventual proposals either appeared less harsh or had come to be expected. This approach was described by Turnbull as one which:

> shows considerable sagacity and cunning on the part of management
> . . . [and is] tantamount to the unilateral enforcement by management of
> changes . . . which need no longer be subject to negotiation or agreement
> (Turnbull, 1986, p. 198).

As will be seen, the implications differed between Lucas sites, but the style of this approach, with clear warnings for other plants, is illustrated by the events surrounding the company's prosecution of the plans to restructure and relocate rotating machine production at the Shaftsmoor Lane plant.

After a series of negotiations on the plans for Shaftsmoor Lane during 1984, which resulted in a failure to agree, the company adopted a high profile tough stance (Turnbull, 1986; McDivitt, 1987). Letters were issued direct to all employees, by-passing the steward committee. These stated that if the plan was not agreed investment would be withdrawn and the plant shut down, and they included an acceptance form to be signed and returned to the company via first level supervision. At the time the senior stewards were in negotiations with the management, and on being told by the company representatives that the workforce had accepted the proposal, at levels approaching 80 per cent in favour, the senior stewards acquiesced. The lessons of this were not lost on stewards and workers in other plants who subsequently faced restructuring and reorganisation.

In contrast, the subsequent introduction of modules at the Great Hampton Street plant was 'gradual'. However, this gradualism did not mean, as Turnbull (1988) implies, that the established union organisation could straightforwardly be mobilised to regulate the changes involved. With the establishment of the first two modules, the unions in the words of one union leader 'took a right dive'. This meant that the JSSC began to address the issue of proper representation of the module workers, made difficult by the recomposition of sectional groupings within the workforce. In particular, the forms of steward representation were reorganised, away from a variety of task and area constituencies to one or more TGWU stewards and at least one AEU steward per module.

The introduction of the module confronted the JSSC with a series of problems. One major issue, mentioned earlier, which was only resolved after the imposition of an overtime ban, concerned the pay and skilled status of material handlers/controllers. A second issue involved the appropriate negotiating bodies to represent the interests of the proposed remanufacturing craftsworkers. This difficulty arose out of the cross-cutting forms of union representation constituted by the central toolsetters negotiating committee and the JSSC; it was eventually resolved in favour of the JSSC but only after the craftworkers on site had been reduced to a residual presence as a result of management policies. Among the substantive issues facing craftworkers was the projected dissolution of the toolroom, and on this issue the unions gained an agreement to maintain the toolroom outside the modules. Finally, much dissatisfaction resulted from the disparity of earnings which arose in the modules because of the protected earnings of some workers. This prompted successful efforts to renegotiate a degree of wage harmonisation.

Many of the initial module workers had relatively little active trade union experience, and though stewards in nearby sections took some responsibility for those workers, it became a matter of concern to the JSSC to ensure that module representation was developed (union records). The development of such representation was not straightforward in these conditions, but despite the relative sectionalism of union organisation it was facilitated by a long history of stewards from different sections and unions working together. Additionally, the main production convenor adopted the practice of more frequent patrols of the production areas, giving support to inexperienced stewards where necessary. These were features of union life that enabled the stewards to respond to the new and more difficult circumstances for trade unionism resulting from modularisation.

When stewards themselves were questioned at the time, they were cautious about these developments, but there were differences of emphasis between production and craft stewards. The production stewards generally appeared more sanguine about the effects of module production on their trades unionism compared to the skilled workers. In general, and for all stewards, the background of recurrent change and crisis imposed increased burdens on unions and activists. Beyond this, the organisational changes have diminished the importance of the allied trades and increased the importance of the operators among manual unions, while the dispersal of staff specialists weakened one strand of occupational collectivity. Nevertheless, the pressures and changes have brought technical and supervisory workers closer together, and the MSF merger seems to have facilitated a trend towards closer co-operation (apart from APEX). The distinct impression was that union organisation remains intact and coping, and even more so, that activists have been working with considerable determination for the survival and development of workplace unionism. Thus, although union organisation remains segmented there is also evidence of continuing co-operation.

The most noteworthy development involving the unions has been the emergence of the TGWU as the key shopfloor union. This heralds an important and in the long-term significant change in trade unionism at the factory, since the TGWU is a production worker-based union, with a still substantial female membership (despite a bias in recent recruitment towards male production workers). With the eclipse of the toolroom and the engineering department the dominance of the craft workers could no longer be sustained. In effect this means the end of a form of unionism based on a defence by male workers of their relative skills and privileges. It suggests the beginnings of more solidaristic forms of unionism than were evident in the past. If this proves to be the case, it is an ironic outcome of a set of managerial inspired changes that had as one intention the neutralising or by-passing of workplace unionism.

CONCLUSION

This analysis of the introduction of modular working at Lucas Great Hampton Street during the second half of the 1980s shows that it was part of a significant process of corporate restructuring which substantially altered patterns of work and occupational organisation within the factory and posed serious challenges to established forms of trade unionism. At the same time the varied, equivocal and often modest changes in the work relations which flowed from these pioneering innovations provide little support for diagnoses of the emergence of post-Fordist forms of flexible working. The actively bargained and sometimes contested character of these changes, coupled with the evidence of a reorientation and renewal of union organisation, support the view that the changes have meant a significant reworking of the established relations between capital and labour rather than any transcendence of those relations.

It is clear that the changes in work relations at Lucas arose out of a crisis of profitability which encouraged a management reappraisal of business performance in the changing market conditions of the 1980s. This reappraisal was orchestrated centrally, through such devices as Task Forces and, most crucially, the Competitiveness Achievement Plans. It prompted a widespread reorientation towards more varied and smaller batch production, combined with management efforts to minimise indirect labour and stockholding costs. In this context the developments at Great Hampton Street clearly illustrate an interplay between broader corporate strategies and monitoring and a tailoring of the pace and character of change by local management according to specific production, market and labour relations contingencies. This points to the importance of parochial 'factory politics' (Jones and Rose, 1986) in conditioning processes of work reorganisation. However, it also underlines the argument of Gough (this volume) and Amin and Robins (1990) that such innovations must be seen as embedded in and regulated by the contradictory and shifting accumulation strategies of large, often transnational, corporations.

Against this background a key argument has been that the introduction of flexible work and employment practices, signalled by such terms as modularisation, has involved quite diverse and uneven patterns of change, usually with mundane implications for work routines, even in such exemplary innovative firms as Lucas. Thus there have been only limited and contradictory changes in patterns of expertise, task rotation, and training, despite a major shift in the balance between direct and indirect workers. There was little evidence that the changes in work relations involved any sustained shift towards multiskilled teamworking or more harmonious relations between workers and management, but rather more of greater work pressure associated with increased responsibilities. In this respect, while the findings parallel those of Turnbull (1986 and 1988), they also underline persistent diversity and unevenness in the patterns and processes of change.

A further important feature of change has been considerable uncertainty, for local management as well as for the workforce. In the wideranging debate about the management impetus for introducing new working practices and forms of work organisation, attention had focused on changes in product markets and to a lesser extent in labour markets (for example Kelly, 1982). The Lucas case confirms the salience of these circumstances for explaining change and variation both at a corporate and a plant or even section level. However, the translation of such pressures into management policies and practices is crucially mediated through the existing social relations within and between management and their workforces. It also involves coping with a variety of persistent tensions between such features as specialisation, the immediate costs of training, and the mobility of labour. This means that such changes require the management of contradictions and uncertainties which remain persistent features of the experience of management, staff and manual workers.

It is evident that the dynamics and directions of change are conditioned by the specific ways in which capital–labour relations have been institutionalised and expressed, not only in terms of the general relations between managers and workers but also in terms of the internal organisation and segmentation of both groupings. Nevertheless, the changes prompted by wider corporate imperatives and informed by concerns to control labour costs and engineer flexible compliance do not simply reproduce these relations. On the one hand, these changes have significantly altered the relations between different occupations and forms of trade unionism. On the other hand, collective organisation and activity have themselves contributed to the recomposition of work relations and the renewal of forms of trade unionism.

An implication of this analysis is that restructuring has involved a shift in the contours and texture of workplace trade unionism. This is a process which has tended to be neglected in assessments of the strengths and weaknesses of unions in the face of flexibility, except in the rather narrow context of discussions of single unionism. It is necessary to consider what these processes of change signify for the possibility of union renewal and reorganisation, not least because unions are active agencies in the process of restructuring even as their bases of organisation are undergoing change (Fairbrother, 1989). In particular, unions are likely to pursue new initiatives, develop different ways of coping, and in the process transform the character of workplace collective organisation and consciousness. To the degree that these developments take place, the new lines of division indicated by flexible restructuring may provide a foundation for revitalised forms of workplace unionism.

7 Management Control and a New Regime of Subordination: Post-Fordism and the Local Economy
Philip Garrahan and Paul Stewart

In a recent review of the changing organisation of modern industry, Wood (1989) firmly concluded that while transformations in work may be occurring, the changes are too diverse to support the notion of a single, linear trend in new developments. This sensible note of caution informs our contribution to the debate about flexibility at the core of recent industrial change, and we address this via an analysis of the Nissan project in Sunderland. Nissan is represented as, and makes the claim for itself to be (Wickens, 1987), a pathfinder in the modernisation of an old industrial region. The Nissan development has been actively encouraged and assisted by UK governments in the 1980s (Garrahan, 1986; Crowther and Garrahan, 1988) and there is a strong resonance here with the Thatcher governments' anti-union legislation. However, the significance of Nissan is not so much in employment creation as in the innovation of new management styles in industry. At the heart of this managerial renaissance are notions of a more flexible, more integrated, and hence more productive set of industrial relations.

Flexibility is partly about changes in methods of production and the technical processes used, but it is also about organisational changes around production. Flexibility is additionally 'an ensemble of social and political relations spanning the spheres of consumption and the state' (Gertler, 1988). The technical/industrial aspects of Fordism were said to be accompanied by corporatist relations between the state, employers, and unions (conflicts could be subject to bargaining, there was agreement on the state's role in managing and regulating economic growth, and support for a notion of full employment). Under a system of flexible production, however, the changes in the technical organisation of production are accompanied by the decline of corporatism and the abandonment of the state's policy of full employment. These interpretations raise a host of questions, not least about the alleged decline of corporatism (is it now just autocratic, whereas once it was consensual corporatism?), and about the homogeneity of the Fordist system under which production is said to have been organised. For the purposes of the present discussion, we have to gloss over these fundamental debates and interpretations, but there is a degree of certainty about one thing, and this is that global economic reversals are having a profound influence on local industrial developments.

There is agreement that world economic upheavals are the driving force behind current industrial change and much theorising goes on at this global level (Aglietta, 1979; Piore and Sable, 1984). Whether they be about long waves of boom, recession, and so on, or whether they have origins in a regulationist school of thinking, all theories of economic restructuring rest on an attempt to explain industrial change. That is, from theorising about global economic trajectories, there are produced explanations of the changing character of industrial production. Following from this, much is derived about the explanations for spatial linkages in the geography of new industrial locations (Schoenberger, 1987; Mair *et al.*, 1988) Spatial phenomena are at issue in debates about industrial districts, local agglomerations, and spatial clustering with vertical integration between manufacturers and suppliers (Amin and Robins, 1989). The allegedly decaying Fordist system of production is associated with spatially discontinuous patterns of production. Hence, a spatially concentrated example of production such as that which is beginning to emerge at Nissan in Sunderland would be regarded in these debates as evidence for 'flexible specialisation' (Piore and Sabel, 1984). Whether it does, is best addressed by examining the organisation of industrial work within given plants. At this level of analysis there is theorising about transformations in the nature of work which is central to the flexible specialisation debate, yet in reality these are the least well researched in terms of detailed examination of empirical evidence. The flexible production or flexible specialisation debate is the context for our investigation, but in many, if not most, instances flexibility is asserted, theorised, and contradicted, but less often examined with concrete evidence. The central question is the pervasiveness of flexible methods of production. It is only when more evidence has become available that the significance of these methods can be assessed.

The research for this chapter was conducted during 1989 and 1990 and used methods of investigation similar to those in studies of the automobile industry in the United States. In one of these studies (Hill, 1988), a research method was used based upon 'qualitative, open-ended interviews with strategic informants'. These informants were identified in a number of ways, including: from the authors' past knowledge of the local area, from '. . . sifting through the written record of events contained in hundreds of newspaper articles, organisational records and government publications; through the use of snowball interviewing techniques whereby one strategic informant leads to another; and, in a couple of instances, through chance encounters'. This research method was employed to study the impact of the Mazda plant in Flat Rock, Michigan and we have also employed it in gathering data about the Nissan development in Sunderland. Contact with local government officers and elected councillors, members of Parliament, the local media, local development corporations, trade unions, manufacturing workers, and company managers have all proved informative. As with the Mazda study, we have entered into a mutual agreement with our interviewees whereby they are not identified in order to protect confidentiality. For the purposes of this chapter, we are examining changes in industrial attitudes and practices brought about at Nissan and rely mostly on recorded interviews with twenty Nissan employees holding positions as technicians and manu-facturing staff. In addition, much valuable material was obtained from company press releases, information and training manuals, and statements by the personnel department. We are assessing the impact Nissan has had, as it is experienced and interpreted by members of its workforce, and the data collected from the interviews are therefore of a qualitative kind.

CIRCUMSTANTIAL EVIDENCE FOR THE SUCCESS OF NISSAN'S PROJECT IN SUNDERLAND

The popular and media acceptance of the validity of the whole new industrial package at Nissan has been practically universal. The most well-known components of this package are: the introduction of team working, the marginalisation of trade union influence, the sharp reduction of job de-marcations and the involvement of management on the shop-floor. All these elements are presented as foundation stones of the commercial success of Japanese companies and the satisfied worker becomes an integral part of that success. The British government has encouraged new local investment from Japan to innovate in the management of labour, not primarily as a job creation policy.

Flexibility, Teamwork, and Quality form the triad of the highly publicised Nissan success story, and we examine the reality behind the rhetoric of these elements in section three. In any plant for industrial production, there remain common imperatives which are not necessarily about flexibility, quality, or teamwork, but are about reducing costs, controlling labour, and ensuring unbroken and reliable production. Yet, the ideological framework at Nissan has become instrumental in publicising different corporate objectives which are themselves sustained by a local consensus on the route to modernisation and efficiency for the local economy. The discredited industrial system which Nissan is said to replace is now ascribed only negative features: deskilling and work intensification, monotonous or repetitive assembly line work, ossified conflict between management and workforce. Under the new ideology, Nissan encourages a 'goal homogeneity' between both sides of the old industrial divide (management and workforce are now in harmony, in a special family relationship); co-operative relationships are said to be the norm, and the workforce benefits from this higher moral ground (after all, who can object to agreement and persuasion, rather than conflict and coercion) (Nissan, 1988). Nissan claims to have introduced multiskilling that enhances or enriches the experience of work; this promotes job satisfaction and egalitarian principles within the plant, it is said (Wickens, 1987).

The relatively few critics of the Nissan development in Sunderland (Hudson, 1988; Garrahan and Stewart, 1989) advocate a more sceptical insight into the motives both of the company itself and of national and local power brokers in bringing the investment to the North-East of England. The characterisation of the area as an old industrial economy leads logically enough to thoughts of modernisation, resurgence of production, and thus a decline in unemployment. Of importance here is Nissan's record as a commercially successful company, the world's fourth largest motor vehicle manufacturer, with operations in almost two dozen countries and an annual output of over 2.6 million vehicles. Yet the recent evidence on the aggregate impact on local unemployment following the inward investment by Nissan and three dozen other Japanese companies is that unemployment is not declining (Smith and Stone, 1989) and economic regeneration is simply absent (Robinson, 1990).

Yet, perceptions of a Nissan-led recovery remain stubbornly in place without much meaningful debate about the reasons why the Nissan project has.worked. In the following section we examine the internal dynamics of the plant, based on in-depth interviews with Nissan employees at representative seniority levels. From the outside, however, the circumstances in which Nissan works remain the same. The company has forcefully, yet exploitatively, located in an area which has seen high unemployment, and thus low wages, for most of the last two decades. High unemployment persists and is only momentarily masked by constant revisions of the official procedures for measuring unemployment (Tyne and Wear R & I Unit, 1989). Low wages play an important part and best estimates suggest that Nissan rates of pay are up to one fifth lower than in the other major car manufacturers such as Ford UK. Regional disparities aside, the two year pay agreement reached in January 1989 did little to establish Nissan as a leader in the national car industry pay league. Finally, high labour turnover at Nissan is not officially acknowledged, Nissan refusing to publish figures such as those available from other companies like Jaguar, but levels were given by our interviewees at between fifteen and twenty per cent of the workforce. This is masked by the sharp rise in the total workforce from around fifteen hundred to more than three thousand between 1989 and 1992.

Finally, it must be added that the disastrous economic collapse experienced in the North-East from the mid-1970s onwards has encouraged the area's traditionally conservative trade union movement and elected labour councils to regard any investment in jobs as beyond critical questioning. This does not distinguish the North-East from any other area which has undergone radical industrial change in recent years, but neither does it mean we should ignore explanations proffered for the reception given to new inward investment with controversial management styles. Instead, our objective is to investigate what it is that makes these new management approaches work successfully in this particular context. Concentrating solely on the vagaries of the external labour market may tell us when and where investment occurs, but not how and why it succeeds. This has more to do with the interaction between the internal and the external environments.

A NEW REGIME OF SUBORDINATION?

It is clear that the introduction of new production arrangements is dependent upon a particular configuration of local social and political factors. When considering the case of Nissan, it becomes clear that in Tyne and Wear there are too many aspects of a local political environment central to new style industrial relations for Nissan's choice of Sunderland to have been fortuitous. These are: a greenfield site; a local political consensus; an acquiescent workforce and union; a young workforce unused to conflictual industrial relations; a relatively geographically dispersed workforce; high local unemployment; and an external labour market which is competitive and dependent. Nevertheless, we argue that this configuration of forces, which in this case is Nissan's strength, in the long term represents its weakness. It is one thing to countenance high labour turnover and rigid internal discipline when the company is expanding in an area of high unemployment, but quite another when the workforce stabilises and the expectations and commitment of the employees are dashed or become soured. According to Wickens (1987, p. 93), both labour turnover and sickness absenteeism are indicators of levels of employee commitment to the company. Labour turnover at Volvo, which is no worse than Nissan's, leads Wickens to infer that commitment levels at Volvo must be low. Since the available indicators (labour turnover, sickness absenteeism) suggest that commitment at Nissan is currently no better than elsewhere in the car industry, everything depends on the successful application of the team concept in providing the internal social and organisational unity.

Our analysis here draws on research into the experience of the US auto industry which began to rely on teamworking and new management strategies about a decade before the UK (Parker and Slaughter, 1988; Garrahan and Stewart, 1991). To try to assess the development of the contemporary production arrangements in the context of the 'new flexibility' and flexible specialisation debate, it would be reasonable to view changes in four distinct but related elements:

1. Management practice, including the nature of the labour process; the response of workers.
2. Work intensity and 'Management By Stress' (Parker and Slaughter, 1989).
3. Worker attitudes to existing trade unions.
4. Limits and horizons of employee dissent.

These four elements are often overlooked in the discussion of new flexible production arrangements. It is almost as if, following Murray (1989), restraint and subordination are temporary aberrants, only really a short-term problem for peripheral workers, but more so where Fordist anachronisms prevail.

Core workers can defend the social and economic life chances of marginal employees precisely because the new flexibility will create innovative and enhancing forms of work and work experience. We have argued elsewhere (Garrahan and Stewart 1990a, b; 1992) that the new flexibility, whatever else it does, seems to reconstitute the terms of employee subordination. In part, this is achieved by utilising much more than the Human Relations School ever did in their employee involvement programmes. The success of Nissan's innovations in its production arrangements depends upon what we term self-subordination. The configuration of the four elements registered above has for some observers been the most important development in managerial initiative. These are crucial for an adequate understanding of the character of current forms of flexibility, yet they continue to be overlooked because insufficient attention has been given to the interdependence between them. It is clear that the work Piore and Sabel (1984) and Amin and Robins (1989) continue this discussion, in their very distinct ways, without any reference to two interrelated and vital processes: the socio-political relations of the external labour market and the local economy and the relation between these and the micro-social relations of the internal labour process.

Academic observers and industrialists alike speak of transition in the organisation of contemporary manufacturing, and this moment of change provides the opportunity for examining whether a fundamental shift is occurring. If Fordism represented a form of labour subordination under a specific regime of accumulation (Lipietz 1986; Clarke 1988) what, if at all, will the new regime of accumulation change, for it is still a regime of subordination? This takes us away from what is a quite sterile discussion about whether post-Fordism has arrived (Elger, 1989) because the main issues are to do with (a) the terms and conditions of continuity and discontinuity, and (b) how the forms of control in the new regime of subordination actually work.

It is with these parameters in mind that we can look at Nissan in Sunderland. Field research here raises a number of problems for theories of change from Fordism to post-Fordism (or flexible specialisation/new flexibility) which ignore (a) and (b) above. Theorists of post-Fordism are trapped in a formalistic a priorism. The prescriptive ennunciations of post-Fordism discussed by Amin and Robins (1989) obscure the grey areas where what matters in manufacturing is not so much production (notwithstanding our emphasis on the labour process) but how production is achieved at the social and political level. We can address this in relation to post-Fordism's emphasis on two connected levels of change:

1. The end of mass production and moves towards niche marketing, made available by flexible specialisation of capital and labour. Related to this;
2. Employee involvement and participation in production as the organisational *sine qua non of* (1).

The End of Mass Production and the Rise of Flexible Specialisation?

Obviously, the move towards niche marketing and customised production is not a case against the existence of mass production. Clearly, what is being suggested by flexible specialisation theorists is the development of production *en masse* of customised goods with even greater time savings than standardised products based on what they term Fordist standardised production cycles. Most commentators, including the trade press, recognise that only car plants producing over 200 000 units per year are viable. There are many of these and with Eastern Europe opening up, one can only guess at how large production runs will be. Developments in manufacturing processes, encapsulated by the potential of some technological innovations in production, make possible faster production changes with shorter time sequences in the change from one product to another on the same line. This view is by now well known, as is the example of Honda that is used to bolster the case for the existence of flexible specialisation in automation, where three different products can be made in sequence and on runs of varying lengths (rear or front or four-wheel drive). But the development of technical and production innovation is nothing new, although arguments about the extent to which customised production is customer-led are problematical without some convincing evidence that the era of advertising and market-led sales have been superseded.

Of more certainty is the automotive industry's continued dependence upon mass sales of standardised small and saloon models, as against the relatively marginal runs of high performance models (the VW Golf apart). It is important to understand that it is the market rather than the customer which has precedence in determining the kind of automobiles produced, appearances about the determining role of the consumer notwithstanding. The latter, in fact, depends upon assumptions implied by the logic of the supposed capacities of new technologies of production and their assumed organisational and social virtues (new forms of quality circle and team working). This technological determinism presumes that certain social and organisational forms are implied by, and will arise from, particular technological forms. Both the determining role of the customer and the pre-eminence of technology in shaping social relations are questionable, and to the extent that changes are occurring they need to be noted (Elger, 1989; Tomaney, 1990). However, the fundamental difficulty arises when potentially short term trends are confused with long term structural change, that is when niche marketing with its associated organisational innovations is represented as the new dominant form of production.

Employee Involvement and Participation?

Technological determinists (Murray, 1988 and 1989; Piore and Sabel, 1984; Sayer, 1985) assume two things about employee involvement and participation: first, that these grow naturally out of the capacity for organisational innovation inherent in the technology and second, that they somehow mean employee control and determination, however small. But these assumptions still beg at least two further questions. Why would a consensus need to be achieved with such practices as teamworking if it were inherent in the production process, and if it is not, where does consensus end and coercion begin? Are these new forms of teamworking really new and if they are, what is their role in establishing consensus? In other words, how much is consensus achieved by the social and organisational form of the new flexible working environment? Is it necessary precisely because of the rigours imposed on employees by assembly line work in this era of flexible specialisation?

A sociologically broader and more appropriate approach to the new production arrangements than that offered by the technological determinists is suggested by Tomaney (1990, pp. 35–6) when he says:

> Participation can, therefore, be seen as coerced rather than a voluntary consensus. Total Quality Control and Quality circles ensnare workers themselves into this system of intensification. In practice, and contrary to a widespread myth, Quality Circles are less concerned with product than with process innovations, principally the elimination of wasteful 'activities'.

In the context of Nissan, we have to be clear about what 'flexibility' means. Nissan (1988), in their 'Facts against Fallacies', and Wickens (1987) attempt to pre-empt criticism of their work organisation when they say that flexibility does not mean moving around the factory. At the same time they argue that what occurs is a process of what we would call 'skill accretion'. This suggests the enlargement of skills or even upskilling, but what we see is neither. In this respect our findings are largely congruent with Elger's (1989) that point out that what often looks like (and is sold as!) upskilling is really a process of task enlargement. Elger's discussion is based upon a wide ranging survey of literature on manufacturing. Bearing in mind our emphases on the automotive industry and Nissan in particular, if we address the crux of the claims made by the protagonists of flexible production arrangements and their social consequences, a less sanguine picture emerges.

CONCLUSIONS

The objective of this chapter has been to scrutinise post-Fordism carefully in the light of empirical evidence from one of the largest manufacturing companies in the world. The changes in the organisation of production in this car firm raise four central aspects about social organisation and control.

First, the process of job enlargement, where manual skills involve dexterity across a range of cognate tasks and where multi-skilling (as the company calls it) occurs, tends to be vertically downward. For example, technicians clean up the work environment or move stock. The change is geared towards task accretion.

Second, task accretion ensures work intensity (Elger, 1989; Pollert 1988a). Where obstacles to production cycles occur due to insufficient sectoral staff levels, the ability to distribute labour rationally throughout the organisation becomes vital to organisational and production continuity. Task accretion constitutes and in itself depends upon:

Third, work intensification. This depends on a reduction of the porosity of the working day to a minimum. In this sense the task cycles within teams on the line depend upon a principle of no standard-task-time. The existence and variability of predefined daily quotas of production obviates the practice of standard-task-times, since management needs to vary work cycle time to meet these quotas. Thus, the task cycles within teams on the line depend upon a principle of non-standard-task-time. The result is that employees work towards lower time sequences for tasks. This requirement is institutionalised through Kaizen (continuous improvement) meetings. These are about 'quality', but are also concerned with a quality-and-effort principle, whereby faster work cycles can be assessed for their impact on variability in product. The Kaizen are a means by which problems in product arrangement or quality can be transferred to employees via team meetings and quality circles. The meetings are also a system of worker peer surveillance, like the 'Neighbour Watch' code. Neighbour Watch involves adjacent workers both up and down the line checking one another's performance, thus substituting worker-imposed for supervisor-imposed discipline (Garrahan and Stewart, 1989 and 1991). 'Quality' problems are seen to be caused by individual misunderstanding or lack of finesse in handling line speed-ups. That is why minimum and optimum standard times are absent.

Fourth, extra-technical forms of subordination. The Kaizen, in turn, depend upon company-centred ideologies of legitimacy. If the ideologies of togetherness and co-operation did not exist, they would have to have been invented (Garrahan and Stewart, 1989 and 1991). The fact that they do exist suggests something about the character of assembly-line work which theorists espousing the positive character of new production arrangements need to address. Kaizen and team working at Nissan are essential to the manufacture of consent for subordination in production. Whatever else these new social and organisational arrangements create at the level of new flexible working arrangements, we can interpret them as constituting essential mechanisms for a new regime of subordination.

In Nissan, employee autonomy, upskilling and knowledge enhancement are important elements in managerial strategies and they link to new manufacturing techniques. Subordination at work is enhanced by the particular form of association in the organisation and it is characterised by the four features above which are indices, not of employee empowerment, but the enhancement of employer power and control.

The four aspects have implications for the post-Fordist debate about flexibility and relate directly to employee autonomy, upskilling and knowledge enhancement. Any argument concerning the social nature of flexibility should be judged in relation to these aspects, because they link directly to the question of power and control in the workplace. The post-Fordist thesis assumes that there is potential for worker empowerment in terms of employee autonomy, upskilling and knowledge enhancement arising from new developments in manufacturing. However, the evidence from Nissan belies both the academic theorists and the industrial relations departments of industry.

8 Gender, Technology and Flexibility in the UK Mail Order Industry

Steve Leman

This chapter's purpose is to contribute to the body of empirical evidence by which the tenets of post-Fordism and flexible specialisation may be judged. This evidence, coming not from manufacturing but from the distribution sector, does not disprove these tenets in general. However, it provides an example of an industry to which they apply only partially.

The evidence supports Clarke's contention (this volume) that despite rapid change during the 1980s we are by no means witnessing the terminal crisis of Fordism. The mail order industry cannot be described as post-Fordist since its ever-increasing logistical systematisation represents a thoroughgoing implementation of Fordist and Taylorist principles. Furthermore, the only significant move towards flexibility is the introduction of new shift patterns which extend working hours into the evenings and weekends. There is little evidence of functional flexibility.

Developments in the industry are best understood in terms of technological innovation and gendered patterns of employment. In this connection, particular attention is paid to the case of telephone ordering or 'fastphone' departments, where telephonists use video display units to enter details of orders.

The theoretical relevance of the modern mail order industry lies in the fact that whilst it belongs in the service sector, it straddles the fields of information handling and goods handling in a unique way. It utilises computer systems for the control and monitoring of work which are similar to those used in the manufacturing industry. This has far-reaching implications for the labour process, which has undergone rapid change in both warehouse and office during the last two decades.

Evidence for these developments is drawn from interviews and group discussions facilitated by the Union of Shop, Distributive and Allied Workers (USDAW), with women and men working in offices and warehouses at four establishments in the North of England. By arrangement with managements we also spoke to personnel, training and operations managers.[1]

A FLEXIBILITY STRATEGY?

The Market Context of the Industry

The leading advocates of the flexible specialisation thesis identify the transformation of markets as the source of contemporary change (Sabel, 1990). The most obvious market transformation in the UK retail sector during the 1980s has been a move towards a segmented marketplace, although the importance of this trend in mail order has been exaggerated even by key participants such as George Davies, former Chief Executive of the Next/Grattan conglomerate (Davies, 1989). Davies based his mail order development strategy on the assumptions that the affluent consumer required exclusivity and individuality, and that market diversification would be both rapid and very extensive. However, these assumptions turned out to be over-optimistic in view of the unexpected persistence of the industry's traditional shape. To investigate the issue of whether or not the industry has moved towards flexible specialisation, it is necessary first to set the scene by describing that traditional shape.

The catalogue mail order industry in the post-war era depended for the maintenance of its market share on several factors which protected its niche in the retail sector. Firstly, from the 1940s to the 1970s it represented a particularly accessible form of credit for the working class at a time when bank-based credit facilities were not generally available. Secondly, the mail order industry took full advantage of this credit factor by including a wide range of goods in catalogues. The typical bulky, weighty catalogue encompasses most household goods and lays special emphasis on clothing. Thirdly, it utilises a network of agents, almost all women, selling on a part-time basis to family, workplace colleagues and friends. Fourthly, there used to be a convenience factor in that some goods available on mail order could not be bought in the High Street. This factor was offset by the 28-day delivery cycle which used to be the norm, and generally speaking the High Street nowadays offers an alternative way of purchasing identical or equivalent goods. The convenience factor for the modern mail order industry lies in the possibility of ordering goods by telephone at most hours of the day or night.

At the onset of the early 1980s recession, the mail order industry suffered disproportionately. The sector's problems were thrown into sharp relief against its buoyancy and vigorous expansion during the 1970s. The worst year was 1981, when mail order's share of total UK retail sales fell to 3.6 per cent (MSI, 1987). This was especially marked with respect to the mail order industry's traditional working class customer base.

The reduction of disposable income in this key customer group resulted in falling sales, an increased incidence of bad debt and more returns (mail order companies are obliged to take back unwanted items returned within a specified period, and refund the customer's remittance). The mail order companies were accustomed to setting their prices approximately six months in advance due to the lengthy production schedule of the catalogue, and were therefore not in a position to respond to price competition from High Street retailers. Considered globally, High Street prices in 1982 were 20 per cent lower than mail order prices (Jordan & Sons, 1983). The most serious long-term threat, however, came from the expansion of High Street credit (ICC, 1988). Mail order was no longer unique as a source of credit for its traditional customer base. Many of those customers were experiencing hard times; but even those who were not, were less likely than before to turn to mail order as an automatic choice.

Two of the 'big five' mail order companies (Great Universal Stores, Grattan, Empire Stores, Littlewoods and Freemans) suffered losses in 1983: Grattan at £1.1m and Empire at £1.13m. The restructuring of the industry accelerated in response to these problems. The major companies were showing high profits by the late 1980s (*Retail Business*, 1989), although they have proved vulnerable to the UK retail recession of 1990, Grattan having been particularly hard hit.

The Restructuring of the Industry

The perception by the directors of the major mail order companies that their traditional customer base was being eroded led to a drive towards diversification aimed at bringing in new sectors of the buying public through the introduction of new marketing techniques.

One of the new marketing techniques is the use of 'Specialogues'; smaller catalogues aimed at well-defined sectors of the market. Another is 'Personal Shopping'; this concept emphasises direct dealing with customers as an alternative to the traditional use of an agent as intermediary. Next Directory, which guarantees delivery within 48 hours, is the best-known example of the Personal Shopping approach. A third is the incursion of the 'Big Five' into the Direct Response and Direct Mail markets, formerly the preserve of smaller, specialised companies. Direct Response uses advertisements in colour supplements and women's magazines, often for a single item; a customer's response is followed up by the despatch of a specialised catalogue. Direct Mail is targeted, unsolicited, to potential customers on a mailing list generated from a computer database; the material is usually in the form of leaflets or small catalogues. It is the existence of large, easily interrogated databases which makes possible the targeting of individual consumers in an increasingly segmented marketplace. The atomisation and individualisation of social formations under advanced capitalism has a particularly symbiotic relationship with new technology in this area.

Despite the well-publicised launching of ventures such as Next Directory, these new forms of marketing are not replacing the large general catalogue listing a broad variety of products and sold through agents, on credit, to lower income groups. The traditional system of selling through agents remains largely intact. It is still responsible for 85 per cent of sales at Empire Stores (Collins, 1989), and has been estimated as nearly 90 per cent of the total home shopping sector (Urry, 1988). One of the companies has withdrawn from the specialogue market for the time being following the failure of an ill-considered scheme. Another firm has made a positive decision not to deploy a segmented marketing approach and to stick to its traditional downmarket niche. Futuristic assumptions about the segmented marketplace led to companies overreaching themselves during the mid-1980s. Specialised marketing has enhanced marginal profitability for some companies, but more important structurally are the demands it makes for flexible and complex technological and information handling systems.

Another aspect of restructuring is the takeover of small firms in an already highly-concentrated industry, whose oligopolistic tendencies are restrained only by the Monopolies and Mergers Commission. The MMC demonstrated in 1983 that major moves to concentrate the industry further would not be tolerated, when it forbade the takeover of Empire by GUS. There have been smaller takeovers in the 1980s, for example Grattan's acquisitions of Kaleidoscope and Scotcade, but these are peripheral and there is little scope in the industry for major restructuring of capital through mergers and acquisitions. The merger of Grattan and Next in 1986 created a large conglomerate spanning mail order and the High Street, seen at the time as a fusion of Next's marketing flair with Grattan's systems expertise, but the stock-market's expectations of continued spectacular growth proved largely unjustified.

The industry is, then, unable to enhance profitability significantly by playing the corporate merger game, and the gains expected from specialised marketing have only partially materialised. For the directors of the Big Five, the most promising route to profitability appears to be to pursue a rigorous containment of costs by continuing to target the well-established working-class marketplace with the traditional comprehensive catalogue, but to reduce the unit cost of despatching the goods. This containment of costs is being achieved through the enhancement of systems and the through labour process changes; productivity is being increased through the introduction of new technology and through the intensification of labour. Such a strategy is best described not as flexible specialisation, but as an extension of Taylorism.

The Applications of New Technologies

The technological base of the catalogue mail order industry has undergone very extensive change during the 1970s and 1980s. Infrastructure and jobs have altered significantly in both warehouse and office.

Office automation is universal. Typically the initial computerisation of data in mail order firms took place in the 1970s and early 1980s. The database facilities maintained by the computing arms of Grattan and Great Universal Stores have space, typically, for eighty lines of data on every adult in the UK. This level of detail facilitates selective mailshots.

The late 1980s have seen the introduction of performance-monitoring techniques, which incorporate data capture into the software so that the productivity of individuals and departments can be determined very precisely. Separate data capture facilities are not required – simply the software to interpret the operator's keystrokes in a manner useful to management.

Work measurement and individualised bonus systems, long familiar in the warehouse, are being implemented in the office. The monitoring of office work in minute particulars facilities internalised discipline through pay incentives as well as providing information for external discipline through supervision. The firm can exert precise control over labour costs by paying a bonus rate exactly matched to the number of item sales processed by the operator.

Where data entry and typing do not involve discretion, the work is measured relatively simply, by the number of items processed. More conflict has arisen from management attempts to measure work which requires higher degrees of discretion. The main example of this is the work undertaken by general office staff who utilise in their VDU work a broad, general, experience-based and intuitive knowledge and grasp of the company's operations. If a difficult problem such as a customer complaint is being dealt with, it is inappropriate to apply simple work measurement methods.

In general clerical work the extent to which work can be measured is contingent upon the degree of discretion involved in the work, but we have firm evidence that work study officers are developing methods of assessing even the most unusual and difficult situations that experienced workers have to deal with. This involves working out the likely frequency of such situations, setting appropriate pay rates, and then implementing pay incentive schemes just as deterministic as those now applied to workers engaged on basic typing and data entry. The more experienced office workers we spoke to felt that this process was an insult to their conscientiousness. It is a mistake to assume that 'VDU work' represents an homogeneous stratum of employment.

Modern Warehousing Systems

Orders placed by mail are of shrinking importance and electronic media have largely taken over. The fastphone department is now effectively the heart of the operation in terms of information processing. However, the companies do not yet have available to them the infrastructure for automating the ordering process altogether. Human telephone operators are still necessary. Interactive electronic ordering has not yet taken off due to the market failure of Prestel, in contrast to France where the Minitel package – including keyboard, screen, and modem – is given free to telephone subscribers. British mail order companies have prototype systems – the full Kays catalogue of 35000 items can be read on Prestel – but the number of subscribers is so low that significant sales through such media have yet to materialise. The involvement of Next/Grattan in British Satellite Broadcasting seems to indicate that the industry is looking seriously at new technologies but for the moment the telephone remains the most important medium for the placing of orders.

On the physical side of warehousing there are various modern systems. The broad shift is away from the traditional knowledge/commonsense method. Traditionally, workers had some discretion to choose their route around the warehouse, picking items, using their initiative to optimise their own efficiency, and picking the whole of a customer's order. Such methods partially persist in some of the smaller warehouses, but in even the most traditionally organised warehouse we saw, workers now pick items according to a route determined by the computer and printed out on a picking slip.

Cockburn (1985) describes how modern warehousing systems represent gendered oppression, designed by men and operated predominantly by women. The warehouse workforces in all the firms are mixed, but usually mostly female. This is reflected in the trade union, most branch secretaries being female. Only one of the major firms has a predominantly male workforce in the warehouse, and male trade unionists in senior positions. This company has the highest wage rates in the Northern England mail order industry for both warehouse and office workers. It is difficult to account for the gender composition of this workforce other than by attributing it to company tradition, since two other large mail order companies are based in the same conurbation and both of them conform to the usual, feminised model.

In large warehouses dealing with a general catalogue, the pickers now only partly fill a customer's order. If it is 'gondola' system, they work in a specific aisle and have to pick the required items in time to put them in the appropriate container or gondola before it disappears to another department or floor. Pickers told us that this machine-paced work was stressful, and in at least one workplace there was a high proportion of temporary workers in the picking department. In the case of a 'carousel' system the operator does not move around at all, the items being brought to the workstation by the conveyor system. Again, the work is machine-paced.

These technologies represent an intensification of work and an erosion of autonomy. In one company where a gondola system had been introduced, the faster pace of work had led to increased absenteeism and health problems. Automation of bulk warehousing is less widespread but is being diffused rapidly. It involves the introduction of Automated Guidance Vehicles (AGVs) for picking and transporting bulk stock from an automated warehouse.

Technological change, then, is facilitating the intensification of work by two means: computerised monitoring of work, and machine pacing.

Skill: Moving the Goalposts

One workplace we studied has modern telephone and computing equipment, but the warehouse provides an example of an earlier stage of technological development because it deals with a single product range – shoes. Management has taken the view that capital investment in gondola or carousel systems is not justified at this stage because there is less need for flexibility than in warehouses at other sites owned by the group which deal with the full product range. There has however been some technological innovation in this warehouse and one of the changes has provoked a conflict which provides evidence for the deskilling versus enskilling debate.

In mail order warehouses there is a Returns department which deals with goods sent back by customers and agents. Before being returned to stock, the goods have to be inspected. The inspection workers in this warehouse used to record the details of each item manually. This job has now been divided and the data entry part of it is done at a computer terminal. This data entry function is a new job for work evaluation purposes. There is a reduced number of workers doing the inspection work, since they have less paperwork to do. Some of the former inspection workers had retrained as data entry operators, thinking that they were acquiring useful keyboard and computer skills which would upgrade their job status. It was only after their redeployment from inspection work to data entry that they discovered that in fact they had been downgraded onto a lower pay scale on the grounds that data entry was a deterministic activity which did not require the discretion and skill needed for inspecting goods.

The received wisdom is that whilst jobs are deskilled in one place, reskilling occurs elsewhere – typically in the form of computer skills. This episode, however, demonstrates that ambiguities concerning skill can arise in one and the same job, because employers and employees in the industry have valuations of skill which are structurally opposed. This story was related to us not by aggrieved workers (though they were pursuing an appeal) but by personnel officers, and not without a degree of glee, supporting the view that this supposed deskilling represented a conscious managerial strategy.

THE FASTPHONE DEPARTMENT

Peripheral Forms of Employment

A striking feature of the employment pattern in the industry is that the operational nerve-centres, the telephone ordering departments, are staffed almost entirely by women part-timers. This move into a part-time employment pattern in a vital part of the business extracts maximum employer benefit from the position of women in both the industrial labour market and the domestic division of labour.

It has been asserted for some years (Edwards *et al.*, 1979) that modern industrial societies are witnessing a polarisation of the labour market into a core of skilled workers and a periphery of workers in jobs which have been largely deskilled. Recent evidence suggests that this process is continuing and that the gender divide is an enabling factor. Gallie (1988, p. 30) argues on the basis of data from a major UK research programme of the 1980s, the Social Change and Economic Life Initiative, that:

> It is men above all that have benefited from the progress of skills in the 1980s, while women are much less likely to have seen their skills increase. The central factor connected with this would appear to be the existence of a major sector of part-time female work, in which the existing levels of skill are typically low and which has remained untouched by the processes that have elsewhere contributed to skill enrichment.

Gallie's thesis is partially supported by our empirical findings concerning fastphone departments. An important reservation is that in this case the problem often lies in the systematic non-recognition of skill in female part-time work, rather than a lack of skills as such.

Telephone ordering or fastphone departments are a development of the 1980s. The job itself is new because it involves two simultaneous activities: telephone communication and the operation of a computer terminal. These departments provide an opportunity to test Gallie's thesis because they have virtually one hundred per cent female workforces most of whom work part-time and many of whom are on temporary contracts.

Because telephone ordering is now so central to mail order operations, the companies have devoted considerable resources to the control and monitoring of work in fastphone departments. They have also decided that part-time employment will be the norm in these departments. This is in line with a general expansion of part-time work in the UK retail sector in the late 1980s (Penn, this volume). The marginalising effects of women's part-time work are well-known. There are clear advantages to management in limiting their legal obligations to workers by means of an employment strategy maximising part-time work. The following account also provides evidence that from the viewpoint of capital there are two further advantages in this emphasis on part-time work. These are the facilitation of temporal flexibility, and the avoidance of problems arising from the fact that the operator is 'burnt out' after a typical shift of four hours.

The system depends on very close collaboration with British Telecom. The agent or customer calls what appears to be a local number, and the call is rerouted to the nerve centre of the mail order company. The computerisation of the customer database enables orders and basic enquiries from agents and customers to be dealt with in real time. Credit ratings are checked while the customer is on the phone although the customer is not informed of this. The operators who do this work are simultaneously operating a computer terminal and a telephone.

Instant response is facilitated by the development of very powerful mainframe computers capable of holding extremely large databases in fast-access disk memory. There is a central processing unit at one main site and operators at remote sites are linked with this. Telecommunications are again of vital importance here. If a link goes down the information handling of the company is paralysed. For example, a customer in London wishing to order from a catalogue calls a London number. The call is rerouted to Preston where a fastphone operator keys in the details which are processed by a central computer in Liverpool. The despatch details are sent from that computer to a distribution centre at Crosby. The customer is charged for the call only at the local rate.

Of the several thousand operators in the firms, only two that we knew of were male. There was anecdotal evidence that some years ago there had occasionally been male temporaries in telephone departments, but this had ceased when keyboard skills came to be vital. In all four of the establishments the vast majority of women in telephone departments worked part-time. Management were unanimous in justifying this by reference to the stress of dealing with members of the public many of whom are rude or aggressive, for example when they have been refused credit. This, it was asserted, meant that four hours of this sort of work was enough.

However, our impression from talking to the operators themselves was that whilst there was some truth in this, a more important cause of stress was the intensity of labour and sense of being constantly watched brought about by the individualised work-monitoring facilities of the computer system. Further stress resulted from the effects of VDU work on health. A self-completion questionnaire survey of 202 general VDU workers at one company (a response rate of 34 per cent), revealed 80 per cent of workers reporting muscular discomfort, 90 per cent visual discomfort, and the great majority broadly dissatisfied with their working conditions (Forrester *et al.*, 1989). From the discussions we had with job evaluation staff, there was no evidence that stress was properly reflected in pay rates.

The managerial justification for telephone work being mostly part-time contains some truth, but for operational rather than altruistic reasons. The concern is that if stress begins to tell after four hours, then productivity will be compromised. The companies also depend on the politeness and patience of telephone staff, which could be affected by mental tiredness (the gendered nature of 'niceness' is an additional reason for the employment of women rather than men in this job). Account must also be taken of managerial strategy concerning job design. The stressful nature of the work is not an inevitable corollary of the processes of communicating with the public by telephone and using a computer terminal. The stress is an outcome of the particular system chosen and the way in which it is implemented.

Technologies of Omniscience

The monitoring of telephone work comprises the capture and analysis of data both from the operator's keystrokes at the computer terminal and from the measurement of the time she takes to deal with each telephone enquiry. We saw two monitoring systems in operation whilst interviewing supervisory staff. One was produced by a Swedish microelectronics firm and another by a subsidiary of one of the UK mail order companies, although the latter was available to other firms. The data captured are stored for various purposes, including the determination of bonus pay in most of the firms. Information is also displayed for the supervisor in real time; instantly on the British system, and in 30-second updates on the Swedish one.

Some of this information is global and includes the number of calls being dealt with, the number being kept waiting for more than a given number of seconds, and the number of calls abandoned that day before being answered. Other information is specific to each operator. Operators log on and off with a personal password, so the precise duration of informal breaks is known. The total of personal break time taken is not demonstrated on the operator's screen, so she tends to take less than the 10 per cent typically allowed, for fear of exceeding her time allocation and being disciplined. An individual-ised bonus system using online work monitoring is in place in the telephone departments of three of the firms, and is expected in the fourth. The time spent on each call is recorded and is usually of relevance to the bonus, as is the number of items ordered. The women are expected to do marketing during the call, usually by mentioning special offers. If an operator dis-connects from the telephone to concentrate on the computer terminal – this is known as being 'in work' or 'in clerical' and is sometimes unavoidable – that time does not count towards the bonus.

There are widespread and well-founded concerns about the accuracy of system output. At one workplace using the Swedish monitoring system, a long-established and extremely conscientious worker was recorded as having accumulated toilet breaks of 45 minutes in a four-hour shift. This was universally regarded as impossible.

At another firm the Swedish system had been in operation for some years and the supervisors had confidence in it. The British system had been running in tandem with it for six months – management had been impressed by its friendly, colourful screens – and was giving different information. The two systems rarely tallied and the supervisors were concerned about the accuracy of the information from the British system. These supervisors also remarked that they were 'drowning in information' from these systems and that part of their skill was in knowing what to ignore.

The omniscience of the monitoring technology was in this case ameliorated by the fact that supervisors were often too busy to use it consistently. Where information on individual workers was relevant to pay, the computer sys-tem would impose the consequences of measured 'slackness' automatically, but disciplinary action was not inevitable, still requiring human intervention. The stress level associated with the system is dependent upon supervisory interpretation of monitored statistics. Most supervisors we met were women. There is a high proportion of women supervisors in both warehouse and office, because management prefer to appoint people with long experience of the shopfloor and it is a predominantly female industry. It is however difficult to progress beyond this first tier of line management and there are few women in senior managerial positions.

The question of skill is a complex one because the job, as a hybrid of telephone and clerical work, is relatively new. The extent of skill is contingent upon which separate half of the job we are comparing it with. Clearly, a worker coming into the job with only telephone experience would be gaining VDU skills. However, it is more appropriate to compare the job to VDU work in mail order, since prior to the growth of fastphone departments most of the information handling was done by VDU operators entering orders from documentation such as order forms sent in by agents.

There is still a need for a large number of such VDU operators since not all ordering is done by telephone and issues which are not straightforward, such as customer complaints, cannot be resolved during the course of a phone call. The centre of the operation was formerly the general office staffed by VDU operators but is now shifting towards the fastphone department.

In the general office the training period for simple data entry jobs is about two weeks, but that for *clerical* VDU operators is three to six months. Clerical work is more complex than basic data entry or typing, involving discretion over issues such as which standard letter should be sent to a customer who is in arrears with payments. There is a similar polarisation of skill in the fastphone department. The training period for the basic grade of telephone/VDU operator is, typically, two weeks and she is qualified only for basic order-taking. More complex calls are transferred to workers on a higher grade, who themselves pass issues which cannot be resolved immediately to the VDU-based clerical workers in the general office.

There is, then, a segregation of issues into positions in a hierarchy of difficulty. It is clearly to the advantage of management to extend this process to the point where the more experienced, more expensively trained, and higher-paid workers are dealing with difficult issues all the time, whilst the less knowledgeable workers in the fastphone department deal with the basics. Computerisation enables this, since a job can be passed from one operator to another in a matter of seconds. Workers on both higher and lower grades are conscious of this skill dichotomy. One highly experienced respondent from a general office was very critical of the lack of knowledge displayed by the telephone workers, and a shop steward in a fastphone department felt strongly that the training of fastphone workers was inadequate.

However, despite this targeted and systematised distribution of tasks to workers on different grades within the job, it is by no means clear that the job as a whole represents deskilling. It is more tenable to argue that the skill inherent in the job is not recognised by management. The job involves the simultaneous use of emotional and communication skills (with some customers the job virtually constitutes counselling), keyboard dexterity, and the ability to interrogate a database. That these skills are undervalued in pay terms, is an outcome of the labour market and industrial relations position.

A redesign of the job would involve using the same hardware, but with different software reflecting a different philosophy. It is reasonable enough for global information to be collected, on how well the department is dealing with calls, and indeed it could be made available generally rather than only on supervisor's screens. It is the individual monitoring that causes stress. Respondents in a department where the Swedish system had been introduced six months previously, reported the loss of a previously happy and co-operative atmosphere and a tangible worsening of relationships between operators and supervisors.

Functional Flexibility?

It has been argued (Pollert 1987; Elger and Fairbrother, this volume) that there are limits to the extent of flexibility in practice. Our evidence supports this insofar as functional flexibility is in question. There is *some* degree of functional flexibility. It is common practice in the workplaces we studied for general office clerical workers to do telephone answering work at busy times, on an *ad hoc* basis. Also, some data entry functions are being performed at terminals on the warehouse floor. However, this is developing in a piecemeal fashion. We found little evidence of comprehensive managerial strategy concerning functional flexibility. Indeed, we found evidence of the deliberate erosion of functional flexibility in order to simplify work measurement. The industry as a whole represents a paradigm of Taylorist scientific management in a contemporary form facilitated by information technology. There has been no implementation of quality circles or other post-Fordist devices. Temporal and numerical flexibility are more important than functional flexibility.

Temporal Flexibility

Temporal flexibility is facilitated by part-time employment. Fastphone departments are open long hours for the customer's convenience. Evenings and weekends are covered and some companies run a 24-hour, 7-days-a-week service. The gendered nature of employment and the domestic division of labour clearly facilitate the availability of women for shifts which cover these extended hours. Temporal flexibility is related to the market, reflecting mail order's position in the distribution sector. This may be contrasted (Leman, 1990) with the extension of temporal flexibility in extractive and manufacturing industries, where the usual objective is simply to maximise the return on fixed investment in plant. This is a new form of temporal flexibility, related to changing markets and facilitated by new technology. However, temporal flexibility also takes the more traditional form of overtime. This is highly seasonal; there is a great deal of it in the busy period leading up to Christmas. One personnel officer told us that workers 'found it difficult' to readjust to lower wages after a period of overtime, and that this caused bad feeling.

Numerical Flexibility

Numerical flexibility is a further means to minimise labour costs. It entails the use of temporary labour to accommodate fluctuations in retail demand. One operations manager told us that he favoured keeping core staff to the absolute minimum required at the slackest possible period and accommodating any demand in excess of that baseline with temporary workers. Temporary labour is used in both the warehouse and the office. Retail demand is sensitive to macroeconomic as well as seasonal factors, but the most common time to ditch temporaries is immediately after Christmas or in some cases just before, if the boom is judged to have peaked. At Christmas 1989 there was a heated managerial debate in one firm as to whether or not to get rid of eighty women employed as temporaries in the telephone department in mid-December. The boom eventually arrived and they were kept on, but another day would have seen the immediate end of their term of employment.

We met workers who had been employed as temporaries for up to four separate terms by the same mail order firm. In some cases they had been re-employed a fortnight after being laid off, and it was not unusual for the total time employed to exceed two years. There is anecdotal evidence of warehouse staff being retained on successive temporary contracts for eight years. Obvious conclusions may be drawn concerning the implications of such practices for management obligations under employment law.

Two classic forms of peripheral employment are, then, used in the industry to facilitate flexibility and the containment of labour costs: part-time labour enabling temporal flexibility, and temporary labour enabling numerical flexibility.

The example of fastphone departments shows that the mail order companies have conscious strategies concerning womens' employment. In this case there are three advantages to management in employing women as part-timers. Legal obligations are minimised; performance is optimised because short shifts mean fresher workers; and temporal flexibility is facilitated. The case fits Gallie's thesis insofar as it demonstrates the usefulness to management of an employment strategy involving part-time female employment in a key and growing sector. There are, however, ambiguities concerning skill. Whilst there is some evidence of skill polarisation between different grades within the job, there is equally compelling evidence that the job as a whole involves considerable skill. The very fact that management itself argues that it is difficult to sustain a high quality of work for more than four hours, supports the view that it calls for considerable mental effort and ability as well as communication skills. These qualities remain largely unrecognised by the managers of this 'male order'.

CONCLUSIONS

This chapter's main finding is that the UK mail order industry conforms only partially to theoretical models of flexible specialisation. Temporal flexibility is on the increase in the telephone ordering departments, and is associated with an extension of peripheral, part-time female employment. There is, however, little evidence of functional flexibility or multi-skilling. There is numerical flexibility but this is not new; employment in the industry has always been cyclical, having seasonal peaks towards Christmas and Easter and troughs at other times of the year. There is no evidence of the flexible recombination of industrial units: on the contrary, the industry is an oligopoly with tendencies towards further capital concentration which are held in check only by the Monopolies and Mergers Commission. The restructuring of the labour process in the industry results not from the new pressures of a diversified and segmented marketplace, but from the simple logic of Taylorist scientific management in association with technological options which permit greater precision in the control and monitoring of work.

Women's employment in the mail order industry during the last two decades has been deeply affected by new technologies. Predominantly male systems designers have chosen options for the implementation of warehousing and information technologies which emphasise the control and monitoring of women's work. This is not to assume technological determinism, since the technologies merely facilitate changes in work organisation which are contingent upon strategic managerial choice. The gendered nature of technological innovation, demonstrated by Cynthia Cockburn (1985) in relation to the warehouse, is equally prevalent in the office.

Note

1. I gratefully acknowledge the financial support of the ESRC and the SERC, the help of all concerned in the research on which this chapter is based, and the involvement of two colleagues in the Working Environment Research Group: Brian Jones who was my collaborator in the gathering of data, and Steve Allen who provided invaluable advice and information as well as transcribing taped interviews.

Part IV
New Patterns of
Employment

9 Older Worker Employment: Change and Continuity in the 1980s

Bernard Casey and Frank Laczko

Between 1979 and 1984 the British labour market underwent a profound transformation. Most dramatic was the rise in unemployment which occurred. From a level of 0.74m (4 per cent) in 1979, it had climbed to as much as 1.98m (11 per cent) five years later. This increase had its special impact on older workers and particularly on older male workers, many of whom not only lost their jobs but were encouraged or forced to withdraw from the labour market entirely. The proportion of older people who were in paid employment fell, in some cases quite spectacularly. Table 9.1 presents details for those in the age ranges 55–69. By 1984 only a half of 60–64 year old men were working, and this proportion was scarcely higher than that of women in the five years up to their 'official' retirement age.[1] In the years thereafter, when unemployment peaked and subsequently fell, older people's employment patterns were much more stable, so that in 1989 their employment rates stood at much the same level as in 1984.

What is of interest is whether the fall in employment rates which is to be observed in the first half of the 1980s is associated with a change in the structure of employment of older men. This could involved a change in the industrial distribution of the older workforce, representing either a differential degree of vulnerability to redundancy or a differential access to the opportunity for early retirement. Both of these propositions are merely restatements of the presumption that the character of a group frequently referred to in the literature and in public debate as if it were homogenous is, in fact, heterogeneous. However, the first is also a recognition of the older worker's role as a member of a 'buffer' group, liable to exclusion from the labour force as jobs become less plentiful. Moreover, if it is possible to envisage a process by which older workers are excluded totally from employment, it is also possible to imagine this process being part of a more encompassing one involving a move from more secure to less secure jobs. Those who have been forced out of employment might succeed in returning to work, but it might well be that the jobs to which they return are not only inferior to their previous jobs but are also jobs commonly regarded as

137

Table 9.1   Proportion of older people in employment, 1979, 1984 and 1989
(percentages)

		1979	1984	1989
Men aged:	55–59	88	74	73
	60–64	69	51	50
	65–69	18	13	13
Women aged:	55–59	52	48	51
	60–64	21	20	22
	65–69	7	7	9

Source: Labour Force Surveys; own calculations

'secondary', 'peripheral', or 'marginal'. Accordingly, we recognise the possible existence of a number of dimensions of disadvantage in the labour market, and we wish to examine how many are relevant to the particular group in question.

As well as using the experiences of older workers to illustrate a way in which tendencies for 'marginalisation' might manifest themselves, our study also has a current and practical relevance. There is today much concern about the ageing of the workforce and about substantial declines in traditional sources of labour. Both of these reasons have led government and employers to reassess (or more frequently, to start the process of assessing) their positions with respect to older workers. Such assessment or reassessment can only be aided by a greater understanding of the employment situation of older people, of the changes which have occurred over time and of the trends which underlie these changes.

In the following sections of the chapter, and by reference to data from the Labour Force Surveys of 1979, 1984 and 1989, we shall show: first that there was considerable difference in what happened to older workers depending upon the industry in which they were employed; second that there was a growth in the proportion of older workers occupying self-employed, part-time and temporary jobs, but that this development affected primarily those above the normal retirement age; and third, and on account of these last developments, older men's employment came a step closer to resembling older women's employment. A final section summarises and draws some conclusions for theory, policy and the future.

DIFFERENCE BETWEEN INDUSTRIES

The fall in employment rates described in the introduction was by no means a uniform one. With reference to men in the age range 55–64, for whom the fall was greatest, we were able to disaggregate the data to provide information about developments in 25 industry groups over the years 1979 to 1984, and to look separately at what happened to those in their late fifties and those in their early sixties. For each industry we compared the number in the age group 50–54 (55–59) in 1979 with the number in the age group 55–59(60–64) in 1984, and expressed the change in relative terms by comparing it to the base total. This gave the percentage of a five year cohort which had left employment in the industry over a five year period (or, where a positive figure was recorded, the amount by which a five year cohort was supplemented).[2]

In five of the industry groups the size of the cohort aged 55–59 in 1979 had fallen by more than 70 per cent five years later. The industries concerned were all from the manufacturing sector: coal, steel, mechanical engineering, motor vehicles and textiles. In the service sector, this phenomenon was rather less pronounced, but in central and local government and in quasi-public posts and telecommunications, falls approaching 60 per cent were recorded. In only one industry, hotels and catering, did the cohort grow in size, and there it did so by less than 10 per cent. The fall in the size of the cohort aged 50–54 in 1979 was smaller, but again in coal, steel, mechanical engineering and motors it was most pronounced (c.40–60 per cent). Equally, it was more pronounced in central and local government (c.35 per cent) than elsewhere in the service sector. In two industries net increases in the size of the cohort were to be seen – business services and miscellaneous services – and in both cases these were substantial (40 and 34 per cent respectively).

Our interest was in how much of the decline in older people's employment was the result of the overall employment decline experienced by those industries most badly hit by the recession of the early 1980s. In this respect we were trying to test a version of the so-called 'troubled industry hypothesis' (Jacobs *et al.*, 1987). This suggests that those industries which are contracting might be especially inclined to implement early retirement programmes or voluntary redundancy programmes constructed to attract older workers, both to ensure a smoother rundown and to avoid an over-ageing of their workforces.[3] We ran a simple regression of the percentage decline in a chosen age cohort in an industry against the decline in the industry's labour force and a number of other industry variables.[4] For both of the age cohorts a reasonable fit was obtained showing a strong and significant relationship

Table 9.2   Regression results for tests of the 'troubled industry' hypothesis, men

---

$\triangle$ EO$_1$ = −0.396   + 1.024 $\triangle$ TE − 0.305W   R^2 = 0.774
            (−0.142)   (2.548)   (−2.268)

$\triangle$ EO$_2$ = −42.264 + 1.360 $\triangle$ TE + 0.3275E   R^2 = 0.968
            (−9.735)   (2.251)   (1.357)

$\triangle$ EO$_1$ = change in the number of employees in the industry aged 50–54 in 1979
            and 55–59 in 1984 expressed as proportion of number of 50–54 year olds
            employed in 1979.
$\triangle$ EO$_2$ = same but with respect to those aged 55–59 in 1979 and 60–64 in 1984.
$\triangle$ TE = proportionate change in total employment in the industry 1979–84.
   W = proportion of total employment in the industry that was white collar.
  SE = proportion of 55–59 year olds who were self-employed in 1979.

Figures in brackets are t statistics
Source: Labour Force Surveys: own calculations

between change in cohort size and change in total industry employment. As Table 9.2 shows, each 10 percentage point decline in an industry's total employment resulted by 1984 in a 14 percentage point decline in the size of the cohort aged 55–59 in 1979, and a 10 percentage point decline in the size of the cohort aged 55–54 in 1979. This is substantial evidence in support of the 'troubled industry' hypothesis.

However, considerable differences were also observable between the two cohorts. The regression showed that as far as the older of the two cohorts was concerned there occurred a major secular decline in employment over the five year period. Our results suggest that even without the cutback of jobs which occurred in the first half of the decade we could have expected a fall in the number of this cohort in employment of over 40 per cent. No such tendency was apparent for the younger cohort, at least not as a whole. With respect to the younger cohort, however, what the regression did show was that in more heavily white collar dominated industries, it declined in size faster. Thus, there are also signs of a generalised movement to early retirement, and this might be more pronounced and/or earlier amongst white collar workers. These employees, it is to be remembered, are more likely to be covered by occupational pension schemes, and their schemes tend to have lower retirement ages than do schemes for blue collar workers. Finally, and although of weak statistical significance, it appears that the higher the proportion of older workers who are self-employed, the smaller the decline in the older of the two cohorts. This phenomenon of the older self-employed staying on longer in work is one to which we shall return in the following section of this chapter.

GROWTH OF 'NON-STANDARD' EMPLOYMENT

A second way in which older workers might experience disadvantage was suggested to be a move from permanent to temporary and from full to part-time jobs. An increase in disadvantage might be seen as an increase in the importance of 'peripheral' or 'marginal' jobs. However, since these terms have value laden connotations, we prefer (following Goldthorpe, 1984) instead to use the term 'non-standard employment form' and thereby designate all forms of employment other than full-time dependent employment. The LFS permits three such forms to be identified: self-employment, part-time employment and (first from 1983), temporary employment. These are shown in Table 9.3.

Self-employment

The rise over the first half of the 1980s in the proportion of older workers who described themselves as self-employed closely mirrors the decline in the proportion who described themselves as full-time employees. The increase in self-employment amongst older workers resembles that amongst the generality of workers, for whom it rose from 7 per cent to 11 per cent, but its very high absolute level, especially amongst men and women over pension age, is remarkable. In 1984 nearly 40 per cent of working men aged 65–69 were self-employed, compared to only 15 per cent of all working men. So were 11 per cent of working women aged 60–64 and 18 per cent of working women aged 65–69, whilst the self-employment rate for all working women was only 7 per cent. Although some of these older self-employed are small scale entrepreneurs, many of them are not. It was the proportion of self-employed without employees which grew faster between 1979 and 1984, particularly amongst men over pension age.

The higher than average level of self-employment amongst the very oldest workers has been commented upon before (see Creigh *et al.*, 1986; Dale and Bamford, 1988), but developments over time have not. What is of interest is whether the higher proportion of older workers who are self-employed represents a significant inflow into self-employment, or whether instead it is indicative of the self-employed staying on in the labour market as other categories of worker drop out. These propositions were tested by comparing the number of self-employed in a five year age group with the

Table 9.3 Status of employed older men and women, 1979, 1984 and 1989 (percentages)

	Aged 55–59			Aged 60–64			Aged 65–69		
	1979	1984	1989	1979	1984	1989	1979	1984	1989
Men:									
Full-time employee	89	84	78	86	79	74	31	16	16
Part-time employee	1	2	2	3	5	7	48	44	47
Self-employed	9	14	20	10	16	19	19	39	37
All part-time	3	4	6	5	8	11	53	65	67
All temporary	na	3	3	na	3	4	na	19	15
Women:									
Full-time employee	46	44	42	30	30	23	17	15	11
Part-time employee	48	48	51	61	63	67	71	66	67
Self-employed	5	7	7	8	11	10	10	18	21
All part-time	50	54	57	65	73	74	77	75	83
All temporary	na	4	6	na	8	8	na	11	17

Note The first three rows sum to 100 per cent and are based upon respondents' self-categorisation; the fourth row defines as part-time all those (employees and self-employed) who usually work 30 hours or less per week, the fifth row defines as temporary all those (employees and self-employed) who said their jobs were seasonal, temporary or casual, or on a fixed contract.

Source: Labour Force Surveys: own calculations

Table 9.4   Number of self-employed of a given age in 1984 as a proportion of the number of self-employed five years younger in 1979 (percentages)

	Self-employed		*All employees*
MEN			
Cohort aged:			
50–54 in 1979 and 55–59 in 1984	103	(105)	80 (85)
55–59 in 1979 and 60–64 in 1984	102	(93)	58 (67)
60–64 in 1979 and 65–69 in 1984	70	(60)	18 (25)
WOMEN			
Cohort aged:			
50–54 in 1979 and 55–59 in 1984	148	(92)	77 (82)
55–59 in 1979 and 60–64 in 1984	92	(64)	39 (45)
60–64 in 1979 and 65–69 in 1984	78	(67)	32 (35)

The table is to read as follows: the number of 65–69 year old self-employed men in 1984 was 70% of the number of 60–64 year old self-employed men in 1979.

Key ( ) = number in 1989 as a proportion of number in 1984
Source: Labour Force Surveys; own calculations; ( ) = 1988–9

number in the succeeding five year age group five years later. This is done in Table 9.4, which considers developments between 1984 and 1989 as well as those between 1979 and 1984. As far as women are concerned there was a substantial net increase in the number self-employed in the age range 55–59 between 1979 and 1984. Otherwise, it appears that the number of self-employed, whilst falling, fell very much more slowly than that of workers as a whole. Although not conclusive, this finding does suggest that the self-employed 'hung on' longer in employment than did dependent employees and that this was particularly so in the first part of the decade. Equally, looking at movements over a single year, it can be seen that the overwhelming majority – some 85–90 per cent – of the older self-employed were self-employed twelve months previously and that they displayed rather greater stability than did the totality of the self-employed (some 80 per cent of whom were self-employed 12 months previously). Finally, if we consider not inflows into but outflows out of self-employment and dependent employment, there is further evidence that the self-employed are more likely to remain in employment. Table 9.5 shows that those older men who were dependent employees in 1983 were two to three times more likely to have ceased working in 1984 than those who were self-employed.

Table 9.5 Outflows out of self-employment, men, 1983–1984 (percentages)

	Situation in 1983 (1988)					
	Aged 55–59		Aged 60–64		Aged 65–69	
Situation in 1984 (1989)	Self-employment	Dependent employment	Self-employment	Dependent employment	Self-employment	Dependent employment
Self-employment	94 (92)	1 (*)	94 (91)	* (1)	85 (94)	2 (1)
Dependent employment	3 (5)	92 (97)	* (6)	83 (96)	– (3)	53 (87)
Not working	3 (6)	7 (2)	6 (2)	17 (2)	15 (1)	46 (10)

Source: Labour Force Surveys; own calculations; ( ) = 1988–89

Table 9.6   Proportion of older men changing from full-time to part-time jobs, 1983–1984 (percentages)

	Aged 55–59	Aged 60–64	Aged 65–69
Of those who:			
Stayed with same firm	0	1	6
Changed to a diff. firm	11	‎22	

Source: 1984 Labour Force Survey; own calculations

Part-time Working

As well as the high level of self-employment, a second characteristic of older people's employment patterns is a high level of part-time employment. Although its level is scarcely significant amongst men under retirement age, part-time working is the dominant form of employment amongst men over retirement age, and amongst women too it becomes more important once they are over the age of 65. As far as men above 65 are concerned, the proportion working part-time increased over the first part of the 1980s, from a half to over two thirds. As has been pointed out by others (see Dale and Bamford, 1988; Laczko, 1988), a substantial proportion of men under pension age – a half to one third – who are working part-time can be considered to be doing so 'involuntarily', because of poor health or because no full-time job could be found, but most women and nearly all men over pension age are doing so 'voluntarily', because they did not want a full-time job.[5] Amongst both these latter groups, and particularly the last of them, there is a considerable overlap between part-time working and self-employment. Nearly one in three 65–69 year old self-employed men were working on a part-time basis, although it was still true to say that the self-employed were less likely to be in part-time jobs than were other older men.

Because of the major shift in working patterns that is apparent when those below and those above retirement age are compared, it is worth considering in more detail the transition from full-time to part-time working. Analysing the 1984 LFS for single years of age revealed that there is some step down from full to part-time working at the age of 65 itself. A reduction in working hours can come within the same job or as a consequence of a job change (coupled with a change of employer). From Table 9.6 it is clear that such reductions came about almost exclusively as a consequence of a job change. This is not surprising, since Britain, unlike certain other European countries, is without an institutionalised gradual retirement system.

Over and above this source of inflow into part-time jobs is the inflow from non-employment (unemployment or inactivity). Between a tenth and a fifth of older men who were working part-time in 1984 had been out of employment the year before, although amongst women the proportion was much lower. Looking at those men who re-entered the labour market between 1983 and 1984, one fifth of those aged 55–59, one quarter of those aged 60–64 and almost all of those aged 65–69 went into part-time jobs.

Temporary Working

Again earlier studies have already pointed out the higher than average incidence of temporary working amongst workers over retirement age (Casey, 1988). The difference is most marked amongst men, where between one in five (1984) and one in six (1989) of those working over the age of 65 claimed to have a temporary job. Like those working part-time, most older workers working on a temporary basis were doing so 'voluntarily', that is, they did not want a permanent job, rather than 'involuntarily'. Another even more substantial overlap between different forms of 'non-standard' working stands out in that, with the exception of men below retirement age, almost all older temporary workers were also part-time workers. Temporary as much as part-time jobs provided a route back into employment for those older women and over-retirement age men able or wanting to return to work.

THE EROSION OF GENDER DIFFERENCES

An earlier analysis of the labour market situation of older people (Dale and Bamford, 1988) using data from the 1984 LFS concluded there was evidence that, as they reach the end of their working life, the employment patterns of men came increasingly to resemble those of women. As the previous section has made clear, the incidence of 'non-standard' employment forms is much higher amongst men in their sixties, and particularly amongst men over retirement age, than amongst those of prime age. Below retirement age, however, the large majority of older men who are in employment are still in full-time employment, whilst the majority of women in employment are already in part-time employment. It is only above retirement age that the incidence of part-time working for men becomes substantial, indeed the dominant form of employment.

Our own analysis has enabled us to examine the phenomenon of an 'erosion of gender differences' longitudinally as well as cross-sectionally. As Table 9.3 shows, between 1979 and 1984 the proportion of men in the

Table 9.7   Index of concentration by industry for older workers, 1979, 1984 and 1989

	1979	1984	1989
Men aged:			
55–59	0.276	0.265	0.330
60–64	0.291	0.279	0.327
65–69	0.410	0.495	0.565
Women aged:			
55–59	0.521	0.639	0.581
60–64	0.534	0.640	0.625
65–69	0.626	0.632	0.631

Note   The index is a Gini coefficient. A value of 0 means older workers are equally distributed across industries according to their size and a value of 1 means they are concentrated in only one industry.

Source: Labour Force Surveys; own calculations

five years above retirement age who were working part-time increased from 53 to 65 per cent, whilst for women aged 60–64 it increased only from 65 to 73 per cent and for those aged 65–69 it stayed virtually constant at 77 per cent. Nevertheless, this convergence effectively ceased, and if anything gave indications of a reversal, in the five years that followed. The share of over pension age men working part-time scarcely increased any further, whilst that of over 65 year-old women started to rise.

One further development stands out from an analysis of employment patterns over time. There are clear indications of an increasing concentration of older male workers into a limited number of industries. Such a concentration is generally agreed to be a characteristic of female employment. Measured with the Gini coefficient,[6] the extent of concentration for men aged 65–69 is double that of men aged 55–59. The Gini coefficient for older women, on the other hand, stays constant with advancing age. Without doubt related to the increase in the incidence of part-time working amongst older men over the first half of the decade is the fact that the increase in the degree of concentration as they passed over retirement age was markedly greater in 1984 than in 1979. Between 1984 and the end of the decade there was little further change in this respect. Table 9.7 shows this.[7]

If there are indications of a convergence, it should also be emphasised that, even where they appear to be similar, older men's employment patterns differ from those of older women. The large majority of older women

Table 9.8   Overlaps of different forms of 'non-standard' work amongst older workers, 1984 (percentages)

	Aged 55–59		*Aged 60–64*		*Aged 65–69*	
	Men	*Women*	*Men*	*Women*	*Men*	*Women*
Self-employed:						
Only self-employed	92	62	89	49	47	46
Self-employed and part-time	3	32	7	31	37	42
Self-employed and temporary	4	0	2	1	1	0
Self-employed, part-time and temporary	1	6	3	19	15	12
Part-time:						
Only part-time	35	89	59	84	50	76
Part-time and self-employed	32	4	22	5	22	10
Part-time and temporary	23	6	11	8	19	11
Part-time, self-employed and temporary	9	1	8	3	9	3

Source: 1984 Labour Force Survey; own calculations

working part-time are 'non-standard' workers on one dimension only (see Casey and Creigh, 1989). This is not so for older male part-timers. As Table 9.8 shows, a substantial proportion are 'non-standard' on at least two dimensions. They are either both part-time and self-employed, or part-time and temporary, and in nearly one case in ten they are part-time, self-employed and temporary. To a lesser extent, we can also see that whilst older self-employed men, or at least those below pension age, are almost exclusively only self-employed, older self-employed women are much more likely also to be part-timers or to be part-timers and to be in temporary jobs.

CONCLUSIONS

In this final section we review the relevance of the themes of 'marginalisation' and 'exclusion' which had provided the original impetus to this study. This leads to a discussion of whether recent government policy initiatives might contribute to an amelioration of the position of older people on the labour market. Finally, we ask whether the changing labour market of the 1990s and beyond may not bring its own element of relief to this group.

Exclusion

Both this chapter and its predecessor (Casey and Laczko, 1989) have brought forth evidence that much of the decline in the employment (and activity) rates of older men in the first part of the 1980s was a consequence of the deterioration of the labour market that occurred in the form of a large increase in the number of redundancies declared, a massive rise in the level of unemployment and a severe contraction in the number of job opportunities available. Here we have suggested that those older workers employed in industries which were contracting fastest were most likely to leave employment and, by implication, the labour market. In finding support for the 'troubled industry' hypothesis, we are able to place Britain in a different category to certain other European countries, notably France and Germany. There, according to other researchers (Jacobs *et al.*, 1987), the decline in older people's employment was similar across all industries, growing ones as much as declining ones.[8] This phenomenon they explained by the way in which social policy instruments, perhaps initially developed to respond to problems of (older worker) unemployment, had in the course of time been extended to create a generalised right to early retirement. In consequence, they doubted whether the trend to early retirement was easily reversible.

Insofar as early retirement in Britain does appear to be a product of particular economic circumstances this might be argued not to be the case here. An upturn should at least stabilise or even reduce the proportion leaving work early. However, this is unlikely to be of any consolation to those who have already been displaced, for the jobs that they did have, it is generally agreed, have disappeared forever. The only opportunities open to them are in the growing sectors, involving jobs at rates of pay and hours of work very different from those which they have been used. Whether they would be taken up is a point to which we shall return.

However, over and above this, we also found some signs of a generalisation of early retirement, signs that might well be stronger where older and or white collar workers were concerned. Such early retirement might be favoured both by management, to whom it gives the opportunity to restructure the labour force in a relatively painless fashion, and by employees, who, seeing it repeatedly practised, come to regard it as an acquired right. This last has been asserted by some researchers (Varloam and Bevan, 1987) although contested by other (Casey *et al.*, 1989). If it does prove to be widespread, it presents enterprises with a dilemma. With the supply of young workers contracting, management might want to retain a greater proportion of their older workers in employment, yet be reluctant, given the precedents set in the last decade and a half, to try and do so.

Turning to the growth in self-employment amongst older workers in the course of the 1980s, we have suggested that it is less likely to be due to the pull created by a climate favourable to enterprise or to the push provided by actual or threatened unemployment, and more likely to be due to the superior ability of the older self-employed to 'hang on' to their jobs. Unlike dependent employees, they could not be made redundant, and they could not be tempted by more or less generous early retirement packages. On the other hand, the businesses they were operating were not necessarily rewarding ones. Some might have been running at an economic or even an accounting loss, and so constituted more a source of activity than of employment. For some of the older self-employed, hanging on might have been an economic necessity. They did not have an occupational pension to support them should they have wished to retire (early or otherwise) and so were obliged to carry on working.[9]

Marginalisation

Combining the discussion of the incidence of 'non-standard' working with the previous discussion of early retirement leads us to the question of whether the major upheaval of the labour market in the first part of the decade contributed to an increasing marginalisation and exclusion of older workers. If, following one commentator (Standing, 1986), marginalisation implies not only the occupancy of part-time, temporary or self-employed jobs, but also the occupancy of these jobs on an involuntary basis, then there is little evidence of older worker marginalisation. Where older workers are to be found in part-time or temporary jobs, the large majority have taken them because they do not want full-time or permanent employment. Equally, if an equation is made between 'female' jobs and 'marginal' jobs, and if an erosion of gender differences such that male employees become more like female employees is taken to imply marginalisation, there is also little evidence of older worker marginalisation. Only a very small proportion of older men below retirement age are working part-time, and although this proportion rose in the first part of the 1980s, it did so from a very low base.

Policy Implications

The fact that the proportion of older non-workers returning to employment is very low has long been recognised by pressure groups advocating the interests of the (older) long-term unemployed. They have argued that part-time or temporary jobs might provide the sort of work experience which would facilitate a subsequent transition to full-time employment. Yet the benefits system, by effectively imposing a 100 per cent marginal tax rate on part-time earnings, rules this option out (Ashby, 1989). In response to such arguments, in Summer 1989 the government unveiled a pilot '50 plus Jobstart' scheme permitting those over 50 and out of work for at least a year to claim a £20 per week allowance if they took on a (low-paid) part-time job. Currently the scheme is limited in coverage – it operates in only four local labour markets – and the level of the allowance has been criticised as too low. Nevertheless a more extensive and more generous scheme, as envisaged by some parties (see Employment Committee, 1989), might considerably enhance the incidence of part-time working amongst men below retirement age.

Although it has yet to formulate its proposal in concrete terms, the government has also given general support to the concept of 'a decade of flexible retirement'. This concept is seen to imply the possibility of retirement at some time between the age of 60 and 70, with the level of pension being higher the more retirement is postponed and with opportunities to combine a partial pension with part-time work. It has won considerable support, political and academic and from the (in this country still embryonic) movements representing older people. However, an attractive system of gradual retirement, such as that in Sweden (see Laczko, 1988), would enable older people to reduce their hours of work whilst staying with their current employer and in their current job. At present, according to the LFS, very few of those who move from full to part-time jobs do so in this way. The majority change employer, and for them the move to part-time work is often associated with a move to a lower status job. For the objective of gradual retirement to be achieved on a wide scale, fundamental reforms seem necessary, not only of the state retirement benefits system but also of the personnel policy of individual employing organisations.

Prospects for the 1990s

Finally, we should ask whether our analysis provides support for the expectation that the 1990s will bring about changes in the situation of older workers on the labour market. We have already made reference to the impact of demographic change on the structure of labour supply. Given a sharp decrease in the number of young workers that will only bottom out by the middle of the decade but will not improve thereafter, employers in the worst affected industries and the worst affected areas are beginning to take active steps to use alternative sources of labour. Examples of the initiatives adopted by some of the front line firms include the targeted recruitment of older workers and efforts to encourage those approaching and beyond retirement age to stay on (see CBI, 1989; NEDO, 1989; Rainnie and Kraithman in this volume). Yet if older workers indeed form one of the buffer stocks on the labour market, this too is an expected outcome. The part older workers play for some firms today, or might play as the decade progresses, is no different to that accorded them in the labour hungry 1960s (see Phillipson, 1982). Moreover, the sectors which are leading the way in exploiting older workers as a resource, particularly retailing and catering, are those where part-time working is of considerable importance, so that many of the new older workers are also part-time workers. To this extent, certain of the trends with respect to employment patterns which we identified as developing in the first part of the 1980s might be continued in the first part of the 1990s, despite the fact that the forces giving rise to them are different.

Perhaps the most significant trend for the future has been the growth in self-employment. It is apparent that the self-employed are more likely to stay in paid work beyond state pension age, although the reasons for their so doing are not always positive. If the higher levels of self-employment undertaken by current cohorts of younger and middle-aged workers are sustained into older age, it could mean that future generations of older workers have greater choice of retirement age (Laczko, 1990). The recent increase in self-employment might actually do more to promote flexibility in retirement than recent changes in public policy.

Notes

The research on which this paper is based was financed by the ESRC under Grant R000 23 1236. Thanks are due to Terence Hogarth (PSI) for setting up the 1979 and 1984 Labour Force Surveys for analysis, and to Chris Henson of the Department of Employment for providing some special tabulations from the 1989 Labour Force Survey. Responsibility for the contents lies with the authors.

1. Prima facie, older men were more profoundly affected by the deterioration of the labour market than older women. Their participation rate fell, whilst that of older women stayed more or less constant. It should, of course, be recognised that the latter had been rising in the preceding years and might have continued to do so if the labour market had been more favourable. Nevertheless, it is largely on the more 'spectacular' developments concerning older men that this chapter concentrates.

2. Strictly speaking, leaving employment in an industry is not synonymous with leaving employment entirely or retiring. Some older workers might have left

employment in one industry and taken up employment elsewhere. However, as we shall see, the incidence of older workers changing employer or of coming into employment from unemployment or inactivity is very low.

3. Employers might have been motivated by industrial relations concerns (voluntary redundancies and early retirements were more socially acceptable than compulsory redundancies) and productivity concerns (a policy of compulsory redundancy would tend to increase the proportion of the labour force who were old, since they would normally have greatest seniority). Whether older workers are, indeed, less productive will not be debated here.

4. The regression was weighted by the percentage decline of the industry labour force to counteract the heteroscedasticity present in the initial, unweighed specification.

5. One quarter of 65–69 year old men and just over a quarter of 60–64 year old women who had jobs were working not more than 12 hours per week, the maximum compatible with receipt of a state retirement pension.

6. The Gini coefficient is most frequently used to measure the degree of inequality or equality of income distribution between different groups in a population. Its value lies between 1 (one group enjoys all the income) and 0 (income is divided between groups according to their respective sizes).

7. Although there appears to be little difference between the sexes in terms of the degree of occupational concentration experienced by older workers, there are major differences in terms of the type of occupation in which they are to be found. In particular, a substantial proportion of older men are to be found in managerial jobs, which is associated with the high incidence of self-employment amongst them, whilst a substantial proportion of older women are found in selling and personal service jobs, which is associated with the high incidence of part-time working amongst them.

8. It should be emphasised that Jacobs/Kohli/Rein looked at the period 1971–81 (that is, a different period to us) and used shift-share analysis to explain movements in the relative share of older worker employment in an industry (that is, a different method to us).

9. The LFS does not permit us to examine these issues, but they are certainly worthy of further research.

10 Structure and Sentiment: Family and Rationality Within the Capitalist Enterprise

Ian Roberts and Glyn Holroyd

The relationship between the family and industry has been an issue of concern to social theorists since the beginnings of the industrial revolution. Most observers, even up to the present day, consider that either the development of the material processes involved in capitalist industry or the extension of the formal rationality of capitalism necessarily imply a decrease in the importance of the family in industry. As Marx and Engels saw it:

> The bourgeois clap-trap about the family and education, about the hallowed co-relation of parent and child becomes all the more disgusting, the more, by the action of modern industry, all family ties among the proletarians are torn asunder, and their children transformed into simple articles of commerce and instruments of labour (Marx and Engels, 1848, p. 70).

For Weber also, the extension under capitalism of formal rationality implied the displacement of the family as an element exercising an effect within industry. Thus the extension of formal rationality necessitates:

> the most complete possible separation of the enterprise and its conditions of success and failure, from the household or private budgeting unit and its property interests (Weber, 1947, p. 275).

Smelser (1959) extended Weber's insight in his study of the textile industry. He argued that as textile production increasingly geared towards a cash market the problem of efficiency encouraged specialisation of function and the selection of specialists according to competence rather than traditional kinship duties and obligations. Success came to depend upon assigning specific jobs to the most competent individuals regardless of sentimental or family connections. More recent theories of the changing role of the family consequent upon industrialisation demonstrate a greater sophistication about the diminishing impact of the family in industry substituting an historical 'ebb and flow' for a unitary development.

Thus Joyce (1980), focusing on Lancashire, notes that technical changes during the 1840s weakened family links within the factory and yet in the 1850s further changes strengthened them again, to the extent that 'work household and neighbourhood were characterised by the same pattern of basically familial relations'. However, for Joyce as for others (Smelser, 1959; Anderson, 1971; Foster, 1974) the issue is seen far more in terms of a debate about the period of the break in the link between industry and family than any more radical questioning of the basic structure of events (Harris 1983; Joyce 1980).

It is the purpose of this chapter to question the validity of studies such as those mentioned above. The critique is based on both empirical and conceptual objections. In a final section the continued importance of the family in the small firm, in both its objective and symbolic aspects, is demonstrated. the empirical material used here as illustration is drawn from a study of industrial relations in small firms sponsored by the Department of Employment. The fieldwork was carried out entirely by the authors. A comprehensive account of this project can be found in Scott, Roberts, Holroyd and Sawbridge (1989).

THE DECLINE OF THE FAMILY IN INDUSTRY?

While accounts of the factors contributing towards a decline in the importance of the family in industry may differ, the eventual outcome seems beyond doubts: such a decline was an inevitable outcome of the rise of capitalist industry and the eventual transformation of the family from a unit of production to a unit of consumption. The first point to make is that whilst the debate over the period of the decline of the family in industry has produced considerable sophistication in the categorisation of family forms it has, as yet, not produced an equal sophistication in dealing with the structural forces which affect the interrelationship between the family and industry. Thus, as we have seen for Marx and Weber, the growth of 'modern industry' is seen as a unilinear movement towards the application of ever greater amounts of technology and consequent growth in the size of industrial organisations. As far as the family is concerned this is seen to imply an attack upon its relevance in relation to the roles of both labour and capital.

Such a unilinear conception of the growth and development of capitalism has been challenged by Sabel and Zeitlin who point to the importance of 'Historical alternatives to mass production'. They suggest that even notions of industrial dualism, which attempts to account for the persistence of small firms in terms of a second and contrary form of production being inherent in the logic of mass production itself, do not go far enough. They note that such a theory does not do justice to the economic organisation of many of the most famous industrial regions of the nineteenth century:

> Silks in Lyon; ribbons, hardware and speciality steel in neighbouring Saint-Etienne; edge tools, cutlery and speciality steels in Solingen, Remscheid and Sheffield; calicoes in Alsace, woollens in Roubaix; cottons in Pawtucket, Rhode Island; textiles of all kinds in Philadelphia – the history of all these industries challenges the classical view of economic progress. Small firms in these 'industrial districts' . . . often developed or exploited new technologies without becoming larger: large firms that employed sophisticated and expensive technology from the start did not concentrate on the production of standardised goods (Sabel and Zeitlin, 1985, p. 142).

Their critique of the classical view of economic progress is useful in itself, independent of their proposed alternative of 'flexible specialisation' which has been ably criticised elsewhere (Pollert, 1988a and b; Rainnie and Kraithman, this volume). It alerts us to the notion that the development of capitalism did not always and everywhere result in large firms and establishments with detailed divisions of labour worked by a deskilled proletariat. The structures were more complicated and consequently the relationships between the family and the workplace are unlikely to have assumed any single simple pattern.

Such an objection would not, however, defeat the analysis offered by Smelser (1959) and could in some ways be seen to support his position. For if progressive deskilling of an increasingly homogeneous proletariat was not a uniform occurrence, then the notion of 'specialisation of function' would tend to lead to the 'selection of specialists according to competence rather than traditional kinship duties and obligations' (Rapoport and Rapoport, 1971, p. 276), in the manual labour market as well as in the recruitment of managers. The problem with this type of analysis is that it reduces the social status of skill merely to the property of isolated agents. It fails to understand the importance of the family as an element in the intersection of work and community. The role of the family in the reproduction of the labour force has historically been of considerable importance, particularly in occupational communities such as the English industrial districts of the 1920s described by Marshall, where initiation into skilled work began long before the period of formal apprenticeship.

the mysteries of the trade become no mysteries; but are as it were in the air, the children learn many of them unconsciously (quoted in Sabel and Zeitlin, 1985, p. 152).

More recent work on socialisation into skilled identities suggests that familial patterns are not only responsible for imparting the 'mysteries' of the trade, but also for the socialisation of youngsters into the normative aspects of skilled work.

> This socialisation takes a strongly normative form and is cemented by the close interpersonal relations of craftsmen and apprentices. However . . . socialisation occurs prior to entry into the apprenticeship system at around the age of sixteen. This is because skilled craft work is highly prized within the manual working class. . . . Apprenticeships are often filled by word of mouth and routinely involve sponsorship of a fifteen year old boy by an existing skilled worker. These informal structures lead to the selection into apprenticeships of a certain kind of boy . . . one who has a close relative in skilled work. . . . This familial process of recruitment means that the apprentice will already know a considerable amount about the normative aspects of craft work. He will have heard discussions of fellow workers, various types of other workers and, of course, the nature of industrial management at home and in the wider community (Penn, 1986, pp. 13–14).

The normative aspects of skilled work are neglected in individualist accounts of specialism as a prerequisite for technical efficiency. It should be obvious, however, that individual technical expertise is useless without the associated normative framework which can enable the individual to function as part of the 'collective worker'. Indeed some observers have pointed to such aspects of skill as being of at least equal importance to technical mastery (Cousins and Brown, 1972).

If such issues form the 'enabling' element of the family effect upon the worker as far as the performance of skilled work is concerned, the 'constraining' effect has to do with 'real subordination' within the commodity status of labour, where affective rationality is at least as important as the extension of formal rationality within the employment relationship. In other words, control of the labour process can be exercised through the use of ties of kinship and friendship as well as through the application of more technical and formal modes of control. More will be said about this later.

The classical interpretation of the development of capitalism implies a decline in the impact of the family in industry, with respect to capital as well as labour. The demise of the family firm consequent upon the growing scale of economic units, capital requirements and the developing domination of the joint stock company were seen to produce a decline in the importance of the family for capital which at least paralleled that of labour (Weber, 1947; Sweezy, 1970). There are several objections to this conclusion, however. Firstly, the displacement of the family as the basis of units of capital has not yet been conclusively demonstrated. Indeed the work of Grou, reproduced by Scott (1985) in Table 10.1, shows that even in the world's largest companies the family remains a significant unit of strategic control. Thus, of the world's largest companies in 1978 where majority control can be identified (99 in total), over a quarter remain in family hands. Of those with an identifiable controlling minority (254 in total), 72 are based upon family groupings.

Moreover, Lupton and Wilson in their discussion of the 'kinship' connections of 'Top Decision Makers' found that ties of kinship remain an important aspect within business and political elites. Such ties can exert a real effect, although they suggest that under certain circumstances kinship may act as a divisive as well as a uniting force (Lupton and Wilson, 1970).

The importance of kinship ties as uniting or dividing forces lies in the strength of feeling with which either aspect is integrated into business affairs and strategy. Formal rationality, the development of calculability in relationships in order to maximise profit, may be the overt form of legitimation, but this does not mean that other forms of rationality, traditional or affective, are absent. In other words, the rationale given for a particular course of action will tend to refer to the means used to maximise profit, whereas the action may also be underpinned by a desire to retain a traditional kin relationship or to express an emotional attachment or aversion.

Table 10.1   Strategic control in the world's 487 largest non-financial enterprises (1978)

	Type of controller						
Mode of control	*Family*	*Corporate*	*Bank*	*State*	*Foreign*	*None*	*Totals*
Majority control	25	9	1	38	26	–	99
Minority control	72	33	124	9	16	–	254
No dominant interest	–	–	–	–	–	134	134
Totals	97	42	125	47	42	134	487

The cut-off point for minority control is 5%.
Source: Scott (1985, Table 51)

Indeed, in some cases the substantive rationality (that is, the rationality of the ends pursued) underlying a business may imply either traditional or affective forms equally as well as formal rationality.

The family as one source of traditional and/or affective rationality can serve to underpin, usually covertly, business strategy. Miller and Rice have argued that in family firms in which the boundaries of multiple task and sentient systems coincide, values other than those orientated towards meeting competition for resources and markets can determine the outcome:

> When non-working members of the family want to put more wealth into the family business, there is little problem. But when they have deep interests in other activities for which they want all the money they can get, decisions can be difficult. . . . Decisions about investment and the distribution of profits are then determined by family relationships instead of business needs (Miller and Rice, 1967, pp. 118–19).

Such a view retains a traditional outlook upon the essential opposition of the family and industry. However the situation has often been historically more complicated than this. For there may be material concerns which underlie some of the more 'positive' aspects of family/business interaction. Thus Sabel and Zeitlin have argued that the 'federated family firm',

> emerged typically in the intermediate cases where production, neither so concentrated as in the case of paternalism nor so dispersed as in municipalism, required a loose reliable alliance of medium and small firms specialising in the particular manufacturing operations. . . . The firms often found markets outside the family; but their financial and emotional ties to the lineage made them dependable partners even in difficult times (Sabel and Zeitlin, 1985, pp. 151–2).

Once placed in the material domain of capitalist production, we can see how the traditional and affective ties of family serve as an instrument of survival when times are hard. This is one reason why the dominance of formal rationality, with its objective of maximisation of profit, does not totally obliterate other forms of rationality in a single unitary tendency. The material conditions of capitalism ensure that other forms of rationality based on family, affective relations or traditional loyalties remain of importance especially in times of economic slump. Thus, for example, family ties existing in particular centres of the British shipbuilding industry in the depression of the inter-war period operated as a *de facto* form of vertical integration, bringing together steel making, ship building and ship ownership and providing markets to ensure the survival of particular yards. The importance of such family ties receded somewhat in times of high market demand (Roberts, 1989).

Similarly, even within the largest and most bureaucratic organisations, individual progress up the management hierarchy is rarely exclusively dependent upon formally rational criteria such as achievement and ability, however defined. It has been suggested that the wives of professional and managerial workers often have well-defined duties that are an integral part of their husband's occupations and career advancement can depend upon a wife's behaviour and attitudes (Whyte, 1957; Papanek, 1973).

So far we have concentrated on the importance of the objective aspects of the. family. We have suggested that much of the work of classical sociologists has underestimated the tenacity of the family and to some extent overestimated the strength, and simplified the directions, of the forces pitted against it. Marx and Engels' invective against the 'action of modern industry' as it tears asunder all family ties can be seen as an overstatement. As child labour was regulated and with the rise of the full-time education system, the original factory fodder, children, were increasingly removed from the industrial arena. However, as we have seen, this does not necessarily imply a single shift from the family as a unit of production to a unit of consumption. The family remains important in the reproduction of the labour force, in helping to provide an acceptable normative framework through which the future 'collective worker' can be made operational.

Similarly, Weber's argument about the decline of the importance of the family in industry in response to the rise of bureaucracy and formal rationality fails to appreciate the fragility of the material conditions of capitalism with respect to individual enterprises. The antithesis of maximum accumulation and growth underscored in times of economic slump may be that of mere survival, an important weapon in such a battle being ties based upon traditional and affective appeals. Thus the survival of the objective possibility of the pursuance of formal rationality, that is, the survival of the enterprise itself, lies in the incorporation of apparently opposed rationalities based on relations of family or friends.

It is not only through the ties of kinship that the control of relationships within organisations can be seen as familial. The family is also important as a symbolic form. As Cooper (1971, p. 6) has argued:

> The power of the family resides in its social mediating function. It reinforces the effective power of ruling class in any exploitative society by providing a highly controllable paradigmatic form for every social institution. So we find the family form replicated through the social structures of the factory, the union branch, the school, the university, the business corporation, the church, political parties and governmental apparatus, the armed forces, general and mental hospitals, and so on.

There are always good or bad, loved or hated 'mothers' and 'fathers' older and younger 'brothers' and 'sisters', defunct or secretly controlling 'grandparents'.

How might a more critical understanding of the family be demonstrated empirically and how might the two strands of objective kinship relations and symbolic approaches be structured? This is the task addressed in the remainder of this chapter.

SMALL FIRMS – THE VISIBLE SPECTRUM

From our discussion so far we can see that the 'family' understood as an introjected set of relations, that is, belief in the family as a desirable prototype for other forms of social grouping, has more general relevance than 'family' understood as an objective set of relations. The introjected 'family' often plays a part in all types of organisation, from micro firms employing only family labour, through family firms indicating primarily a relationship of ownership, to massive firms and even state bureaucracies not organised objectively on family relations. Our focus on small firms is a convenient device as it enables us to deal with all levels of objective family/ kinship presence, from total and exclusive family employment to firms with no involvement. We can thus examine in a simplified context the full spectrum of family involvement in industry.

Of the first type of firm, that 'employing' exclusively family labour, we will not say a great deal. It suffices that in such firms there is a fusion of technical and affective relationships. Quite often this includes the hidden employment of a spouse and/or siblings in service of a single status of 'self-employment'. Formal and substantive rationality are merged so that economically the unit may not be reproducing the 'real costs' of labour input. Where this occurs self exploitation can be seen to be happening. However, it is common in such cases for the head of the firm to be the patriarch and therefore 'self' exploitation may be conceptualised as a form of patriarchal dominance.

Far more common than the family as an exclusive unit of production is the family firm. The business is owned and/or controlled by a single family whose members may or may not work within the firm. Again the variety within the small firm sector is instructive in presenting us with examples where the owner(s) and family members work in the firm either exclusively in a managerial capacity or directly in the labour process or with a mixture of both aspects. Finally firms with no objective 'family' structure may incorporate hierarchies, legitimacies and rationalisations which are familial in form. The claim which is advanced by some owner/managers in small firms that we are 'one big family' must be taken seriously on this level.

In order to pursue these issues in an empirical context, we will consider three aspects of the employment relationship in small firms, namely recruitment; the day-to-day management of industrial relations and the labour process; and discipline. The project 'Management and Industrial Relations in Small Firms' carried out at Durham involved a two stage methodology, comprising a relatively large scale interview survey, complemented by a sub-sample of detailed longitudinal case studies. The interview survey covered 400 firms in four locations in England and Scotland across four industry sub-sectors. This was supplemented by a sub-sample of thirty firms which were visited on at least three occasions over a period of twelve months. The material drawn on here is from the second stage of the research, which used a combination of semi-structured interviews with management and workers, critical case study analysis and direct observation. The objective of the study was to analyse the day-to-day industrial relations practices within small firms whilst recognising the heterogeneity of the small firm sector as a whole.

RECRUITMENT

As far as recruitment is concerned, there is a large literature dealing with the recruitment of professional management within family firms (for example, Gibb-Dyer 1986). Often recruitment to the 'family' is experienced as a more traumatic event than 'loss'. As Miller and Rice (1967, p. 121) have commented,

> It is as though the introduction of outsiders might introduce a mechanism that would release the latent violence within the family.

In such cases the introduction of 'professional managers' alters the basis of legitimacy for decision-making and may reorientate the balance of power between family members. Sometimes, Miller and Rice argue, the fear of such changes results in no such appointments being made, even where the price to be paid for such inaction is the demise of the firm itself. In cases involving the employment of non-managerial employees the degree of trauma for the employers may be less, but not necessarily so. Employees, once recruited, may be expected by management to be co-opted into the family and to display exactly the same commitments and values towards the business as family members. This can cause problems of recruitment, as Frankenberg noted in relation to the farming industry:

Even when hired labour is employed, the idea of a family farm persists. Farmers seek other farmers' sons as labourers and treat them as part of the family. This may raise another difficulty in finding volunteers, for a family member is not expected to worry about the hours he works or the wage he receives (Frankenberg, 1966).

The economic unit is reduced to the family as a unit of production, employees are not recognised as such, but are, as far as possible, integrated into the family. The *modus operandi* underlying such relationships becomes the appeal to traditional and affective rationality rather than a more calculative formal rationality within the employment relationship. The legitimacy of such forms is by no means guaranteed, for as Frankenberg points out, finding 'volunteers' can be problematic. In our own research we found that recruitment remains a problem for small firm owners even in very loose labour markets. High levels of 'churning' or labour turnover were evident especially during the first weeks of employment, a period known as the induction crisis. Indeed only five firms of the thirty case studies displayed no labour turnover during the study period. Four of these firms were in the traditional service sector, two of which only employed one or two people, and in each case there was a close link between the staff and owner (friend and family respectively). The other three firms with no labour turnover also employed less than ten people and all were situated in areas of relatively high unemployment. The other 25 firms exhibited varying rates of labour turnover, some very high.

It was the subjective character of employees and their unwillingess to be sufficiently 'flexible' that was criticised by employers, particularly in the traditional sectors. Much of the resistance displayed by the employees amounted to a rejection of traditional and affective appeals. In this context, 'restrictive' practices and behaviour merely represent an internalisation of the formal rationality involved in calculative employment relationships.

Problems with recruitment are often dealt with in small firms, not by a return to employment relations based upon formal rationality, but through recourse to existing social networks. In our research this was more evident in the traditional sectors and involved the use of a recruitment network which moved from family to friends and acquaintances. The importance of such a strategy is that if the owner/manager needs to exert pressure upon an employee he/she can do it indirectly by 'having a word' with either the relative or friend who spoke for the person concerned when the vacancy arose. Pressure is thus exerted through a system of moral obligations, rather than by directly invoking inequalities of power within the employment relationship. Such 'familial' networks can work well for employers, but the extent of such recruitment strategies will be limited by a temporal and emerging social distance between employers and employees. Particularly in the traditional sectors, the longer the owner has been a proprietor, the weaker is his or her direct link to workers in the wider community.

A case study from our research illustrates this point. A graphic design workshop was opened by four partners in 1979 and, by the time of our first visit in 1985, was employing eighteen workers, the majority of whom had been the partners' workmates; all had been recruited on the basis of either direct knowledge or the recommendation of an exiting employee. The year of our visit had been a good one for the firm. They had invested heavily in new equipment and started another firm, instructing their accountant to 'lose some of the profit' between the two businesses. However, between our first and second visits, a period of four months, the workers had got together and decided that their wage rises (individually allotted) were not satisfactory, given the evidently healthy performance of the firm. They approached the partners with a demand for union recognition and collective bargaining. This was eventually acceded to. However, the damage done to internal relationships was said to be 'considerable'. The partners felt 'betrayed' that their workmates had 'turned against them'. In particular, they blamed four individual trouble makers who had left the firm by the time of our second visit. This was seen to have eased the situation somewhat, and the union had become more 'flexible'.

The result of these changes was to make the partners very unsure about recruiting replacement staff, because they no longer had direct contact with other workers; having been employers for eight years, their network had dried up. They needed to be sure that an individual was both capable of doing the job and would be the 'right kind' of worker for the firm. At our third visit, four months after the second, they had advertised the posts and had many replies, but had still not taken anyone on and felt that they just did not know how to ensure that they would get the 'right kind of worker'.

A similar case occurred in another graphic design workshop in the Leeds area. In this firm there was already a union closed shop. However, salaries were negotiated on an individual basis and relationships were very informal. The partners running the firm had served apprenticeships and had previously worked as employees. The majority of their workforce (15 out of 18) were people with whom the partners had worked. Although they recruited using the unions' 'white card' procedure they manipulated this to ensure that they got the people they wanted. A partner explained how this is done:

> we tend to approach somebody at an angle and say 'look, we are thinking of putting a vacancy out, are you interested?' and if they are then we put the vacancy out and they are the first on the list. Most people do this, but the union frowns upon it (Scott *et al.*, 1989, p. 49).

This method of recruitment worked well from the employers' point of view until the year before our study, when they 'ran out of contacts' that they knew first hand. Consequently, when three workers left to set up their own business, they recruited another three workers all from the same large firm where redundancies were threatened. The view of the partner interviewed was that these workers became the catalyst for subsequent developments which occurred during the period of our research. The financial position of the firm had on the whole been improving since start-up, and in the year prior to our research they had invested heavily in new equipment. There was then a move by the workforce to achieve collective bargaining. The Father of Chapel (shop steward) substantiated the owner's claim that the three most recent recruits had been very active, but not solely responsible, for initiating this move. By our second visit four months later, collective bargaining had been instigated. The attitude of the partner interviewed had become noticeably more polarised than in the first visit. He said of the change in the format of negotiation, 'they won, we lost'.

In this firm the basis of the employment relationship had remained hidden behind appeals to a traditional and affective rationale. The informal and personalised recruitment strategy had served to obscure employment relationships and had produced a quasi-familial form of integration. Yet if this approach had produced the prize of integration it had done so at the price of precariousness. For both the external network and the internal system had collapsed, the one due to developing status differences, the other due to changes in the fortunes of the firm (for the better) producing a gap between the aspirations of the employees and the rewards offered by the employers.

Of course it is not only when firms are performing well that aspirations and rewards become mismatched. We saw several examples of firms where poor performance had resulted in labour turnover and recruitment problems. Thus in one swimwear distributor, staff who were referred to affectionately by the owner as friends at our first visit were subsequently described as 'shit' after they had left the firm to go elsewhere. It should be stressed that these examples are critical cases where change had lifted the veil from the employment relationship and had exhausted networks for recruitment. There were of course others where these forms of integration continued to serve management well.

DAY TO DAY CONTROL

Family and affective forms are also important in the day-to-day regulation of the labour process. The strategic location of family members within the labour process complicates capital/labour relations. With the 'owners of the means of production' active in the labour process, any potential for the workforce to institute forms of restriction of output is neutralised and often reversed in the constitution of a 'norm' of maximum output as an objective possibility evidenced in the performance of family members. In addition, the increase in managerial knowledge consequent upon family involvement in the labour process ensures that measures of direct control can be well targeted.

It is the direct presence of the family that ensures the effective performance of the workforce. Whilst some employees identify with the family and are referred to, as in one printing firm we visited, as 'honourary family members', we did not find this to be generally the case. The network recruitment strategies, particularly in the traditional sectors, combined with the family presence in the labour process, can exert direct control on the workforce and can stand as a very effective bulwark against trade union and other forms of collective representation.

If objective relationships imply a coercive form of control the importance of the phenomenological 'family' influence lies rather in its incorporation of dimensions or control as legitimate obligations, recognised as much by the workforce as imposed by management. The importance of patriarchal dominance in the clothing industry with a predominantly female workforce has been pointed to by Scott and Rainnie (1982). However, forms of familial relationship between workers, rather than management and workers, can also be seen to implicate control dimensions of the labour process.

In our research, one case, a transport café, illustrates the point well. The owner (a man) employed predominantly young, female staff and one mature woman. Whilst the older woman did not formally occupy a supervisory role, it became obvious that 'she keeps the younger girls right'. 'Keeping them right' in this sense included making sure that they pulled their weight and defending them from the unwanted attentions of lorry drivers. The role of 'mother' thus included both responding defensively towards 'her charges' and ensuring that, at least to some extent, they behaved responsibly, that is, they did some work. On the basis of our interviews and observations, it appeared that both the older and younger women accepted this state of affairs. When such familial and affective relationships become synonymous with the employment relationship, there can be benefits for management. Work is perceived as a moral duty or individual tasks are undertaken to please another with whom we are bonded familiarly or through affection, rather than as a calculative act. We should not worry about hours worked or wages received. The social structure of the workplace can function to some extent on this basis. However, such a system cannot always respond effectively to issues of discipline where the effect is felt not as a compromising of the moral welfare of a subordinate initiating the act (this situation would typically bring a parental response of 'we are disciplining you for your own good'), but because such behaviour is detrimental to the profitability of the firm.

DISCIPLINE

It is this issue of discipline that proves most difficult in firms where familial or affective models dominate. Thus in the small firms that we studied we confirmed earlier findings that they rarely institute procedures for corrective discipline (Evans, 1985) and that often dismissal was the first and only direct way that owner/managers handled disciplinary issues. The reasons for this were found to lie not in the usual 'common sense' explanation that when someone is not 'performing satisfactorily' the owner/manager must move quickly as small firms cannot afford to carry employees. The opposite seemed to be the case, that when a disciplinary problem arose it was not dealt with immediately, but was ignored. If attention was paid to the problem the approach was at best indirect. That is, the person concerned was not approached for an explanation of their behaviour, but rather their friends or relatives. Furthermore, any pressure exercised by management for change was also indirect: the relative, friend or person who 'spoke' for the miscreant would be asked to 'have a word with them'.

For owner/managers such indirect pressure has both positive and negative aspects. It seeks to exploit the ties of moral obligation felt between the 'troublemaker' and their kin/friends. More negatively, it is the only way the employer can attempt to exert control without overtly invoking power inequalities in the employment relationship. For if the owner/manager has to discipline an employee formally he/she is drawing back the veil from the employment relationship. This inevitably destroys the affective focus of the relationship between the employer and employee. Because of this, even where procedures exist in written form, they will not necessarily be used as a device to regulate relationship within the firm. For as one of the owner/managers in our study put it:

> If a problem gets to the stage that one needs to go through formal procedures it is usually time to call it a day (Scott *et al.*, 1989).

It is because of the incorporation of traditional and affective rationalities in the service of the formal rationality of accumulation within small firms that discipline is such a problem. In our study, owner/managers in all industrial sectors displayed a reticence towards dealing with disciplinary problems and certainly did not move quickly to do so. Where they did act, it was usually by exercising indirect pressure on the individual concerned, through an intermediary. To do otherwise would risk upsetting the imagery of the 'one big happy family'. The reliance upon 'familial' and affective relations as an element in the conduct of industrial relations in small firms can provide management with a potent instrument for control. This form of regulation can prove brittle in the close, and to some extent, rigid context of the small firm. As we have noted above, discipline becomes an explosive issue when 'familial' and affective relations are overlaid on the employment relationship. Similarly it is likely that the transition crisis in small family firms owes at least as much to legitimation crises of father/mother figures as to more technical aspects of the knowledge and abilities of managers.

Whilst most of these phenomena are starkly revealed in the small firms, they are nevertheless also evident in larger organisations, where apprenticeship can equate with the parent/child bond, and trade unionism calls on the legitimacy of brotherhood (or sisterhood). Thus the symbolic power of the family form has been harnessed by both capital and labour in an effort to legitimise their stance in the employment relationship in a way that goes beyond the formal legal status as enshrined in the employment contract.

CONCLUSION

This chapter has called for a re-examination of the linkage between the family and industry. The importance of the family in industry has been undervalued, not only because of the dominance of unilinear conceptions of capitalist development, the increasing scale of organisations and the growth of formal rationality, but also because of a restricted understanding of the family.

Once the importance of the 'family' in its socially mediating function and as a paradigmatic form for the exercise of power is grasped, we can appreciate its import not only in constricting the rationality of capital (Chalmers, 1989), but also in incorporating authority, legitimacy and obligation in the service of capitalist production. The employment relationship can be seen to involve elements of a 'status contract' overlaying and contributing to the more overt 'instrumental contract'. This explains why the family is not to be seen as always and everywhere in opposition to the logic of modern industry. It is ironic that the industrial relations process in the small firm, with the unity of ownership and control personified in the classically entrepreneurial owner/manager, often owes at least as much and sometimes far more to traditional and affective rationality embodied in the obscuring of the employment relationship as it does to a more formal rationality underpinning the 'spirit of capitalism'.

In looking at the family both as kinship and as symbolic form, we have only focused in this chapter on one example where traditional, affective and instrumental rationally in industry are not in opposition but are, as Munch (1988) puts it, interpenetrated. The result of such interpenetration is not however the production of an unproblematic consensus. Rather this analysis suggests that we must strive to unite approaches to industry which recognise the dialectic of conflict and consensus, of structure and action. Insofar as we can do this we should be able to take account not only of the objective changes of large scale historical and systemic tendencies, but also the intersubjective meanings generated by individuals struggling to make sense of their world at work and elsewhere, to deal effectively with structure and sentiment.

11 Over the Threshold? Public and Private Choices in New Information Technology Homeworking

Stephen Lloyd Smith and James Anderson

New technology home working (NHW) provokes discussion of post-Fordist flexibility, the control of the labour process, housing and labour markets, and households. However, NHW forecasts are generally rhetorical, deterministic, and based on the nominal attributes of NHW. Technologists and, to a lesser extent, social scientists, have gone much further than the data warrants.

Several labels cover newly decentralised work: 'telecommuting', 'networking', 'distance working' and 'new homeworking', that is home-based computer work, sometimes linked to other computers. Some have argued that these link-ups have the greatest potential for change (Olson, 1983; Nilles, 1985): a transformation of home and work, a good life combining the city and country, 'flexitime' and 'flexiplace' (Anderson, 1971), bringing gains for the disabled, and among women reconciling domesticity and paid work (Tivers, 1985).

The lure of NHW is tempered by two problems which are explored in this chapter. Firstly, the diversity of NHW arrangements can fit two rival forecasts. Secondly, given the historical advantages to owners of a centralised factory system of office work, why move away from it; why now?

In this chapter we will outline several variants of NHW, drawing on pioneering work by Huws (1984), Holti and Stern (1985, 1986) as well as from our own research – around twenty interviews plus workshop discussions with contractors, trades unionists, government officials, technologists, networkers and academics run by the research consultants Empirica. (See also Kinsman, 1987; Allen and Wolkowitz, 1987; Howe, 1988.) Later in this chapter we question the alleged productivity gains from NHW and the search for ideal occupational traits which might lend themselves to NHW, and comment on some invisible costs. Finally we compare the relative limits of public and private choice.

LABELS AND VISIONS

Interpreting Diversity and Numbers

NHW varies along six dimensions: technology, market, skill, location, gender and contractual status. There are the self-employed; the employees of a single employer; subcontractors to one or more companies on a permanent or irregular, full or part-time basis; female or male; professional or routine workers.

This diversity might suggest that NHW will have a massive employment impact: it appears that it will be flexible enough to cover a large number of diverse workers and organisations. Or, diversity may mean that NHW will have narrow impact on very detailed parts of the workforce, split along all the dimensions specified – especially when the fate of the case-studies is looked at. New homeworkers would never form a clear social group, nor achieve any kind of political nor social cohesion. The second fits the evidence better.

What should be counted as NHW? Strict NHW remains numerically insignificant. The figure of 5000 UK new technology homeworkers is often quoted, implying that our case studies cover 40 per cent. We have not gauged NHW in the unrecorded economy (Mattera, 1985, pp. 34–39). There is a strong case for excluding remote or tele-linked office work from the count. Recent examples within Lloyds Bank, across Ireland, and in Derbyshire, have continued the trend towards tele-linked offices for date-entry and word-processing: conventional factory-like offices relocated beyond costly metropolitan centres. These are recognisably Fordist branch-plants and they are not novel. They constitute the great majority of ex-urban office relocations so the main threat to the future of the urban office comes from the remote branch office, not from NHW.

The USA is comparable. According to the *Financial Times* (24 July 1986), 'Work: the way ahead', 'Only about 40 US corporations organise part [sic] of their work in this way, and there may be only 3000 to 5000 US new technology homeworkers'. Against this view, Electronic Services Unlimited (!) claimed that in 1984 there were 'about 100000 people . . . engaged in formal and informal remote work programs for 450 companies [in the USA]' (Cross, 1986).

Turning to the UK, a growing majority of all homeworkers work in information processing rather than manufacturing. Among women homeworkers, clerical work was twice as important as work in clothing by 1971. There were 37300 clerical homeworkers, compared to 18500 in clothing and leather work (Pugh, 1984). Norwich Union regularly employed home-typists (Holti and Stern, 1985, pp. 90–1), while journalists and sales representatives have often worked from home.

The distinctions between manufacturing and other activities is not especially important. The point is that some NHW grows out of an historically contiguous pattern of domestic production. IT homeworkers were not recorded in the 1981 employment census. Home working was officially two-thirds of a million in England and Wales (excluding 'live-in' jobs). A mere 72000 of these were in manufacturing (Hakim, 1984).

Significantly, 70 per cent of workers 'from home' were men, while 70 per cent of workers 'at home' were women: a strongly, but not overwhelmingly gendered pattern (Table 11.1). These figures are valuable be-

Table 11.1   Gender comparisons between working at home and from home

	At home	From home	Total
Women	178,000	117,000	295,000
Men	73,000	290,000	363,000
Total	251,000	407,000	658,000

cause they suggest likely female/male, at/from home ratios for NHW workers. However, note that men may be less inclined to admit to working 'at home' than women, preferring for status reasons to describe themselves as working 'from home'. See also Allen and Wolkowitz (1987, p. 35) and their discussion of other methodological limits to homeworking surveys.

Some data sources are much less useful than they seem. Higher estimates, based on permissive definitions, often come from suppliers and forecasters. In 1974 the British Telecommunications Long Range Intelligence Unit identified 13.5 million workers whose job could in principle be done from home. A Californian study in 1973 suggested that over a fifth of all occupations could be conducted remotely (Huws, 1984, p. 12). These forecasts are unhelpful because no timescale is given. However the Henley Centre for Forecasting stated that half of all UK employees and almost half the self-employed could be partly teleworking by 1995. The weaknesses of this kind of data can be highlighted if the argument is turned on its head. Many (unpaid) tasks currently performed at home could in principle be done at the office. However this would not be a basis for arguing that the end of housework is at hand. In other words, arguments made 'in principle' do not carry much weight.

Attitude surveys seem to underlie these radical forecasts. An American survey reported that a third of white collar workers would like to work from home (Cross, 1986). This fits UK findings which suggested in 1979 that well over half of those questioned would not want to work from home (O'Brien, 1985). But attitude surveys are a notorious basis for forecasting and are open to similar criticisms as the previous data.

Technological Rhetoric

These forecasts are implicitly rhetorical. NHW is also used as a much more explicit rhetorical device. Optimists look forward to a transformation of the city by electronic cottage telecommuting. Geographical space would become more homogeneous. Flexiplace and flexihours would favourably alter orthodox social time and space. (See *The Independent*, 9 June 1990.)

Rhetorical pessimists compare female new technology homeworkers with old sweated homeworking, and envisage a new round of super-exploitation. Visions of NHW are constructed from diverse ideologies. Feminists wish to recover the equality and communalism of the domestic system; while suppliers appeal to individualism – to be 'your own boss in your own time'. The female manager of IBM's NHW experiment carries the title Equal Opportunity Officer, while Steve Shirley (F-International) argues that 'the computer can do more to free women than the liberation movement'.

Rhetoric presupposes the self-evident; these forecasts are probably not intended to be evaluated.

Contemporary Trends

Webster and Robins (1979) see NHW as a means of reorganising production. By undermining independent producers, factory owners were once able to impose their control on a new and unorganised working-class. In turn, professionalisation and unionisation constrained employers, who may re-invent domestic production to side-step worker organisation. Historically specific employer strategies sweep back and forth across national and international economies in response to particular worker resistance strategies.

This concrete historical perspective makes some sense of the relative decline in conventional full-time employment; the more than doubling of part-time jobs in the last twenty years (Pearson, 1984); growth in the informal economy; increases in subcontracting and self-employment; and internal labour-market segmentation (Leman, this volume). Employers switched to subcontracting in the recession of the 1870s, and homeworking increased.

Homeworking is nominally flexible enough to respond to both labour shortage and redundancy. The computer industry subcontracts in order to tap scarce skills (Huws, 1984, p. 13). NHW is also a way of shedding labour (below). In short, NHW represents one of a range of historically particular solutions to fluctuations in the business-cycle. But why has new homeworking grown so slowly while these other recent changes have been rapid?

Having rejected the rhetorical approach for a more concrete one, we turn to different corporate NHW strategies. What is very striking about the companies we researched is the diversity of their objectives and limits.

EMPLOYER AND MAIN-CONTRACTOR STRATEGIES

Norwich Union: Data-entry and Word Processing among Junior Female Staff, at home

Home-based workers have always been part of the insurance industry. Historically they have mostly been male. They have used portable terminals for a decade, largely as a marketing tool (Abbey Life, Allied Dunbar) and can be classified as new technology home-based workers. However Norwich Union has employed homeworkers for typing and data preparation for much longer. The company currently draws on mostly female workers within the city region; here NHW is a logical extension of a long-standing practice, upgraded from existing mechanical or electromagnetic machines. The primary rationale was also unchanged by the new technology: productivity and workforce flexibility. The overall proportion of the company's clerical tasks performed in this way remains small, probably less than three per cent.

F-International: Subcontracted, Women Professionals, from Home

Steve Shirley devised a scheme in 1962 whereby female programmers worked from home because of childcare constraints. About 95 per cent of the company's UK new homeworkers are women. The total peaked in the mid 1980s at well over fifteen hundred. The programmers are self-employed, managed by salaried staff from conventional head and regional offices. To qualify, prospective subcontractors must have at least three years experience as a computer programmer, analyst or consultant; have not spent more than two years out of employment; and agree to work at least twenty hours a week, including two days a week outside the home.

The company stresses the importance of maintaining face-to-face contact with the central office for progress chasing, controlling standards and reducing isolation. Until 1984 very little use was made of telecommunication links, though some use of them is made now. However the number of subcontractors has been very drastically reduced.

ICL: Directly Employed Female and Male Computer Professionals, Both at and from Home

In 1969 ICL began a homeworking scheme for programmers on the initiative of women employees who wanted to look after children at home while continuing their careers. The scheme covers over two hundred homeworkers, mostly working through modems. Unlike F-International, they are unionised, have employee status and have comparable benefits with office staff (excepting pensions). Most work twenty or twenty-five hours a week. Partly because of the greater use of on-line terminals, the mobility requirements are less strict than at F-International and many ICL homeworkers work only at home.

The trades unions have found them easier to organise than subcontractors. While the number of new homeworkers in this scheme has remained steady, there has been a marked proportional shift towards males – now half are men.

Rank Xerox: Sub-contracted Mostly Male ex-office Managers, from Home

Rank Xerox administrative HQ is in central London. Homeworking, or networking, began in 1982. The aim was to cut overheads by shedding senior and middle management specialists. Originally they remained Rank Xerox employees, but this 'was expensive in management time' and within two years all were self-employed. Rank Xerox stressed that subcontracting avoided many of the managerial difficulties associated with directly employed home-based workers. They preferred to have no direct control. Using psychological tests, entrepreneurial, autonomous personalities were distinguished from collectivists. The latter were discouraged from NHW, to minimise the management of networkers.

In the first year, 50 per cent of a networker's business was guaranteed by Rank-Xerox. About fifty became networkers. An association of subcontractors, Xanadu, was established to reduce isolation and identify new business. The company reported large savings, and most networkers reported significantly improved real earnings. Ten percent went bankrupt. However, Xerox have recently reduced office costs more conventionally by moving a greater number of jobs to an office in Marlow.

Centralised New Technology for mostly male Home-Based Workers: British Telecom 'Network Nine'

A fifth distinct model for NHW was Network Nine, a subsidiary of British Telecom. It traded between 1985 and 1990, copying similar US companies. Network Nine leased electronic office accommodation to independent home-based businesses at a prestigious central London address. Additional room space could be hired as required. Users valued the Central London image. There were a handful of directly employed workers. Their skills were included in leasing costs of around £800 per month. An employee explained how she worked:

> Well, you could say I'm a personal secretary for fifty clients. The trick is when you answer the 'phone and they start talking, you have to think through who they want to talk to. To some clients image is of the utmost importance.   ·

The users did not use the technology as much as expected. Legal restrictions prevented Network Nine from acting as a telephone exchange. It was described as 'a market place for inter-client trading', a halfway house between the new technology office and NHW. There are two other similar UK organisations including London Group in Kingston. Network Nine again shows that technology is permissive; it also shows that the image value of an office (Network Nine's primary value) can be directly quantified in rent. This is important because, notwithstanding Rank Xerox's carefully quantified 'overheads' case for office closures, Network Nine reveals the normally hidden image value of an office.

Although financially successful, it shut in August, 1990, because British Telecom decided that property management was too far outside the company's main business.

Self-Employed Word Processing and Desk top Publishing Agencies, at Home

Certainly the largest group of new homeworkers are those substituting wordprocessors for typewriters, without changing workplace. Small agencies can sell 'higher value-added' word-processing and desk-top publishing services. Labour productivity is less important than this qualitative shift. Growth depends directly on a continuation of the trend towards subcontracting begun in the 1970s. But home clerical work was already well established before this. Unfortunately we cannot quantify these sectors as they do not have an employment census classification. Of the homeworkers we interviewed, it was a household in this category which came closest to the ideal sharing of domestic production between wife and husband. Table 11.2 provides a summary of these NHW strategies.

EVALUATION

As we have seen, productivity, labour flexibility, marketing and reduced overheads are given as main reasons for NHW. Increased control of labour is never offered. Why is this?

Productivity

In the USA dramatic productivity increases of 20 per cent or greater (40 per cent, Cross, 1986) were claimed. New homeworkers in the UK considered that their own productivity had risen (interviews, and workshop discussion). But productivity is difficult to measure, particularly outside manufacturing. It is therefore advisable to be cautious about NHW productivity forecasts.

There are also important conceptual difficulties. Productivity can be defined as output achieved for hours worked. But this need not directly concern main contractors, unless workers' labour power has been directly purchased for a wage or salary. Rank Xerox quickly switched away from direct employment of new homeworkers because of the increased difficulties of managing the labour power they started by buying at a distance. The clear implication is that the introduction of direct employment NHW brings no increases in managerial control and may sharply increase managers' problems.

On a cautious note, it may be that Xerox's perception of the comparative success of the two regimes turned on who 'owned the problem' of management, rather than on the workers' productivity as such. Regardless of the productivity of the two systems, subcontracting brings a welcome reduction in managers' workload by side-stepping the need for conventional management altogether.

Companies clearly differed over which type of contract was best. While Rank Xerox moved from direct employment to subcontracting, ICL moved the opposite way. However while direct employment came up against

Table 11.2 The diversity of new homeworking: a summary

	Norwich Union	F-International	ICL	Rank Xerox	Network Nine	Self Employed
Skill	Low	High	High	High	High	??
Gender	Female	Female	Male/female	Male	Male	Female
At/from home	At	From	From	From	From	At
Contract	Employee	Sub-contractor	Employee	Subcontractor	Subcontractor	Subcontractor
Unionised	??	No	Yes	No	No	No
Location	Local	National	South-East	South-East	South-East	National
Rationale	Flexibility	Flexibility	Flexibility	Overhead	Marketing	Marketing
	Childcare	Skill shortage	Skill shortage	Savings		
		Childcare	Childcare			
Outcome	Stable	Drastic cuts	Stable	Stable	Closed	??

management limitations at Rank Xerox, subcontracting will generate its own limits.

Where the finished piece, rather than labour power is purchased, what is bound to be both more important and more apparent to the main contractor is output quality and quantity against contract price paid. This is also (though less correctly) used to measure the productivity of new technology homeworkers. And this is where main contractors are certain to confront an 18th century constraint which will seriously restrict the growth of NHW. Because freelance new homeworkers can earn much more than office-based counterparts, they can reach a satisfactory standard of living while producing less. According to Marglin (1980) satisficing by outworkers, that is, producing at a satisfactory rather than maximal level, was one of the major reasons for the original development of the factory system. Overseers found it difficult to force their outworkers to produce more. Satisficing could only be controlled through buying the producers' labour power (ability to labour) outright and subjecting it to factory control.

What is important to note is that the relations of production among 18th century outworkers were very similar to NHW subcontracting today. The historical lesson is that the popularity of NHW subcontracting schemes among large companies will be dented because of the power it gives subcontractors when demand is high.

There are striking historic technical similarities too. Marglin notes that there was little difference between domestic and early factory technology. And there is not much difference between office- and home-based systems today. Both then and now, technology had few specific social effects. Social considerations remain paramount.

For Rank Xerox,

Technology began as the major issue in the mind of the planners . . . and ended as the least significant . . . technology is the most minor aspect of the entire exercise (Judkins *et al.*, 1986, p. 61).

Overheads and Telecommunications Costs: Spatial Effects?

NHW saves the employer office space, heating, lighting and maintenance costs. Subcontractors may bear telecommunications costs. Could these factors shift growth away from cities through NHW?

Judkins, West and Drew explain,

of every £100 of the cost of our headquarters locations . . . during 1982 just under one-third was bound up in facilities and related internal support facilities . . . basic salaries . . . a similar proportion, and the costs of employment . . . national insurance contributions, company pension and benefit contributions accounted for a further 15 per cent. Everything else (24 per cent) was divided [evenly] between data processing costs, and miscellaneous expenditure, chiefly travel. . . . By facilities costs we mean . . . rent and rates, . . . depreciation, maintenance, energy costs, security, etc. . . . The first building [was] disposed of . . . in 1983; it originally housed 42 staff, [allowing] . . . overhead savings of a third of a million pounds each year (Judkins *et al.*, 1986, pp. 17–19, 24).

But NHW means forgoing equipment depreciation and training allow-ances. At least one main contractor was lobbying Government on the latter. Workers will be reluctant to accept NHW if their perceived costs rise sharply. Lost fringe benefits are balanced against favourable tax allowances for self-employment.

The cost and accessibility of telecommunications vary. Huws claimed that:

Except in the case of very highly paid professional and managerial staff, it was simply not cost-effective to employ home-based workers when the only means of communicating was British Telecom's expensive telephone network . . . in most cases it remained cheaper to shift the workers to their offices every day than to send the information to their homes (Huws 1984, p. 14).

Yet Rank Xerox networkers' telecommunications costs

are, in practice, trivial. . . . Most professional or managerial work . . . [does not] involve . . . lengthy use of a database or keyboard work, but more usually initial accessing of a database, downloading relevant data on to a local processor, manipulating the selected data locally, and finally submitting a report. The actual time the micro is telecommunicating . . . may typically be as little as five or ten minutes a day, so that the . . . charges . . . are absolutely minimal when set against a £17000 overhead cost saving per £10000 of salary (Judkins *et al.*, 1986).

It is safe to say that telecommunications pricing structures only constrain NHW in a small way (and in no case is the telephone network 'the only means of communicating'). Cities have a mild technical advantage over peripheral regions in the UK. Many UK subscribers only have access to the Public Switched Telephone Network (PSTN) with distance-based charges. The Packet Switched Digital Network (PSDN) is a more reliable, volume-priced system, ideal for transmitting data long distance, but access is re-stricted. PSDN is not generally available in peripheral areas, excepting the Scottish Highlands.

In the light of Huws' and Judkins' comments, extending PSDN would barely have any effect on professional workers' spatial distribution, and would marginally increase the potential for integrating some low skilled peripheral workers into NHW for some core companies. A Cornish group campaigned for a direct link into the London local call area charged at the local rate (Holti and Stern, 1985, p. 105). Clearly they considered data communications costs to be a constraint. But there is no real evidence of impending spatial shifts. Late developments include a large EC regional development grant to upgrade the Northern Ireland Telecommunications infrastructure. On the mainland, British Telecom is itself evaluating the feasibility of using NHW for their directory enquiries service. A mere sixteen operators are involved at the time of writing.

ROBUST DESIGNS OR ORGANISED OPPOSITION?

Different NHW arrangements generate specific limits. These limits are primarily social rather than technical though it would be quite wrong to explain the general stagnation of NHW as if it were caused by anything like a social movement. The immediate barriers are mundane, *ad hoc* and need no mobilisation. For example, researchers clearly agree that tasks involving frequent face-to-face interaction, brain-storming, close co-operation or supervision cannot lend themselves to NHW. Our respondents all agreed. Individuals who are 'natural' collaborators do not take to NHW, as Judkins states. Even if a task is amenable to NHW, it may be that the individual currently performing that task is not. Moreover, jobs which are nominally suitable for NHW may call for reorganisations which are costly in non-financial terms, requiring co-ordination with jobs which remain in the office but which also have to change. Tasks may have to be specified more fully in advance and new forms of monitoring and quality control, methods of payment, and intellectual property rights may have to be settled.

The Search of Ideal Traits for NHW

What job characteristics suit NHW? Contractors will look for regimes that are at least robust enough to work in the medium term. The companies showed no pattern, insisting that their particular strategy worked for them. But a small American survey of 20 women and 12 men, in clerical, technical and managerial occupations (Olson, 1983) claimed that some common characteristics were found. Olson cautioned that 'These traits are relatively independent from the technology employed or the job level'. They included minimum physical and space requirements, individual control over work, planned completion dates (excepting data-entry jobs), well-defined contracts and the ability to concentrate for extended periods. However, the amount of supervision needed varied considerably and no ideal could be defined. Perhaps surprisingly, Olson claimed that data-entry workers needed less supervision than programmers. To the extent that office-based data-entry work is frequently associated with very direct management control, we might have expected comparatively intense managerial control of non-professional new homeworkers.

A more careful definition of control in each case might have resolved the ambiguity. Baran has argued (1985) that NHW may conflict with management strategies to introduce more personal forms of control. These comments should be compared with Leman's chapter in this volume, describing automatic office surveillance systems in data-entry software. Could automated managerial control be incorporated into NHW? We did not find this; the Fordist branch plant offers the greatest scope for direct control. (For good discussions see Downing, 1980; and Wilkinson, 1983).

Ad hoc opposition seems more important than organised opposition. In the case of Rank Xerox, newly established, male homeworkers were often embarrassed by their neighbour's suspicion that they had become unemployed! They also felt their status declined among former colleagues. Managers may oppose directly employed NHW because new homeworkers are reckoned more difficult to supervise than on-site employees.

Both American and European trades unions fear NHW may replicate the sweated labour and insecurity of old homeworking. In Britain most unions have adopted a wait-and-see policy; some officials suggested that there were too few new homeworkers to constitute a serious trade union issue. However, Manufacturing and Science has recruited new homeworkers at ICL.

NHW was successfully resisted by local authority workers in Lambeth in 1985 when the local authority proposed NHW to minimise staff shortages. This is the only case of successful resistance we know of. Trades unionists also unsuccessfully opposed a Greater London Council work centre because it was difficult to recruit members there. Unions in the USA and Germany (see 'At the centre of a new fight: Homework', *New York Times*, 20 May 1984) have called for a blanket ban on all NHW, but it is difficult to see how it could be implemented.

Household Logics

While new homeworkers have more control over their own time-budgeting than office workers, they face obstacles which they cannot change. New homeworkers make decisions against, rather than with the activities of the household and neighbourhood. These problems are not comparable with pre-industrial households because earlier producers worked under a very different universe of values and household relationships. Historically the home was a centre for shared production as well as shared consumption. Children worked from an early age and were not required to develop literacy and numeracy, nor were they formally educated. Adulthood was less clearly demarcated from childhood, paid work from housework, work time from leisure time. Households worked as units.

It is inconceivable that these regimes could be extensively copied today. Child-labour at computer terminals would clearly be resisted in the metropolitan economies and work cannot be spread around the household. Getting out of the house was itself an important motive among those questioned by Tansey and Moran (1985). Men remain particularly keen to go out to work.

THE PUBLIC-PRIVATE DIVIDE

Decisions and Non-Decisions

Public policymakers have contemplated incorporating NHW within industrial development and employment policies. New technology homeworkers may eventually contribute privately to the public good by marginally relieving traffic (Nilles *et al.*, 1976). The Henley Centre estimates (1988) of a 17 per cent reduction in road casualties and a £700m saving in commuting costs by 1992 seem extremely unlikely. We have already seen that the impact of private NHW schemes is very limited. But it is even more difficult to envisage NHW as an explicit objective of public policy on any scale. If the state is contributing to NHW, it is probably doing so indirectly through failures in other areas.

For example, failures to control traffic congestion or to improve nursery provision amount to non-decisions which increase the constraints on conventional women's employment. These non-decisions which have already been taken, may increase the appeal of NHW as a private response among women. The Highlands and Islands Development Board have subsidised the introduction of digital telecommunication in order to increase the competitiveness of the region and stem decline, and the Irish Republic has done the same. This reduces one minor cost-barrier to NHW. Some explicit public decisionmaking has taken place around NHW. The Department of Industry subsidises the technology costs of over fifty disabled people who work for private employers. The scheme is open-ended but has not grown quickly.

Work Centre Compromise

The public 'neighbourhood work centre' has had a very limited impact. Here subcontractors and employees of different companies work under the same roof. They are brought together on the basis of proximity to their place of residence, avoiding the isolation of orthodox NHW. Social access would be maximised with the inclusion of childcare and other communal facilities. Local authorities in London and Sheffield have considered them and one is being established in Hope, Derbyshire, in an attempt to revitalise the local economy.

Work centres have not spread. According to Holti and Stern (1985, p. 114), there were then only two neighbourhood work centres in continental Europe: one in West Germany, the other in Sweden. The Swedish work centre was operated by the Nordic Institute for Urban and Regional Planning between 1982 and 1984, as an experiment in 'a new geographical organisation of work' (Sahlberg *et al.*, 1986). Located in a commuter town outside Stockholm, it housed high status, mainly male specialists and low status, mainly female clerical workers. For the high status workers it was considered relatively successful. But for the clerical workers, for whom it was their only workplace, it provided insufficient social or professional contact. This was because work times were highly variable and unco-ordinated (Holti and Stern, 1985, pp. 117–18). Flexibility defeated social solidarity.

Establishing a work centre requires political commitment, co-ordination between local authorities, diverse workers and companies, and investment by possibly all three. Anti-collectivism will curtail their development and it is unsurprising that conventional, private homeworking schemes are more common.

CONCLUSIONS

Predicting the future of NHW is difficult not because the data are incomplete, but because the outcome of household and corporate decisions and conflicts cannot be known beforehand. 'It is a liar who foretells the future, even if proved right.' We have concentrated on eliciting current policies and practices. These are extremely diverse, underlining the dangers of forecasting.

Optimistic and pessimistic visions can be rejected because of their technological determinism and rhetorical urgency. It is also necessary to accept that a series of disparate events such as skill shortages, increases in direct data capture (OCR, Barcoding) and changes in taxation and public service provision could combine to significantly shift the balance of advantages and disadvantage of NHW in unpredictable ways.

This is not to argue that the future is open-ended. The very specific advantages and limits, the mixed outcomes, the uniqueness of each of the schemes described, are consistent with very minor, uneven increases in NHW. The effects are unlikely to be dramatic. Residential suburbanisation is already well developed, so the effects of NHW on housing markets will be immeasurably small. The Henley Centre forecast that NHW would increase house prices by up to 15 per cent outside London is far-fetched. Decentralisation of routine clerical work has continued to take the more orthodox branch plant route instead: we are not seeing growth in data preparation by NHW. The tightest control of labour is still to be found in the Fordist office; there are certainly no control advantages for employers from NHW.

Face-to-face contact will remain particularly important for large sections of non-routine workers. Tele-conferencing has failed to substitute for meetings.

All this is reinforcement for existing spatial and organisational patterns. Different companies making different strategic decisions are most likely to produce modest increases in NHW, and a workforce segmented in terms of skill, status, gender, age and contractual conditions.

The variety of NHW models might prefigure substantial increase in homeworking, but it is safer to argue that the changes companies are making are distinctive, but narrow and numerically small and they have either stagnated or collapsed with few imitations. The historic work satisficing problem also lies in wait, if homeworking were to become more widespread.

Finally NHW should not be thought of as being particularly revolutionary. It is one among many frameworks for production that have swept the developed economies. And like all frameworks, it generates its own limits. To mimic Marx, the contradictory nature of the social relations of production thus count both for and against new homeworking, depending on the historically specific, concrete actions of contractors and new homeworkers.

Bibliography

ACAS (1987) 'Labour Flexibility in Britain: 1987 ACAS Survey' (London: Advisory, Conciliation and Arbitration Service).

AGLIETTA, M. (1979) *A Theory of Capitalist Regulation: the US Experience* (London: Verso).

ALLEN, J. and MASSEY, D. (eds) (1988) *The Economy in Question* (London: Sage).

ALLEN, S. and WOLKOWITZ, C. (1987) *Homeworking: Myths and Realities* (London: Macmillan).

AMIN, A. and ROBINS, K. (1989) 'Industrial Districts and Regional Development: limits and possibilities', mimeograph from the Centre for Urban and Regional Development Studies, Newcastle University.

AMIN, A. and ROBINS, K. (1990) 'Global integration, local fragmentation', presented to the British Sociological Association's Annual Conference, Guildford, UK, April.

ANDERSON, J. (1971) 'Space-time budgets and activity studies in urban geography and planning', *Environment and Planning*, vol. 3, pp. 353–68.

ANDERSON, M. (1974) *Sociology of the Family* (Harmondsworth: Penguin).

ASHBY, P. (1989) Evidence of Mr P. Ashby, in *The Employment Patterns of the Over 50s*. Report of the House of Commons Employment Committee, vol. II, Session 1988–1989 (London: HMSO) pp. 32–41.

ATKINSON, J. (1984a) 'Manpower Strategies for Flexible Organisations', *Personnel Management*, August, pp. 28–31.

ATKINSON, J. (1984b) 'Flexibility, Uncertainty and Manpower Management', Institute of Manpower Studies, Report No. 89, Sussex University.

ATKINSON, J. (1985) 'The Changing Corporation', in D. Clutterbuck (ed.), *New Patterns of Work* (Aldershot: Gower).

ATKINSON, J. and GREGORY, D. (1986a) 'A Flexible Future: Britain's dual labour force', *Marxism Today*, April, pp. 12–17.

ATKINSON, J. and GREGORY, D. (1986b) 'New Forms of Work Organisation', Institute of Manpower Studies, Report No. 121, Sussex University.

ATKINSON, J. and MEAGER, N. (1986) *Changing Working Patterns: How Companies Achieve Flexibility to Meet New Needs* (London: NEDO).

BARAN, B. (1985) 'Office automation and women's work: the technological transformation of the insurance industry', in M. Castells (ed.) *High Technology, Space and Society*, Urban Affairs Annual Reviews, vol. 28 (Beverly Hills: Sage) pp. 143–71.

BASSETT, P. (1986) *Strike Free: New Industrial Relations in Britain* (London: Macmillan).

BEAUMONT, S. (1989) 'Why Today's Workers Are On the Move', *Personnel Management*, April.

BEYNON, H. (1973) *Working for Ford* (Harmondsworth: Penguin).

BOYER, R. (1986) *La Théorie de la Régulation* (Paris: La Découverte).

BOYER, R. (1988) *The Search for Labour Market Flexibility: the European Economies in Transition* (Oxford: Clarendon Press).

BRAVERMAN, H. (1974) *Labor and Monopoly Capital: The Degradation of Work in the Twentieth Century* (New York: Monthly, Review Press).

BURNHAM, P. (1990) *The Political Economy of Post-War Reconstruction* (London: Macmillan).

BURROWS, R. (1991) *Deciphering the Enterprise Culture* (London: Routledge).

CASEY, B. (1988) *Temporary Employment: Practice and Policy in Britain* (London: Policy Studies Institute and the Anglo-German Foundation).

CASEY, B. and BRUCHE, G. (1983) *Work or Retirement? Labour Market and Social Policy for Older Workers in France, Great Britain, the Netherlands, Sweden and the USA* (Aldershot: Gower).

CASEY, B. and CREIGH, S. (1989) '"Marginal" groups in the labour force survey', *Scottish Journal of Political Economy*, vol. 36, no. 3, pp. 282–300.

CASEY, B. and LACZKO, F. (1989) 'Early retired or long-term unemployed? The changing situation of non-working men from 1979 to 1986', *Work, Employment and Society*, vol. 3, no. 4, pp. 509–26.

CASEY, B., EDWARDS, S. and WOOD, S. (1989) 'State Policies, Firm Policies and Early Retirement in Britain' (London: Policy Studies Institute and London School of Economics) mimeo.

CAVENDISH, R. (1982) *Women on the Line* (London: Routledge and Kegan Paul).

CBI (1989) *Workforce 2000: An Agenda for Action* (London: Confederation of British Industry).

CHALMERS, N.J. (1989) *Industrial Relations in Japan: The Peripheral Workforce* (London: Routledge).

CLARKE, S. (1988a) 'Overaccumulation, Class Struggle, and the Regulation Approach', *Capital and Class*, no. 36, pp. 59–92.

CLARKE, S. (1988b) *Keynesianism, Monetarism and the Crisis of the State* (Aldershot: Edward Elgar; and Vermont: Gower).

CLARKE, S. (1990) 'New Utopias for Old', *Capital and Class*, no. 42.

COCHRANE, J.L. (1979) *Industrialism and Industrial Man Revisited* (New York: Ford Foundation).

COCKBURN, C. (1985) *Machinery of dominance: women, men and technical know-how* (London: Pluto).

COLLINS, R. (1989) 'Mail order survives a catalogue of troubles', *The Guardian*, 18 Jan. 1989.

COOPER, D. (1971) *The Death of the Family* (Harmondsworth: Pelican).

CORRY, B. and BLANCHFLOWER, D. (1987) 'Part-time Employment in Great Britain: An Analysis Using Establishment Data', Research Paper Number 57 (London: Department of Employment).

COUSINS, J. and BROWN R.K. (1972) 'Patterns of Paradox: shipbuilding workers' images of society', University of Durham Working Papers in Sociology, no. 4.

CREIGH, S., ROBERTS, C., GORMAN, A. and SAWYER, P. (1986) 'Self-employment in Great Britain', *Employment Gazette*, vol. 93, no. 9, pp. 183–94.

CROSS, T.B. (1986) 'Telecommuting – future options for work', *Oxford Surveys in Information Technology*, vol. 3 (Oxford: Oxford University Press).

CROWTHER, S. and GARRAHAN, P. (1988) 'Corporate Power and the Local Economy', *Industrial Relations Journal*, vol. 19, pp. 51–9.

CSE/STAGE ONE (1976) *The Labour Process and Class Strategies* (London: CSE/Stage One).

DALE, A. and BAMFORD, C. (1988) 'Older workers and the peripheral workforce: the erosion of gender differences', *Ageing and Society*, vol. 8, no. 1, pp. 43–62.

DAVIES, G. (1989) *What Next ?* (London: Century).

DAVIS, M. (1978) ''Fordism' in crisis: a review of Michel Aglietta's 'A Theory of Capitalist Regulation'', *Review*, vol. II, no. 2, pp. 207–69.

DAVIS, M. (1986) *Prisoners of the American Dream* (London: Verso).

DOWNING, H. (1980) 'Wordprocessing and the Oppression of Women', in T. Forester, *The Microelectronic Revolution* (Oxford: Blackwell).

DUNFORD, M. (1990) 'Theories of Regulation', *Society and Space*, vol 8., no. 3, pp. 297–321.

DUNNETT, P. (1980) *The Decline of the British Motor Industry: The Effects of Government Policy, 1945–1979* (London: Croom Helm).

EDWARDS, P. and SISSON, K. (1989) 'Industrial Relations in the UK: Change in the 1980s' (London: Economic and Social Research Council).

EDWARDS, R.C., REICH, M. and GORDON, D.M. (1979) *Labor Market Segmentation* (Lexington, Mass: D.C. Health).

ELAM, M. and BORJESON, M. (1989) 'Languages of workplace reform and the stabilisation of flexible production: observations on the identity of Swedish post-Fordism', European Association for Evolutionary Political Economy Conference, Newcastle-upon-Tyne, September.

ELGER, T. (1989) 'Change and Continuity in the Labour Process', paper presented to the Work, Employment and Society Conference, Durham University.

ELGER, T. (1990) 'Technical Innovation and Work Reorganisation in British Manufacturing in the 1980s: Continuity, Intensification or Transformation?' *Work, Employment and Society*, Special Issue, pp. 67–101.

ELIAS, P. (1989) *A Study of Trends in Part-Time Employment, 1971–1986* (Institute for Employment Research, Warwick University).

EMPLOYMENT COMMITTEE (1989) *The Employment Patterns of the Over 50s*, Report of the House of Commons Employment Committee, Session 1988–1989 (London: HMSO).

EVANS, S. (1985) 'Unfair Dismissal. Law and Company Practices in the 1980s', Department of Employment Research Paper, no. 53 (London: HMSO).

FAIRBROTHER, P. (1989) 'Workplace Unionism in the 1980s: A Process of Renewal?', *Workers' Educational Association Studies for Trade Unionists*, vol. 15, no. 57, July.

FORD, H. (1922) *My Life and Work* (Garden City, New York: Doubleday).

FORRESTER, K., LEMAN, S. and WINTERTON, J. (1989) *Preliminary Report of a Workers' Investigation into New Technology in Mail Order*, report no. 11, Working Environment Research Group, University of Bradford.

FOSTER, J. (1974) *Class Struggle and the Industrial Revolution* (London: Methuen).

FRANKENBERG, R. (1966) *Communities in Britain* (Harmondsworth: Penguin).

FRIEDMAN, A. (1986) 'Developing the managerial strategies approach to the labour process', *Capital and Class*, no. 30, pp. 97–124.

GAFFIKIN, F. and NICKSON A. (n.d.) *Jobs Crisis and the Multinationals: De-Industrialisation in the West Midlands* (Birmingham Trade Union Group for World Development and Birmingham Trades Union Resource Centre).

GALLIE, D. (1988) *Technological Change, Gender and Skill*, Working Paper no. 4, Social Change and Economic Life Initiative of the UK Economic and Social Research Council.

GAMBINO, F. (n.d.) *Workers' Struggles and the Development of Ford in Britain* (London: Red Notes).

GAMBLE, A. (1988) *The Free Economy and the Strong State* (London: Macmillan).

GARRAHAN, P. (1986) 'Nissan in the North East', *Capital and Class*, no. 27, pp. 5–13.

GARRAHAN, P. and STEWART, P. (1989) 'Post-Fordism, Japanisation, and the Local Economy', paper presented to the CSE conference, Sheffield Polytechnic.

GARRAHAN, P. and STEWART, P. (1990a) 'Auto Industry Unions: Sayonara?', *International Labour Report*, issue 38, March–April, pp. 21–3.

GARRAHAN, P. and STEWART, P. (1990b) 'Nothing New About Nissan?', in C. Law (ed.) *Restructuring the Central Automobile Industry* (London: Routledge).

GARRAHAN, P. and STEWART, P. (1992) 'Working for Nissan', *Science as Culture*, forthcoming.

GARRAHAN, P. and STEWART, P. (1991) *The Nissan Enigma* (London: Cassell).

GEDDES, M. (1988) 'The capitalist state and the local economy: "restructuring for labour" and beyond', *Capital and Class*, no. 35, pp. 85–120.

GERTLER, M.S. (1988) 'The Limits to Flexibility', *Transactions of the Institute of British Geographers*, no. 13, pp. 419–32.

GERTLER, M.S. (1989) 'Resurecting flexibility? A reply to Schoenberger', *Transactions of the Institute of British Geography*, no. 14, pp. 109–112.

GIBB-DYER, W. (1986) *Cultural Change in Family Firms* (London: Jossey-Bass).

GOLDTHORPE, J. (1984) 'The end of convergence: corporatist and dualist tendencies in modern western societies', in J. Goldthorpe (ed.), *Order and Conflict in Contemporary Capitalism* (Oxford: Clarendon Press) pp. 315–43.

GRAMSCI, A. (1971) 'Americanism and Fordism', *Prison Notebooks* (London: Lawrence and Wishart).

GREATER LONDON COUNCIL (1985) *The London Industrial Strategy* (London: GLC) Introduction.

HAKIM, C. (1984) 'Homework and Outwork: national estimates from two surveys', *Employment Gazette*, Jan. 1984, pp. 7–12.

HAKIM, C. (1987) 'Trends in the flexible workforce', *Employment Gazette*, vol. 95, no. 11, pp. 92–104.

HALL, P. (1985) 'The Geography of the Fifth Kondratieff Cycle', in P. Hall and A. Markusen (eds) *Silicon Landscapes* (London: Allen and Unwin).

HALL, S. and JACQUES, M. (1989) *New Times: the Changing Face of Politics in the 1990s* (London: Lawrence and Wishart).

HARRIS, C.C. (1983) *The Family and Industrial Society* (London: Allen and Unwin).

HARVEY, D. (1982) *The Limits to Capital* (Oxford: Basil Blackwell).

HARVEY, D. (1989) *The Condition of Postmodernity* (Oxford: Basil Blackwell).

HEALY, G. and KRAITHMAN, D. (1989) 'Woman Returners in the North Hertfordshire Labour Market', report commissioned by the Training Agency, Local Economy Research Unit, Hatfield Polytechnic.

HENLEY CENTRE FOR FORCASTING LTD (1988) 'Tomorrow's Workplace: Harnessing the Challenge of Homeworking. The development of Teleworking, an economic and social cost-benefit analysis' (British Telecom and the Confederation of British Industry).

HERTIS (1988) 'Hertfordshire Skill Shortages', mimeo, Hatfield Polytechnic.

HILL, R.C. (1988) 'Flat Rock: Home of Mazda: the social impact of a Japanese

190 *Bibliography*

company on an American Community', paper presented to the Eighth Annual International Automotive Conference, University of Michigan.

HOLTI, R. and STERN, E. (1985) 'The Origins and Diffusion of Distance Working', FAST Project Working Paper no. 3 (London: Tavistock Institute of Human Relations).

HOLTI, R. and STERN, E. (1986) *Distance Working in Urban and Reserve Settings* (London: Tavistock).

HOWE, J. (1988) 'Housebound', in J. Zerzan and A. Carnes, *Questioning Technology: A Critical Anthology* (London: Freedom Press).

HUDSON, R. (1988) 'Labour Market Changes and New Forms of Work in an Old Industrial Region', in D. Massey and J. Allen (eds), *Uneven Redevelopment* (London: Hodder and Stoughton) pp. 147–66.

HUWS, U. (1984) *The New Homeworkers: new technology and the changing location of white collar work*, pamphlet no. 28 (London: Low Pay Unit).

HUXLEY, A. (1955) *Brave New World* (Harmondsworth: Penguin).

HYMAN, R. (1987) 'Strategy or Structure', *Work, Employment and Society*, vol. 1, no. 1.

ICC INFORMATION GROUP LTD (1988) *Business Ratio Report: Mail Order and Catalogue Houses*, 4th edn (London).

INCOMES DATA SERVICES (1987) 'Flexibility at Work', Study 360 (London).

INCOMES DATA SERVICES (1989) *Incomes Data Services Report*, no 8, September.

INDUSTRIAL RELATIONS REVIEW AND REPORT (1984) 'Lucas Electrical Restructures for Survival', *Industrial Relations Review and Report* no. 331, 6 Nov., pp. 7–11.

ITOH, M. (1990) 'The Japanese model of post-Fordism', Conference of Socialist Economists, Sheffield, July.

JACOBS, K., KOHLI, M. and REIN, M. (1987) 'Testing the Industry-Mix Hypothesis of Early Exit', discussion paper IIVG/87–229 (Berlin: Wissenschaftszentrum).

JESSOP, B. (1989) 'Conservative Regimes and the Transition to Post- Fordism: the cases of Great Britain and West Germany', in M. Gottdeiner and N. Komninos (eds) *Capitalist Development and Crisis Theory: Accumulation, Regulation and Spatial Restructuring* (New York: St. Martin's Press).

JONES, B. and ROSE, M. (1986) 'Re-Dividing Labour: Factory Politics and Work Reorganisation in the Current Industrial Transition', in K. Purcell, S. Wood, A. Waton and S. Allen (eds) *The Changing Experience of Employment: Restructuring and Recession* (London: Macmillan) pp. 35–57.

JORDAN & SONS LTD. (1983) *Jordans Survey: Mail Order*.

JOYCE, P. (1980) *Work, Society and Politics* (Hassocks: Harvester).

JUDKINS, P., WEST, D., and DREW, J. (1986) *Networking in Organisations: The Rank Xerox Experiment* (Aldershot: Gower).

KELLY, J. (1982) *Scientific Management, Job Redesign and Work Performance* (London: Academic Press).

KERR, C. *et al.* (1962) *Industrialism and Industrial Man* (London: Heinemann).

KINSMAN, F. (1987) *The Telecommuters* (Chichester: Wiley).

KRAITHMAN, D. and RAINNIE, A. (1989) 'Recruitment in Crisis? The Hertfordshire Labour Market in the 1990s', Local Economy Research Unit, Hatfield Polytechnic.

LACZKO, F. (1988) 'Partial retirement: an alternative to early retirement? A comparison of phased retirement schemes in the United Kingdom, France and Scandinavia', *International Social Security Review*, vol. XLI, no. 2, pp. 149–69.

LACZKO, F. (1990) 'Early retirement and the employment of older workers in the 1990s', *Ageing International*, forthcoming.

LAING, R.D. (1971) *The Politics of the Family* (London: Tavistock).

LASH, S. and URRY, J. (1987) *The End of Organised Capitalism* (Oxford: Polity Press).

LEMAN, S. (1990) 'Wisdom, Knowledge or Information? Work-monitoring techniques in the coalmining, clothing manufacture and mail order industries', *Industrial Tutor*, Autumn issue.

LEVIDOV, L. (1990) 'Foreclosing the future', *Science as Culture*, no. 8, pp. 59–79.

LIPIETZ, A. (1986) 'New Tendencies in the International Division of Labour', in A.J. Scott and M. Storper (eds) *Production, Work, Territory* (London: Allen and Unwin) pp. 16–40.

LIPIETZ, A. (1987) *Mirages and Miracles* (London: Verso).

LUCAS INDUSTRIES PLC (1984) *Chairman's Review to Shareholders and Employees.*

LUCAS INDUSTRIES PLC (1988) *Report to Shareholders.*

LUPTON, T. and WILSON, C.S. (1970) 'The Kinship Connexions of Top Decision Makers', in Worsley, P. (ed) *Modern Sociology* (Harmondsworth: Penguin).

MAIR, A., FLORIDA, R., KENNEY, M. (1988) 'The New Geography of Automobile Production: Japanese transplants in North America', *Economic Geography*, vol. 64, pp. 352–73.

MANDEL, E. (1980) *Long Waves of Capitalist Development* (Cambridge: CUP).

MANIFESTO FOR NEW TIMES (1989) in S. Hall and M. Jacques (eds) *New Times* (London: Lawrence and Wishart).

MARGLIN, S. (1980) 'The Origins and Functions of Hierarchy in Capitalist Production', in T. Nichols (ed.) *Capital and Labour* (London: Fontana).

MARKETING STRATEGIES FOR INDUSTRY (1987) *MSI Database: Mail Order UK* (Mitcham: MSI (UK) Ltd).

MARTIN, J. and ROBERTS, C. (1984) *Women and Employment: A Lifetime Perspective* (London: HMSO).

MARX, K. and ENGELS, F. (1848) *The Communist Manifesto* (London: Lawrence and Wishart).

MATTERA, P. (1985) *Off the Books: the rise of the underground economy* (London: Pluto Press).

McDIVITT, W. (1987) 'Module Production: Lucas Electrical', in P. Fairbrother (ed.) *From Productivity Deals to Flexibility at Work*, Monograph in Labour Studies, Department of Sociology, University of Warwick, mimeo.

MEACHAM, L. (1972) *The Origins and Operations of the Unofficial 'Toolgroup' Negotiating Committee in the Joseph Lucas Combine,* MA Dissertation, University of Warwick, mimeo.

MEAGER, N. (1985) 'Temporary Work in Britain: Its Growth and Changing Rationales', Institute of Manpower Studies, report no. 106, University of Sussex.

MEYER, S. (1981) *The Five Dollar Day* (Albany: SUNY Press).

MILLER, E.J. and RICE, A.K. (1967) *Systems of Organisation* (London: Tavistock).

MUNCH, R. (1988) *Understanding Modernity* (London: Routledge).

MURRAY, R. (1988) 'Life After Henry Ford', *Marxism Today*, Oct., pp. 8–13.

MURRAY, R. (1989) Interview in *Interlinks, Journal of the Socialist Society*, February–March, pp. 11–14.

NEDO (1989) *Defusing the Demographic Time Bomb* (London: National Economic Development Office).

NILLES, J.M. (1985) 'Teleworking from Home', in T. Forester (ed.) *The Information Technology Revolution* (Oxford: Basil Blackwell).

NILLES, J.M., CARLSON, F.R., GRAY, P., and HANNEMAN, G.J. (1976) *The Telecommunications-Transportation Trade-off: Options for Tomorrow* (New York: John Wiley).

NISSAN MOTOR MANUFACTURING UK LTD (1988) *Information Pack*.

O'BRIEN, P. (1985) 'From the Automated Office to the Electronic Cottage: A Logical Step?', Society and Technology Honours Project, Middlesex Polytechnic.

OEEC (1952) *Some Aspects of the Motor Vehicle Industry in the US* (Paris: OEEC).

OLIVER, N. and WILKINSON, B. (1988) *The Japanisation of British Industry* (Oxford: Basil Blackwell).

OLSON, M. (1983) 'Remote Office Work: Changing Work Patterns in Space and Time', *Communication of the ACM*, vol. 26, no. 3, March.

PALLOIX, C. (1976) 'The Labour Process: from Fordism to neo-Fordism', in CSE Pamphlet 1 *The Labor Process and Class Strategies* (London: CSE/Stage One) pp. 46–67.

PAPANEK, H. (1973) 'Men, Women and Work: Reflections on the two-person career', *Amercian Journal of Sociology*, vol. 78, pp. 852–72.

PARKER, M. and SLAUGHTER, J. (1988) *Choosing Sides: Unions and the Team Concept* (Labour Notes/South End Press).

PARKER, M. and SLAUGHTER, J. (1989) 'Sparks Fly on the Factory Floor', *New Internationalist*, May, pp. 24–5.

PARNABY, J. (1987a) 'Competitiveness via Total Quality of Performance', *Progress in Rubber and Plastics Technology*, vol 3, no. 1, pp. 42–51.

PARNABY, J. (1987b) 'Practical Just-In-Time – Inside and Outside the Factory', *The Fifth FT Manufacturing Forum* (London) mimeo.

PARNABY, J. (1987c) 'The Need for Fundamental Changes in UK Manufacturing Systems Engineering', Advanced Manufacturing Summit 87, Birmingham, mimeo.

PEARSON, R. (1984) 'Briefing on Labour Market Trends', Planning for Home Work Conference, Housing Associations Charitable Trust, London, May.

PELAEZ, E. and HOLLOWAY, J. (1990) 'Learning to bow', *Science as Culture*, no. 8, pp. 15–26.

PENN, R.D. (1986) 'Socialisation into skilled identities', Organisation and Control of the Labour Process Conference, Aston/UMIST April.

PENN, R.D. (1991a) 'Technical Change and Skilled Work in Rochdale and Aberdeen', in R. Penn, M. Rose and J. Rubery (eds), *Skills and Occupational Change* (Oxford University Press) forthcoming.

PENN, R. D. (1991b) 'Contemporary Relations Between Firms in a Classic Industrial District: Evidence from the Social Change and Economic Life Initiative Research in Rochdale', in J. Rubery, J. Sewel and F. Wilkinson (eds) *Employers' Strategies in the 1980s* (Oxford University Press) forthcoming.

PENN, R.D., SCATTERGOOD, H. and MARTIN, A. (1991) 'Textile Employment, Gender Relations and Technology', *Sociology*, forthcoming.

PHILLIPSON, C. (1982) *Capitalism and the Construction of Old Age* (London: Macmillan).

PIORE, M.J. and SABEL, C. (1984) *The Second Industrial Divide* (New York: Basic Books).

POLLERT, A. (1987) 'The flexible firm: a Model in Search of Reality or a Policy in Search of Practice?', Warwick Papers in Industrial Relations, Warwick University.

POLLERT, A. (1988a) 'Dismantling flexibility', *Capital and Class*, no. 34, pp. 42–75.

POLLERT, A. (1988b) 'The Flexible Firm: Fixation or Fact?', *Work, Employment and Society*, vol. 2, pp. 281–316.

POLLERT, A. (1991a) *Farewell to Flexibility? Questions of Restructuring* (Oxford: Basil Blackwell).

POLLERT, A. (1991b) 'The Orthodoxy of Flexibility', in A. Pollert (ed.) *Farewell to Flexibility?* (Oxford; Blackwell).

PUGH, H.S. (1984) 'Estimating the Extent of Homeworking', Working Paper no. 15 (London: Social Statistics Research Unit, The City University).

RAINNIE, A. (1989) *Industrial Relations in Small Firms* (London: Routledge).

RAINNIE, A., CHARLESWORTH, J. and HOLLYWOOD, J. (1989) 'Skill Shortages in High Technology Industries in the Welwyn/Hatfield District', Report Commissioned by Welwyn/Hatfield District Council, Local Economy Research Unit, Hatfield Polytechnic.

RAPOPORT, R. and RAPOPORT, R. (1971) 'Family roles and work roles', in M. Anderson (ed.) *Sociology of the Family* (Harmondsworth: Penguin).

RED NOTES/CSE BOOKS (1979) *Working Class Autonomy and the Crisis* (London: Red Notes/ CSE Books).

RENFRO, W.L. 'Second Thoughts on Moving the Office Home', in T. Forester (ed.) *The Information Technology Revolution* (Oxford: Blackwell).

RETAIL BUSINESS (1989) *Retail Trade Review* (London: The Economist Publications).

ROBERTS, I. P. (1989) 'A Question of Construction: Capital and Labour in Wearside Shipbuilding since the 1930s', Ph.D. thesis, University of Durham.

ROBINSON, F. (1990) *The Great North?*, Centre for Urban and Regional Development Studies, Newcastle University.

ROSE, M. and JONES, B., (1985) 'Managerial Strategy and Trade Union Responses', in D. Knights *et al.* (eds) *Jobs Redesign: Critical Perspectives on the Labour Process* (Aldershot: Gower).

SABEL, C. (1982) *Work and Politics* (Cambridge and New York: Cambridge University Press).

SABEL, C. (1989) 'Flexible Specialisation and the Reemergence of Regional Economies', in P. Hirst and J. Zeitlin (eds) *Reversing Industrial Decline* (Oxford: Berg).

SABEL, C. (1990) 'Skills without a Place: The Reorganisation of the Corporation and the Experience of Work', presented to the British Sociological Association's Annual Conference, Guildford, UK, April.

SABEL, C. and ZEITLIN, J. (1985) 'Historical alternatives to mass production', *Past and Present*, no. 108, pp. 133–76.

SAHLBERG, B., ENGSTROM, M-G., and PAAVONEN, H. (1986) *Tomorrow's Work in Today's Society: A full-scale experiment in Sweden* (Stockholm: Swedish Council for Building Research).

SAUNDERS, P. (1986) *Social Theory and the Urban Question*, 2nd edn (London: Hutchinson).

SAYER, A. (1985), 'New Developments in Manufacturing: the Just in Time System', *Capital and Class*, no. 30, pp. 43–72.

SCASE, R. and GOFFEE, R. (1989) *Reluctant Managers* (London: Unwin Hyman).

SCHOENBERGER, E. (1987) 'Technological and Organisational Change in Automobile Production: spatial implications', *Regional Studies*, vol. 21, pp. 199–214.

SCOTT, J. (1985) *Corporation, Classes and Capitalism* (London: Hutchinson).

SCOTT, M., ROBERTS, I., HOLROYD, G. and SAWBRIDGE, D. (1989) *Management and industrial relations in small firms*, Department of Employment Research Paper no. 70 (London: HMSO).

SCOTT, M.G. and RAINNIE, A.F. (1982) 'Beyond Bolton: Industrial Relations in the Small Firm', in J. Stanworth and J. Cameron (eds) *Perspectives on a Decade of Small Business Research* (Aldershot: Gower).

SENNET, R. (1979) 'Destructive Geimenschaft', in R. Bocock (ed.) *An Introduction to Sociology* (Glasgow: Fontana).

SMELSER, N. (1959) *Social Change in the Industrial Revolution* (London: Routledge and Kegan Paul).

SMITH, I. and STONE, I. (1989) 'Foreign Investment in the North', *Northern Economic Review*, no. 18, pp. 50–61.

STANDING, G. (1986) 'Labour flexibility and older worker marginalisation: the need for a new strategy', *International Labour Review*, vol. 125, no. 3, pp. 329–48.

SWEEZY, P. (1970) *The Theory of Capitalist Development* (London: Monthly Review Press).

TANSEY, J. and MORAN, R. (1985) 'Notes on Questionnaire Data', FAST Networking Programme, Women's Studies Unit, Irish Foundation for Human Development, Dublin.

TIVERS, J. (1985) *Women Attached: the daily lives of women with young children* (London: Croom Helm).

TOMANEY, J. (1989a) *The Reality of Workplace Flexibility*, Centre for Urban and Regional Development Studies, Newcastle University.

TOMANEY, J. (1989b) 'Workplace Flexibility in the North East', *Northern Economic Review*, no. 18, pp. 16–29.

TOMANEY, J. (1990) 'The Reality of Workplace Flexibility', *Capital and Class*, no. 40, pp. 29–60.

TRY, P. (1985) *The Changing Role of the Mechanical Engineering Craftsman and its possible effects on Industrial Relations within the Automotive Engineering Industry: an assessment based on two case studies – Austin Rover and Lucas Electrical*, MA Dissertation, University of Warwick, mimeo.

TURNBULL, P. (1986) 'The "Japanisation" of production and industrial relations at Lucas Electrical', *Industrial Relations Journal*, vol. 17, no. 3, pp. 193–206.

TURNBULL, P. (1988) 'The Limits to "Japanisation" – Just-In-Time, Labour Relations and the UK Automotive Industry', *New Technology, Work and Employment*, vol. 3, no. 1, pp. 7–20.

TURNBULL, P. (1989) 'Industrial Restructuring and Labour Relations in the Automotive Components Industry: "Just-In-Time" or "Just-Too-Late"?', in S. Tailby and C. Whitson (eds) *Manufacturing Change: Industrial Relations and Restructuring* (Oxford: Basil Blackwell) pp. 124–61.

TYNE AND WEAR R&I UNIT (1989) *The Effect of Changes to the Unemployment Count, 1979–1989*, mimeo, Newcastle City Council.

URRY, M. (1988) 'Trying new ideas', *Financial Times*, 19 Sept.

VAN DE VLIET, A. (1986) 'Where Lucas Sees The Light', *Management Today*, June, pp. 39–45, 92.

VARLAAM, C. and BEVAN, S. (1987) *Patterns of Retirement*, Institute of Manpower Studies report no. 134, University of Sussex.

WEBER, M. (1930) *The Protestant Ethic and the Spirit of Capitalism* (London: Unwin).

WEBER, M. (1947) *The Theory of Social and Economic Organisation* (New York: Free Press).

WEBSTER, F. and ROBINS, K. (1979) 'Mass Communications and Information Technology', *Socialist Register*, pp. 285–313.

WHYTE, W.H. (1957) *The Organisation Man* (Harmondsworth: Penguin).

WICKENS, P. (1987) *The Road to Nissan* (London: Macmillan)

WILKINSON, B. (1983) *The Shop-Floor Politics of New Technology* (London: Heinemann).

WILLIAMS, K., CUTLER, T., WILLIAMS, J. and HASLAM, C. (1987) 'The End of Mass Production?', *Economy and Society*, vol. 16, no. 3, pp. 405–39.

WOOD, S. (1989) *The Transformation of Work* (London: Macmillan).

ZWEIG, F. (1961) *The Worker in an Affluent Society* (London: Heinemann).

Author Index

Subject Index